THE COMPLETE
M&A HANDBOOK

THE COMPLETE M&A HANDBOOK

*The Ultimate Guide to
Buying, Selling, Merging, or Valuing
a Business for Maximum Return*

TOM TAULLI

PRIMA VENTURE
An Imprint of Prima Publishing

Published by Prima Publishing, Roseville, California. Member of the
Crown Publishing Group, a division of Random House, Inc.

PRIMA VENTURE and colophon are trademarks of Random House, Inc.
PRIMA PUBLISHING and colophon are trademarks of Random House,
Inc., registered with the United States Patent and Trademark Office.

Library of Congress Cataloging-in-Publication Data
Taulli, Tom.
    The complete M & A handbook : the ultimate guide to buying,
  selling, merging, or valuing a business for maximum return /
  Tom Taulli.
       p.   cm.
    Includes bibliographical references and index.
    ISBN 0-7615-3561-6
    1. Consolidation and merger of corporations–Handbooks, manuals,
  etc. 2. Corporations—Valuation—Handbooks, manuals, etc. 3. Corporations—Finance—Handbooks, manuals, etc. I. Title: Complete M
  and A handbook. II. Title.
  HG4028.M4 T38 2001
  658.1'6—dc21   2001055405

02 03 04 05 HH 10 9 8 7 6 5 4 3 2 1
Printed in the United States of America

First Edition
Visit us online at www.primapublishing.com

CONTENTS

ACKNOWLEDGMENTS

I want to thank editor extraordinaire Mark Baven for his verbal acumen, organizational prowess, and marketing savvy. Mark's additions, subtractions, multiplications, and divisions were invaluable in helping to produce a book that fulfilled my vision. I also thank David Richardson, Andrew Vallas, and Andi Reese Brady of Prima Publishing.

This book would not have been possible without my parents. They've always been supportive of whatever I wanted to do—no matter how crazy. And, of course, I thank my wife, Shauna. She is by far the best!

INTRODUCTION

Welcome to *The Complete M&A Handbook*. If you are interested in buying or selling a business, you've found the best resource for your needs—a comprehensive guide that covers virtually every type of M&A situation. Until now, there has been no one-stop manual presenting a panoramic picture of the M&A process. I should know: As an M&A professional, I had long noticed this glaring gap in business literature. After years of expecting someone to fill this hole, I decided to do it myself.

I've experienced M&A deals from both sides of the fence: first as an entrepreneur starting and selling three high-tech businesses, and later as an M&A adviser. Since the mid-90s, I have facilitated or advised on the sale of more than a dozen M&A deals. Today I work at a registered broker-dealer, NetCap Ventures, in Newport Beach, a firm that brokers deals for small- to medium-sized businesses. I also write about M&A for Forbes.com, MSN Investor, *Bloomberg Personal Finance,* and other publications and appear as a regular guest commentator on CNBC, CNN, and Bloomberg TV.

I've seen too many people jump into M&A deals without knowing what they're doing. The results, predictably enough, are often unsatisfactory—and sometimes disastrous. Not only is the sale or purchase of a company a very high-stakes proposition, but it's also an incredibly complicated process. Virtually every aspect of business comes into play: negotiation, financial analysis, marketing, personnel management, regulations, contract law, strategic assets, competition, evaluating intangibles, positioning, and more. Of all commercial activities, M&A is perhaps the most skill- and knowledge-intensive. A savvy businessperson would never want to attempt such an endeavor without understanding the process.

Anyone aiming for the best outcome—seller or buyer—must understand how the other side thinks and operates. *The M&A Handbook* will help you understand both sides of the process. M&A deals should be win-win propositions, but that's possible only when both parties know what they're doing. In these pages, I frequently specify exactly how sellers and buyers can use the information and advice. I don't play favorites; I want everyone to come out ahead.

Although the *Handbook* assumes very little business knowledge on the part of the reader, it's not merely for beginners. Even those with substantial M&A experience may benefit from the review—or may learn something new. As several of the anecdotes in these pages illustrate, it's dangerous in the M&A game to let your vigilance slip. Each deal is different, and subtle nuances can tip the balance.

Take note that this book should *not* be considered a go-it-alone manual. As I emphasize throughout the chapters, M&A deals are nothing if not complex, and it would be folly to attempt one without the help of one or more specialists. (Perhaps after you've done a handful of deals, it will be a different story.) Like all business, M&A is a team sport. The better dealmakers know how to work effectively with numerous participants. They tackle M&As with a combination of delegation, decision-making, trust, oversight, wariness, patience, guts, and faith. In short, they know how to collaborate with their advisers and negotiate with their partners on the other side.

For ease of use, this book is organized in a roughly chronological sequence. ("Roughly" because many of the steps in an M&A deal occur concurrently or overlap, and each deal has its own variables that affect the timing and order of operations.) I recommend that everyone, regardless of whether they'll be buying or selling, read through the first nine chapters. Perhaps some people will skim over a few sections, but going through the entire set will provide an excellent overview of M&A activities.

The opening two chapters cover the issues facing sellers and buyers, respectively. In these, I describe the considerations that are peculiar to each side of the table and outline a general "order of operations" that leads to a finalized deal. They also contain many insights concerning psychological factors that can have a huge impact on many deals.

Each of the following seven chapters then covers in detail a major stage, process, or subject—such as due diligence, valuation, regulations, negotiations, post-deal integration, and so on. Depending on the nature of your own deal, some of these chapters may be more essential for you than others. Again, I urge you to at least skim the sections of less immediate interest, so you get a complete picture.

The last handful of chapters covers special cases—hostile takeovers, going private, strategic partnering as an alternative to M&A, and so on. With these chapters, the reader can stick to the subjects that pertain to his or her situation. Someone engaged in coping with a hostile takeover generally doesn't need to read about going public. Then again, you never know. Perhaps there are options in some other chapter that you didn't consider but which could save the day—such as an employee buyout.

My greatest hope for this book is that it contributes to your ultimate success and satisfaction in all your M&A activities.

CHAPTER 1

SELLING YOUR COMPANY

Over the course of 30 years, you've put a huge amount of time and effort into your business, called Tux Deluxe. In the past five years, you have enjoyed a nice income—as your business has generated growing profits that have reached about $2 million annually. The business affords you an important role in the community. You have created hundreds of jobs, and some of your people have been with you for more than 20 years.

But the tuxedo field is not an easy one. After all, a person rents out a tux, on average, about once every 10 years. And business growth has slowed in the last year because of industry consolidation—shifting from regional to national players. Clearly, the next few years will be a challenge. But you'll be turning 65 in five months, and grueling competition is not what you had in mind. As much as you love the business, you've been giving a lot of thought to retirement.

Unfortunately, there's no one to take your place. You've been the sole driving force of the business. None of your three kids have an active role in the business, nor want one, and your general manager has no interest in owning the shop.

You're trying to get a handle on some very tough questions: Should you sell out? If so, to whom? How do you do it? What about the taxes—will they decimate your profit? How do you diversify your wealth?

———+———

Following a great American tradition, you dropped out of college to start a high-tech company based on a cellular technology you and a classmate had devised. In its first year, the company has grown ferociously, garnering $50 million in top-flight venture capital as well as a strategic investment from Cisco. Yet you still do not have any revenues. The company's key product won't be launched for another full year, and profitability is projected (optimistically) to come two years out from the rollout. Meanwhile, your company is burning through $3 million per month.

At the same time, you're facing some tough competition. Four other companies with similar technology under development have received $50 million or more in venture capital. You know you are in a hot market, with a potentially explosive product and a very skilled engineering team. But can the company really survive?

Investment bankers are courting you to go public, claiming that you can raise $200 million at minimum. But you're wondering whether you could raise enough to run the company if the IPO market heads south, as it's threatening to do.

Then again, several big companies have already offered to buy the business for between $1 billion and $2 billion, which would make you and the shareholders rich. But if there is a successful IPO, the company could be worth $5 billion or $10 billion. What should you do?

You are the CEO of a billion-dollar corporation that distributes generic drugs. The company, which has been around for over 30 years, is currently trading on the New York Stock Exchange at $20 per share. But the stock has barely moved in the past two years. In the land of the health-care giants, the company is ignored by investors and analysts—despite a 15% annual growth rate. Basically, the company is stuck.

To make it into the "big leagues" requires that it purchase other companies. But the stock valuation is too low to buy other companies. And with investors uninterested in buying equity and the company already saddled with substantial debt, raising the required capital would be extremely difficult.

Even though you do not want to sell the company, it appears to be an option that needs to be considered very seriously. But if there is a buyout, who should it be with, and at what terms? Will you remain CEO? And will the company retain its autonomy?

Selling your business can be a wonderful, gratifying, lucrative experience. For many businesspeople, selling their companies served as a springboard to even greater achievements. But it is by no means a simple process.

There is a lot to know, and the more you understand about the process, the better it's likely to turn out for you.

After all the work and care you've poured into your enterprise, you absolutely *deserve* to get the best deal possible when you sell. And what exactly does that mean? It means that you won't leave anything on the table. Once you've sold your business, it's gone, and there's no way to recoup any shortfall from what you *could have* gotten. This reminds me of a friend of mine who sold his company. He said to me, "You want to know the main reason I sold?" He pulled out a picture from his wallet, and it was of him and his wife on an exclusive beach in Fiji. "By the way, I had to write two big checks because of the transaction. One was for my investment banker, and the other was for April 15th."

Unfortunately, many times sellers don't get what they deserve. Buyers tend to be more experienced in these types of transactions, which puts sellers at something of a disadvantage. Even if you've been a savvy business player for many years, it is *extremely* advisable to retain the services of several professionals during this process. In this book, I will provide you with the know-how to secure the appropriate and skilled helpers and to make the best use of them.

The critical factor is preparation—you should know what to expect and give yourself enough time to arrange your business and personal situation to help obtain an optimal deal. As an owner or CEO of a company, the possibility of selling it should never be far from your mind. Perhaps it seems like a far-fetched idea at the moment, but markets can move extremely fast, and an excellent M&A opportunity might present itself sooner than you expect. When it does, you want to be ready to move fast and skillfully.

Just like anything in business, there are no clear-cut answers, no one-size-fits-all solutions. Every situation is unique. However, there are definitely ways to approach these situations. That's what we will explore in this chapter.

I begin with an overview of the sequence of actions involved in selling a business. Then I proceed through the various stages, offering detailed guidance about how to handle all these activities, many of which will be unfamiliar to anyone who has not previously sold a company. The information, knowledge, and advice you glean here and in the other related chapters will be a source of power for you as you proceed through this exciting undertaking.

ORDER OF OPERATIONS

For sellers—especially first-time sellers—the M&A process is sometimes frustrating, often confusing, and virtually always more drawn out than they anticipate. To avoid feeling that the whole project has slipped out of your control, it's extremely valuable to understand how the M&A process typically unfolds.

However, there is no single, set sequence that all sellers follow in their M&A deals. Each transaction is different: Some will involve conducting an audit, for example, while others won't. Sometimes negotiations begin as the buyer is still conducting due diligence, and sometimes the buyer insists on waiting until his people have inspected every financial record and given the seller's physical plant the full white-glove treatment.

Nevertheless, most deals proceed along similar lines. For example, the letter of intent must precede the merger agreement, not the other way around. Fortunately, it is possible to sketch out a general order of operations that most sellers are likely to follow. The following outline should provide you with your bearings—but remember, it's intended as a loose guide rather than a rigid schedule.

DANGER POINTS—WHERE, WHEN, AND HOW DEALS GO BAD

In my experience, the most common pitfalls sellers fall into are the following:

Cheapness. The founder doesn't want to shell out to hire professionals to help sell the company. It's downright foolish to hire bargain-rate amateurs instead because they often make serious mistakes—such as shopping the deal—that can end up costing the owner a couple of years. As the saying goes, "You get what you pay for." This is especially true in M&A.

Stubbornness. The founder doesn't accept what potential buyers offer, believing the bids to be too low. At the same time, the owner refuses to get a valuation. The upshot of such an impasse is rarely favorable for the owner.

Nonadherence. Entrepreneurs tend to be cowboys and to disregard some of the drudgery of following sound business practices or principles. They don't necessarily do anything downright fraudulent, just improper or inadequate documentation or procedures. Such problems often lead to a big mess during due diligence, resulting in failed deals. All this can be avoided, however, if owners take the advice of a good CPA.

Unrealistic integration goals. The postdeal integration phase can be very tricky, especially in earn-out situations. If an owner agrees to unrealistic integration goals, he or she might not get paid.

Inadequate resources. M&A is more expensive than many sellers realize. Sometimes an owner doesn't have adequate money available and ends up holding the bag.

Some of these steps can occur in a different order than presented here, and some can occur simultaneously.

MAKE THE DECISION. This is the first moment of truth, the culmination of all your soul-searching and consultations. Perhaps you've discussed the matter with some of your shareholders, top managers, and even your family—stressing the need for confidentiality, of course. You have consensus, and you're committed to following through. (See page 12, "Making the Decision: Why Sell" for a discussion of the motives for selling.) Now you start telling people, in an appropriate order, about your decision (see the "Informing Others" section).

HIRE A BROKER (OR INVESTMENT BANKER). Some owners wait until they've done some preparatory work on the company before taking this step, but it's a good idea to get a broker (or investment banker for big-ticket deals) involved to help you figure out what needs to be done to bolster the company's value in the eyes of a potential buyer. A good broker should be able to tell you how long it will take to make your business shipshape for the best possible deal. The broker gives you a proposal of what steps he'll be taking. Many times, they'll put together a book—a document you can send out to potential buyers. So when you're looking for a broker, ask to see some of the books they've done.

HIRE AN ATTORNEY (AND CPA). Even if you have in-house counsel, a corporate attorney is not the same as a deal attorney. It's wise to hire a lawyer specializing in M&A as early as possible. You need to know what information you should give out to potential buyers, for example, and the attorney will also offer useful real-world advice. The preliminary consultation needs to be only three or four hours. (You'll start racking up the legal hours later, after the Letter of Intent.) Some brokers are

BROKER OR INVESTMENT BANKER?

The distinction between brokers and investment bankers (IBs) is clear-cut. It's all about size.

Brokers usually work out of one office and comprise three or four people. A good company will do a terrific job on smaller deals—certainly up to the $10 million range. And because their overhead is quite low, brokers represent a very cost-effective solution for sellers of small to medium-size companies. Also, there is intense competition in the broker domain. The fact that so many firms are vying for deals helps drive down prices. So never accept a broker's first quote; you can virtually always do better if you hold out a little.

An investment banker, however, is registered as a broker/dealer and runs several offices, with at least 20 or 30 employees. The firm will have in-house analysts, accountants, and other experts. With its extensive infrastructure, an IB is a logical choice for larger deals. There is a cutoff point—often tagged at around $50 million—beyond which it no longer makes sense to go with a broker. The resources you'll need to conduct a deal of that scale should be easily accessible and thoroughly integrated within the M&A process. That is where an IB shines.

If your deal is over $10 million but less than $50 million, you could potentially go with either option. Most sellers in that range ultimately opt for the IB, but there is at least one reason—other than the lower price—to consider a broker instead: Because brokers can do only a limited number of deals at any one time, they provide more TLC to a seller than a large, widely dispersed investment bank. So if the personal touch matters a lot to you, going with a top-tier broker might be a better choice over an IB.

also attorneys, but there is more objectivity if you go to a different professional.

As for the accountant, the one you already use is fine, assuming it's an independent, third-party firm. But if you have had your accounting done in-house, then you need to hire someone outside.

VALUATE. This is optional—some owners opt out of this step entirely. For example, a lot of smaller companies in fluid, less efficient markets, where valuations are all over the dial, decide against it. Public companies, and larger companies using investment bakers, must valuate. For some others, valuation is performed on a regular basis, perhaps once a year. For entrepreneurs who have an inflated sense of their company's worth, a third-party valuation is a very useful reality check, which ultimately helps them. Aside from selling considerations, valuating is a good idea for estate purposes as well. To have a valuation done, you will hire a third-party valuation firm; it's a one-time deal, and the cost for a medium-size company might be in the $20,000 range. (See chapter 3.)

GET YOUR HOUSE IN ORDER. With the help of your broker, you're ready to start "corporate cleanup." (See the section "Corporate Cleanup" in this chapter for a thorough discussion.) By now, you've started to hear about some issues you hadn't considered—what about that lawsuit? or that other licensing problem? Your goal is to take care of problems and ensure that the company's affairs are in good order. So this is when you go to your accountant to discuss your books and to your (outside) lawyer to address licensing deals, articles of incorporation, and so on. This is also when you want to figure out what kind of deal is best for you—what type of transaction is best for your company, given its unique circumstances, and what impact it will have on your tax situation. (See chapter 5.) Another step you might take at this point is to have your employees sign nondisclosure agreements.

FIND THE BUYER. Finally, the real fun begins. Well, not so fast: Even before putting the word out and soliciting bids, you need to have done some research. First, to ensure you get the best price, you want to know more about your industry than you ever have before. For example, how does your company's valuation stack up against your competitors? Brokers often help owners conduct some of the research that the owner doesn't know how to do. This is when you and the broker actively seek a potential buyer. Hopefully, your broker already has some warm leads to go to—but make sure he goes further than just that.

PRELIMINARY NEGOTIATIONS. You hold in-person meetings with parties interested in buying your business. Here it's fairly easy to weed out any unsuitable potential buyers. Many issues are discussed—price, deal structure, financing considerations, and everything else relating to the deal. You might even end up with an "auction" between two or more bidders. (See chapter 4.)

LETTER OF INTENT (LOI). Once you and the buyer have settled on a price, you sign an LOI—even if the details aren't thoroughly worked out. The LOI often stipulates "pending due diligence." Although LOIs are usually not binding—especially concerning the price—some clauses will be binding, such as a covenant not to shop the deal or to disclose confidential information. This is a very critical document, and having a sharp attorney goes a long way toward protecting your interests. The stakes are especially high at this point if you own a public company because you're required to issue a press release indicating you've inked an LOI. The problem is that if it goes sour, then that will have to be disclosed as well— which is a nightmare for the seller, even if it was the buyer who proved to be the bad candidate. (See chapter 4, which contains a section on the LOI.)

DUE DILIGENCE. You will be spending a lot of time with the prospective buyer as he conducts due diligence on your company. Negotiation is still going on, and the buyer will have loads of probing questions based on the due diligence. You will have to "open your kimono," as we say, and this is usually *not fun* for the seller. At the same time, it's key that you conduct some due diligence on the potential buyer. It probably won't be as rigorous as the process applied to you, but it is crucial, especially as it pertains to stock. After you have spent a big chunk of your life building your company, the worst thing that could happen would be to sell it to a fraud—and lose everything. (See chapter 6 for a full discussion of due diligence.)

SIGN MERGER AGREEMENT. This is where the deal is made official. Merger agreement is the generic term; the actual document is more likely to be an asset sale agreement or purchase agreement. Sometimes the seller must receive shareholder approval before the document can be signed. After the signatures, there is usually an exchange of certificates, for cash or other forms of assets.

POSTDEAL INTEGRATION. After the transaction, there's an all-important transition period, and the seller is often obliged or encouraged to play a role. In fact, many deals contain earn-out provisions whereby the former owner has a financial stake in the continuing performance of the company. Also, nowadays it's quite common for a seller to partially finance the deal by floating a loan to the buyer. Also, some deals stipulate the seller will stay on as a "consultant" for a certain amount of time. It's increasingly rare that a seller can simply wash his hands and walk away with the pile of cash. (See chapter 8.)

MAKING THE DECISION: WHY SELL?

Deciding whether to sell your company is a very tough, ongoing challenge. Most owners and CEOs have invested so much of themselves that it is virtually impossible to see things objectively. Yet, you must. Because even if you do not want to sell the business, it may be the only smart move. In the world we live in now, where there's a lot of capital and a lot of private equity buyout funds, the big players can see a trend and jump on it faster. So you can't count on retiring with the same business you started and ran.

And it can work in the opposite direction, too, when a business owner is spurred to sell by lush visions of yachts and a life of ease. But reality is often less cushy. Most acquisitions these days are structured as cash/stock deals, and many times an owner actually has to partially bankroll the buyer with a loan against the sale price. So a few weeks on a tropical isle—no problem. But don't expect to buy the island.

Another point is that the trend is for buyers to find ways to handcuff founders so they don't fly the coop; this is a result of too many bad experiences where a buyer found that the founder had been key to a business's success or even survival. The continuity of a former owner's ongoing involvement can help ensure the company endures.

Exit Strategy

Though any reason for selling a company can be termed an "exit strategy," some make for more graceful exits than others. It's a better feeling to sell your company from a position of strength than weakness. An example of strength would be when you see that your market is getting its turn to skyrocket, and you decide to strike when the iron is hot. In a situation like that, you're likely to make a killing; the only question is whether you could have done even better by keeping the company. An example of weakness would be if your company's stock is falling fast, your technology is outmoded, and the big consolidator in your industry offers to buy you out for a reasonable sum. This was the situation independent video stores were in when the majority of them opted to sell to Blockbuster.

Sometimes, this crucial decision can be a toss-up. Take Yahoo. Early on in the company's existence, founders Jerry Yang and David Filo got a $5 million buy-out offer. In interviews, they've said that at the time they would've sold for $7 million. The rest is history.

What it comes down to is many owners end up selling because it's so hard to go it alone. With the failure rate for start-ups so very high, founders must think deep and hard about their exit strategies. The cycle in many industries is similar: soaring growth, followed by a brutal shakeout when a dominant player wields its lower cost structure to drive out the independents. If your company comes to face that rough choice—sell or die—it's best to negotiate while you can. After all, the big players generally prefer to buy you out because it's usually cheaper to buy a company than to chase it down to the bitter end.

Your own situation might have little in common with the scenarios I just described. There are a lot of other reasons to sell, and it's worth looking at a full range. Here are some of the most common motivations for selling:

RETIREMENT. Enough already! You want to kick back and work on your golf game or go hiking in the Amazon (the jungle, not the Web site). It's been a great ride, but there's more to life than working until you keel over.

NO CHOICE, NO CONTROL. If you do not have majority control, your shareholders may force you to sell the company.

NEED THE MONEY. Sometimes company founders will live extravagant lifestyles, taking on quite a bit of debt. When income begins to fall, a founder may consider selling the company in order to avoid going bust.

ESTATE BILL. Another common predicament is when the founder dies and the heirs are hit with a huge estate bill.

BOREDOM. It was fun to build the company, but now you're itching to take on a new challenge—perhaps to start another business in an unrelated industry. An excellent example is Ely Callaway, who first became a textile mogul, sold that off, and proceeded to launch his world-class business, Callaway Golf Co.

FAILURE. You gave it your best shot, but the business has not taken wing. This really smudges the line between exit strategy and survival.

INDUSTRY CONSOLIDATION OR HOT MARKET. Your industry is starting to coalesce, and you recognize an excellent opportunity to fetch a high price, whereas if you wait, you're likely to lose your shot. A prime example was PointCast, which was one of the pioneer Internet companies in the mid-1990s. In 1997, Rupert Murdoch offered to buy the company for $450 million, but PointCast wanted to go public. The company did manage to file, but the timing was unfortunate: In the face of very rough market conditions, the IPO was pulled. By May 1999, PointCast sold out to the Idealab! venture fund for approximately $10 million.

LOGGERHEADS. Management difficulties are forcing you to sell. These can take many forms: family flare-ups, dissent among the owners, or investor pressure. Shareholders might insist you actively solicit or accept any buyout offers, especially if you hold only a minority stake.

CAPITAL SQUEEZE. You don't have the money to grow your company to the next level, and you're already extended with too much debt to get loans.

Size Matters

Reasons for selling are also determined by a company's relative size. Business dynamics are very different for a $75 million company than for a $3 million one; for one thing, the larger company will have active investors, whereas the small one is likely owned by one person or family.

Here are some representative examples, organized by business size:

Small Business (up to $10 Million in Revenues)

With companies in this bracket—many of which are family owned—the problem is that you hit a plateau. Usually, to grow a company beyond the small-business level requires expansion capital. Do you have the contacts and the know-how to do so? And if you can come up with the bucks, do you have the managerial expertise to run a fast-growing business?

In most cases of small businesses, the founder still has primary control over the company. Maybe the founder is getting close to retirement and wants to cash out. Meanwhile, his kids don't have the skills or inclination to continue managing the company.

By the same token, sometimes a death in the family is the cause for selling. In a small business, everything might hinge on one or two people, so any disruption involving these players means it's the end of the road.

Also, small businesses are inherently vulnerable, and turns of events can rapidly change their outlook for survival. For example, if a slightly larger competitor opens a shop next door and reduces prices substantially, trying to match the other operation's prices could kill your profits. And if a massive chain store drops anchor in your town, your little business could be capsized in a flash. The ultimate example of this is Wal-Mart, which brandishes its economies of scale to crush the competition.

Let's look at another type of situation. In the high-tech world, there are many examples of small new companies with huge potential. Perhaps you're a gifted young MIT engineer who has come up with an idea to revolutionize cell phones. Even though your company has no customers, it still may be worth many millions because the intellectual property might translate into massive revenues. Though you were able to develop the technology for a mere half million dollars, you will need to raise substantial capital to make the company work. You also must have a top-notch management team. But, as an engineer, this isn't your forte. So you might instead prefer to sell out and move to the next thing.

In short, if you are unable—or unwilling—to find ways to take your company beyond a small business, it is definitely a good idea to look at the possibility of selling it.

Medium-Size Business ($10 Million to $100 Million in Sales)

It's a whole different ball game at this level. Business matters are far trickier and more complex than at a small company. And there's a lot more at stake, financially; if you make a mistake, it could cost you $50 million. You can find yourself in bankruptcy right quick if you don't watch it. Not many owners have the skills to run a growth company. That's why so many business failures occur when a medium company tries to grow into a large one.

Also, you're more of a target than a small company. So when the big player in your industry sends you a threat, you pay attention.

Quite a few companies in this bracket are still family owned. And once the business has grown to this level, the pie gets a lot bigger, so greed takes over. Family members or partners start to disagree over important issues—company "vision" or marketing strategies. Or some family members have become disgruntled, sometimes because of a divorce, and they want to cash out—despite the fact the company has great prospects.

There also can be terrific opportunities. In this size bracket, valuations can fluctuate widely. Much depends on prevalent conditions in your particular sector. If your company is in a mature industry that grows 5% per year, do not expect a high valuation. But if your industry is red hot, the valuation can be substantial.

But even if the company is in an industry that is strong, this does not mean the company will continue to be a success. Many medium-size businesses fail. You must continually take a hard look at the competitive environment. Is the product line strong? Where will the growth come from? Can management get the company over $100 million in sales and even beyond $1 billion? Will there be a need for a substantial investment in R&D? If so, where will the money come from?

Any of these factors or questions can be the basis for a decision to sell.

Big Company
(over $100 Million in Sales)

Very few companies achieve such "big time" status. But as is the case with any stage of the life cycle of a business, there are many potential dangers. A few wrong steps, and a big company can go into freefall.

One of the most pressing issues is whether the company has enough growth potential to become public. Or does it make more sense to merge into another, bigger company since the market is really a niche?

PSYCHOLOGICAL FACTORS

As anyone with experience in the world of M&A knows, the toughest adversary most sellers face is themselves. It's true—your cast of mind is likely to be the most crucial factor in determining how well the transaction goes. And there's a good reason why I address this topic before I even discuss the sell decision: Psychological factors can, and often do, seriously undermine owners during the preliminary stages. Most commonly, business owners or executives who *should* sell decide against it, and down the road they bitterly rue the missed opportunity.

You might think of yourself as a clear-headed, savvy businessman, one who is accustomed to competitive stress, adversarial negotiations, and difficult decision making. But the process of selling your company is apt to push buttons like nothing else. Even rational, well-balanced businesspeople have certain blind spots, ego issues, or mixed feelings that come to the fore when they decide to sell their companies. You are so identified with the business that it is nearly impossible to be objective.

In fact, the great difficulty for most owners to put aside their psychological baggage is among the best arguments for hiring a broker. Hiring one or more advisers to help sell the company will greatly increase your chances of success. (Besides, most business owners have little day-to-day experience with the complexities of M&A.)

As they say, "Forewarned is forearmed." So I'll fill you in on the main mental traps to look out for—in yourself and in the other partners or executives.

"Separation anxiety." In a way, the business you have created is tantamount to your baby. Leaving the business—even if you make a lot of money from the sale—is still tough. You may have spent many years of your time and effort building the company. Now, someone else will be in control of your creation. Sometimes an owner will end up sabotaging a deal because he can't bear to let go.

Anxiousness. It's common for business owners to become too anxious during the selling process, either because of worry, stress, or even sheer excitement. As a result, you may tend to immediately blurt out your plans and reactions. The problem is that buyers will see you as desperate to sell or as vulnerable to poor judgment.

Unrealism. Nearly every owner thinks his or hers is the best little business in the country. Most commonly, they overestimate what the company could fetch. Often this tendency is coupled with a stubborn streak, so they refuse to even have the company valuated. As a result, the business stays on the block for years and grows more and more tarnished in the eyes of the market.

Oversensitivity. When talking to advisers or potential buyers, you will hear criticisms. They will inevitably find faults with your business. After all, this is what a buyer is *supposed* to do in order to lower the valuation. And advisers will point out faults to show that their services are needed. Which they are. Remember, these professionals spend every day doing such deals. And since no business is perfect— there are always problems—you *want* your advisers to point out the weak spots. While it is tempting to be defensive, this is usually counterproductive. So try to thicken your skin, at least temporarily.

(continues)

(continued)

Guilt. Once your people know you're looking to sell, a certain amount of apprehension is natural, from the shop floor or mailroom on up to your top managers. After all, new ownership always entails the risk of layoffs—and if you're selling to a larger business planning to "absorb" your company, odds are even higher some people will lose their jobs. This can complicate situations and color your judgment, especially if you have enjoyed a mutually loyal relationship with your employees.

Contrariness. If you stay with the company after the acquisition, you'll face a huge, fundamental adjustment. So expect some chafing. Previous owners find getting used to working for someone else takes time—even if you and the acquiring company share the same cultural values. Sometimes former owners become highly "difficult" to deal with, which can be self-destructive—especially in earn-out situations. One well-known example is H. Ross Perot, who proved to be a holy terror at GM after he sold them EDS. Ultimately, he made out all right—but don't assume you'll be so fortunate.

At this level, the dynamics involve a complicated matrix of interests: Investors often play a huge role in the sale or stay decision.

INFORMING OTHERS

At every stage of the selling process, communication is key. That might sound obvious, but faulty communication is often a source of problems. In selling a company, timing is critical. It should not be rushed. You need to be mindful of both the quantity and the quality of the information you share—who and how much you tell and how you tell them. A good adviser will help you time your announcements strategically and craft your tone for each one.

Here are the key points about communication:

MAINTAIN STRICT CONFIDENTIALITY. The last thing you need is for your intentions to leak out before you're ready. If you have doubts about someone's reliability at keeping information under their hat, try to keep them out of the loop, if possible. If the market knows you're planning to sell long in advance, by the time you make the move, your deal might already seem stale. Confidentiality is vitally important, especially between the seller and buyer. One tricky area is for small public companies that are selling out. For example, suppose a small company trades about 1,000 shares per day and news of a buyout leaks out. Then in the next few days, volumes surges to 100,000 per day and the stock soars. The buyer would likely walk away from the deal. (In chapter 6, we present guidelines for negotiating and setting up confidentiality agreements.)

DON'T KEEP PEOPLE IN THE DARK. This is the flip side to the above advice. Even if you're a sole proprietor, other people need and deserve to know your plans as they take shape—especially investors, key managers, and family members. Neglecting to inform people is a great way to sow dissent and resentment. Rumors are likely to be circulating anyway. Furthermore, making a decision in isolation can be very dangerous. As you discuss the potential sale with your business and personal contacts, you're likely to gain valuable insight.

ATTEND TO DIFFERENCES. Base your "message" on the audience at the time. In the early stages of planning, for example, you will need to share information with your junior partners and accountant that you do *not* want to divulge to customers yet.

NEVER APPEAR DESPERATE (ESPECIALLY IF YOU ARE). If a potential buyer thinks you need to sell as soon as possible, that could instantly slice 25% off the bid. No matter how much you're sweating it, maintain your cool. If it's not your disposition to do so, then have your broker or another negotiator serve as your public face.

Of course, following the above four principles involves a lot of judgment calls. In general, err on the side of safety—that is, reveal a little less to the world than you might be inclined to. With anyone you don't trust implicitly, let on a bare minimum.

Here are some more specific suggestions on how to communicate with different constituents:

THE BOARD. As soon as you decide you want to sell the company, you should notify the board. Since they represent the interests of shareholders, this is often a legal requirement. The best way is to convene a special meeting to discuss your motives and rationale for the sale. Hopefully, the board composes a diverse group of people who can offer useful suggestions (or criticisms) and can help you come up with a game plan. Even if your mind is made up, it's wise to adopt a consultative tack with your board.

INVESTORS. With the board aware of your plans, you usually needn't notify investors until an actual offer is on the table. Remember, even promising M&A deals often fail to materialize. So telling investors too early could generate unwarranted excitement since they will probably realize a gain on their investment.

CUSTOMERS, SUPPLIERS, AND COMPETITORS. As a rule of thumb, you don't want these players to know until it's a done deal. There is too high a risk the information could lead to nasty repercussions—especially if the deal falls through. For example, suppose you're negotiating to merge your company with XYZ Inc., and one make-or-break stipulation is that your firm will have to use XYZ's suppliers rather than your current ones. If your suppliers tell of this during the negotiation phase, they might well decide to drop you now. If the deal falls through, your company could be in big trouble.

As for informing customers, it's usually a poor idea to do so until the deal is done. Even if the prospective sale would benefit your current customers, news that a deal is in the offing could shake their confidence. Regardless of what you claim, they're likely to wonder, Is the company in trouble? Is our account in jeopardy? And if the deal falls through, then customers may consider you to be in a worse situation.

An important point: If either the seller or the buyer is a public company, the question is probably moot. Disclosure is prohibited in most cases because it could be grounds for selective disclosure—that is, a violation of the full-disclosure rule or even insider information.

With regard to competitors, obviously it's best they do *not* hear about any discussions you're having with potential bidders. Again, this points to the necessity of ensuring both parties keep the talks confidential.

HIRING A BROKER

Just as you would use a broker to sell your house, the same goes for selling your business. You could try to do the deal on your own, but M&A requires so much specialized knowledge that it would be foolish not to avail yourself of a broker's expertise. The bottom line is that even after paying for the broker's service, you will almost undoubtedly come out well ahead of where you would if you tried to sell your company by yourself.

Many of the most tragic tales of sellers getting burned could have been averted if the owner had hired a professional to help out.

Let's face it: Most CEOs and founders have little experience with selling companies. Having a broker—one that is skilled—can be very helpful. They understand the many pitfalls of a transaction and will be helpful in providing a valuation for the company, finding buyers, getting a good price, and negotiating terms. A good broker will have a team, which includes valuation experts, analysts, and deal makers who can find buyers and negotiate a good deal.

One key difference between a real estate broker and the M&A variety is that you generally pay a retainer when you hire a good broker. So you shouldn't hire one until you're ready to sell. Generally, an owner is foolish to merely "test the waters"; word *will* get out, and since most industries are close knit, you run the risk of "shopping your deal."

When retaining a broker, you need to be careful and do your own research (as described in the next section). Just as there are many incompetent home brokers, the same goes for M&A brokers. Interestingly enough, there are no official licensing regulations for brokers. Basically, anyone can print some business cards, set up a telephone (and probably a Web site), and hang out the proverbial shingle as a broker.

The seller also must beware of unscrupulous brokers. Legally, a broker is an agent that represents the company, known as the principal. As a result, the broker owes a fiduciary responsibility to the company. That is, the agent must act in good faith, disclose all potential conflicts of interest, present all offers to the seller on a timely basis, and disclose material facts to both parties. Thus, a broker would have to disclose if it has a fee-based agreement with a buyer. If not, the seller has the right to deny the broker any fees from the transaction or

TERMS AND JARGON

Like every business specialty, M&A has its own trade jargon—phrases instantly understood by the players but not necessarily by the outside world. Throughout the book, we'll highlight the important ones. Here's the first batch:

"Open the kimono." This pungent phrase refers to the aspect of due diligence in which the prospective buyer probes the seller's company, looking for warts (or worse).

"Cockroach theory." The assumption, during due diligence, that if you find one problem, there are probably hundreds of others to uncover.

"Shop your deal" or "Become shopped." This is when a seller's company is overexposed and, as a result, becomes devalued in the eyes of the market. Example: An owner who merely "puts out feelers" rather than seriously pursuing a deal. When a business is up for sale for a while, others quickly wonder what's wrong with it.

even to sue the broker in the case of an "inside deal." Note that the seller's broker must act in good faith with any potential buyer as well.

Moreover, it is customary that a broker gets paid when he or she locates a buyer that is ready, willing, and able to carry out on the seller's terms.

Another point: Brokers typically are involved in smaller deals—say, below $50 million. For larger-value deals, the companies involved will retain investment bankers (explained in much more detail in chapter 2). Investment bankers have much more organizational

THIRD-PARTY SOURCES FOR BROKERS

In your search for a broker, it is a good idea to look at third-party sources. Here are several useful professional resources.

International Association of Merger and Acquisition Professionals *(www.imap.com)*. This group provides information and networking opportunities for brokers. It publishes a quarterly newsletter on M&A that you can download from the Web site.

Institute of Business Appraisers *(www.instbus app.org)*. Established in 1978, IBA is the oldest professional society for the appraisal of closely held businesses. The Institute provides its 3,000-plus members with technical support, market data, and education programs. IBA offers a Certified Business Appraiser (CBA) accreditation. To qualify, candidates must have four years of college, provide references, and complete a four-hour, proctored exam covering the theory and practice of business appraisal. Finally, they must submit two comprehensive business appraisal reports.

International Business Brokers Association *(www.ibba.org)*. IBBA membership comprises more than 900 business brokers and intermediaries in the United States, Canada, Mexico, and Europe. The association offers a Certified Business Intermediary (CBI) accreditation. Candidates must have at least three years' experience as a broker, complete 60 credit hours of courses—and score at least 75% on each exam.

resources available, and of course they charge much higher fees.

Finders

Another adviser that might play a role in the early stages of the selling process is a finder. Finders are only rarely involved in big-ticket deals. Most finders work with or for brokers. Such a finder continually puts out feelers for businesses that might be looking to sell and tries to connect any live prospects to a broker, who then pays the finder a fee. A finder might have relationships with any number of brokers, and a broker might have dealings with any number of finders. They work in conjunction, with the finder playing a decidedly junior role.

Because of the limited role (really it is about introducing parties), a finder has no fiduciary relationship of trust with the seller, although there is a contract between the two parties. If a transaction is completed, the finder gets a fee. But since the services and duties are not as onerous, the fees tend to be smaller—perhaps equivalent to 5% to 10% of the broker's fee. A finder incurs no legal liability for making a reference, even if the broker is paying him a fee for his trouble, *unless* the finder lies or misrepresents.

Many sellers prefer dealing only with a broker to avoid building in extra fees. Note that even if a finder locates a buyer, the seller usually will still need to retain a broker for the negotiation phase.

It's no surprise that the lines of demarcation can get tricky: If a finder also *negotiates* a deal on your behalf, the relationship may transmute into a broker structure, in which case the fee will be higher and fiduciary trust will be involved. It's not always easy to determine when such a shift occurs.

Choosing the Right Broker

For CEOs of small companies, locating any number of brokers or finders is rarely a problem. When the market (in a given industry) is strong, a business owner can expect to get hit up quite frequently—perhaps once a month—by a finder or broker. In fact, they can get downright pesky.

As in life in general, a large percentage of contacts between sellers and brokers are made via word of mouth, especially in smaller deals. Firms that have brokered a lot of deals in a particular industry gain renown and a well-known reputation. But even if a broker comes highly recommended, you still owe it to yourself to conduct a full interview and of course draw up a full contract. You never know—the firm might have recently lost its best professional, the one who had been chiefly responsible for its stellar reputation.

Brokers often specialize in particular niches, such as high tech, auto dealerships, and so on. There's no question that it's a good idea to go with a firm that knows your market inside and out. Even though all M&A transactions are fundamentally similar, nuances can be very significant. A broker's knowledge of your particular industry's unique aspects—such as changes in state regulations or valuation metrics—will be critical for the success of your deal.

No matter what, do your research and interview candidates very closely. It's usually a good idea to speak to more than one broker before making a decision. And even if the broker comes highly recommended from a trusted colleague, solicit some additional references from the firm—and follow up with these.

If you must choose among several good firms with excellent reputations, the deciding factor is likely to be personal chemistry. One personality trait to watch out for is pushiness. You don't want to hire a broker that uses high-pressure tactics on you. Brokers have a reputation for being pushy characters, but this can hinder a deal. While you obviously wouldn't want to retain a wishy-washy broker, there's a fine line between persistence and overaggressiveness. A good broker should know how to toe that line, particularly in his initial dealings with you—a prospective client.

Qualifications

In seeking a broker, you can look for certain types of qualifications:

REAL ESTATE BROKER'S LICENSE. Real estate and business brokers share many of the same duties. In fact, some states require business brokers to have a real estate license because acquisitions often involve real estate. So if you hire a broker and later find that he doesn't have a state-mandated real estate license, you probably have the right to terminate the contract and not owe any fees.

SERIES 7. This is the National Association of Securities Dealers (NASD) license allowing people to sell securities to the public. Although Series 7 is meant mostly for selling public stocks and mutual funds, the advantages for you are the fact that the qualifying test is quite rigorous and the license requires members to uphold high standards for clients.

Interviewing

When interviewing a broker candidate, you should ask the following questions:
- How do you screen buyers?
- How many people work at your firm?
- Do you have other offices?
- How many people will work on my deal?

- How many deals have you completed in the past year?
- At what prices?
- What were the general terms?
- How long did the deals take?
- How did you get leads for these sales?
- Did the sales come from your network?
- Do you advertise?
- How much do you spend on advertising?
- Where do you advertise?
- Will you advertise for my deal?
- Can you show me examples of the advertisements?

Screening buyers is at the heart of a broker's responsibilities. Any good broker should have a very detailed list of criteria. When you work with a broker, you can streamline the search by specifying the type of buyer you want.

You want to work with a firm that has conducted at least five deals in the past year because that would show they know how to execute. The general terms and prices should be in line with the industry. It might seem curious, for example, if you find all the deals included earn-outs.

You definitely want a deal shop that completes deals expeditiously. The last thing you need is an overshopped deal, as that can pull the price down dramatically.

The broker's industry contacts should include key players; preferably, the broker has done deals with the industry's movers and shakers. The wider the broker's base of industry contacts, the better your deal should be. Good contacts also confers credibility on your deal. In the M&A business, particularly with regard to brokers, reputation is very important. As the old saying goes, "You are only as good as your last deal."

In general, your deal is much more likely to be sold through the broker's network of contacts rather than through advertisements. So be sure the broker doesn't spend an excessive amount on ads. Also, check to see that the firm targets the right publications for your company. Ask to see a couple of ads. You may want to restrain the broker from overdoing the ad angle, perhaps by setting a dollar cap. More than $10,000 is probably too much.

Confidentiality Agreement

The broker has a duty to keep your proprietary information confidential. It would be horrendous if your broker approaches competitors of yours and then ends up disclosing material information to them. Consequently, the first document you must have is a confidentiality agreement. This will stipulate, for example, that you have the right to review what information the broker will show to a prospective buyer before he approaches them. (See chapter 6 for detailed tips about confidentiality agreements.)

The Broker Agreement

The document defining the mutual obligations, expectations, terms, and conditions of the seller/broker business relationship is called the broker agreement. Since your broker is likely to be *the* key business companion in your M&A journey, it is critical to draw up the agreement with the utmost care. This section will offer you invaluable advice on how to do it, but do not think this eliminates the need for a lawyer. A poorly constructed broker agreement can cause you untold headaches and stress.

If asked about the single most important component of the agreement, I would say it's termination. The contract *must* provide you an "out" if you find the broker is underperforming. Quite often, I've seen sellers hog-tied by an exclusivity clause, unable to break free of an unsatisfactory broker relationship.

Now, the first question is, Who should draft the contract—you or the broker? As per a rule of thumb, the drafter has a little more leverage in the negotiations, so I recommend you take the opportunity to draft this covenant—unless you're short of money. Because when I say "you," I of course mean your attorney, who might typically charge as much as $5,000. Needless to say, be sure to note the date of the draft and that your side authored it.

There is no standard organization form for a broker's agreement; its layout can take many shapes. But virtually all agreements must cover a similar set of basic contingencies. To provide a suitably detailed exhibition of pertinent clauses, we'll use an actual broker agreement—one inked in October 1998 between Women.com and BT Alex. Brown.

Services Rendered

Somewhere in the first few paragraphs, the contract should define the basic agreement. This will be phrased something like this: "The broker expressly agrees that it shall perform the services to . . ."

In the Women.com contract, the services include

> . . . services with respect to the exploration of strategic alternatives that may lead to a possible transaction, through (i) a minority investment in the Company or (ii) a sale, merger, joint venture, or otherwise, whether effected in a single transaction or a series of related transactions, in which 50 percent or more of the voting power of the Company or all or a substantial portion of its business or assets are combined with or transferred to another company (excluding reincorporations or similar reorganizations).

The contract then sets forth more specific services to help Women.com reach its desired goals. In the event of a conflict that needs adjudication, if no such terms are specified, then it is left up to the courts to decide, and this can be quite unpredictable. And defining very specific performance tasks helps sync expectations for both parties.

In the Women.com agreement, the services were listed extensively:

(a) BT Alex. Brown will familiarize itself to the extent it deems appropriate and feasible with the business, operations, properties, financial condition and prospects of the Company;

(b) Assist the Company in identifying and evaluating candidates for a potential Transaction with the Company;

(c) Assist the Company in the preparation and implementation of a marketing plan and in the preparation of a memorandum (together with exhibits, the "Memorandum") describing the Company and its business operations for distribution to potential parties to a Transaction;

(d) Contact potential candidates which BT Alex. Brown and the Company believe to be appropriate for a potential Transaction. In rendering such services, BT Alex. Brown may meet with representatives of such candidates, as are approved in advance by the Company, and provide such representatives with such information about the Company as may be appropriate, subject to customary business confidentiality;

(e) BT Alex. Brown will advise and assist the Company in considering the desirability of effecting a Transaction, and, if the Company believes such a Transaction to be desirable, in developing a general negotiating strategy for accomplishing a Transaction;

(f) BT Alex. Brown will advise and assist management of the Company in making presentations to the Board of Directors of the Company concerning any proposed Transaction; and

(g) BT Alex. Brown will advise and assist the Company in the course of its negotiation of a Transaction and will participate in such negotiations.

Again, each deal is different, so the above list is not necessarily what you should include in your own contract. For example, you might want the broker to conduct a valuation and compare the results to industry standards. Or you might require the adviser to produce at least three or four prospective buyers. Or you might stipulate the adviser must spend at least a set amount on advertising.

Remember that the duties listed are terms of a contract. So if there is a breach, then the contract may not necessarily be enforceable and the fees may not be due. Then again, the seller has duties, too. You need to disclose the necessary information—financials, goals, risk factors, and so on—to facilitate the adviser's performance.

Generally, the broker will want an exclusive listing. This means that for a fixed period of time, the broker gets a commission regardless of who buys the business. That commission amount will be based on the same formula as if the broker itself had sold the business. Try to limit this time period—to, say, six months.

Transaction Fees

Unless otherwise specified in a contract, a broker is entitled to a fee if, from his efforts, he introduces a buyer to the seller and a merger results. In this circumstance, it does not matter if the broker negotiated the deal. A broker is also entitled to compensation if, from his efforts, he introduces a buyer who is ready, willing, and able to purchase the seller's company on the seller's terms—even if the deal falls through.

In both cases above, the broker is considered the "procuring cause" of the transaction.

However, disputes sometimes arise. For example, suppose a broker introduces you to a buyer, but negotiations result in no deal. A year lapses, and then talks begin again. A deal is consummated, but on different terms from the original proposed deal. In this case, the broker may not be considered a "procuring cause" and does not get a fee.

Now, the above need not be the case with your broker's contract. Rather, you negotiate these points. For example, the phrase "ready, willing, and able" is quite vague. You can, in the contract, set forth what this means. This may mean that the deal is 10% cash and the rest in Nasdaq or NYSE stock. The minimum price is $5 million. There must also be an employment agreement (for three years at $100,000 per year) and some type of bonus structure (over, say, the next three years you can make 30% of the purchase price of the company). Also, you can say that payment is made only if a deal is closed. Thus, the terms can be very creative. And, by being specific, you can help reduce potential disputes.

The most common compensation schedule in brokers' agreements is the Double Lehman Index, wherein the fee is a percentage of the transaction that decreases incrementally as the transaction amount goes higher. Here is a sample:

12% for the first $500,000

10% for the second $500,000

8% for the second $1,000,000

6% for the third $1,000,000

4% for the fourth $1,000,000

2% for any amount more than $4,000,000

Yet again, you can modify these any way you want. Maybe your company will sell for at least $30 million, and for any price above this, you are willing to pay no more than 0.25%.

This was the fee structure and terms for the Women .com deal:

> The Company shall pay BT Alex. Brown for its services hereunder a cash fee equal to:
>
> In the event of a Minority Investment, a cash fee at closing equal to five percent (5%) of the Aggregate Consideration payable to the Company or its security holders in such Transaction, but in no event less than $1,000,000. In addition, the Company agrees that BT Alex. Brown shall have the right to reinvest an amount equal to half of the fee earned hereunder pursuant to five-year non-cancelable warrants to purchase common stock exercisable at 120 percent of the common equivalent price per share of the securities sold in the Transaction.
>
> In the event of a Sale, payable at closing of such Transaction a cash fee of $1,000,000.

Expenses

The broker may be required to travel, seek the advice of counsel, and incur other out-of-pocket expenses. Consequently, the broker will likely propose an "expenses clause" that pays for reasonable expenses. Also, it is a good idea to specify a fixed amount that must be approved by the seller.

Here's the expenses clause for the Women.com deal:

> Section 3. Expenses. In addition to any fees that may be payable to BT Alex. Brown hereunder and regardless of whether any Transaction is proposed or consummated, the Company hereby agrees, from time to time upon request, to reimburse BT Alex. Brown for all reasonable fees and disbursements of BT Alex. Brown's counsel, if any, and all of BT Alex. Brown's reasonable travel and other out-of-pocket expenses incurred in connection with any actual or proposed Transaction arising out of BT Alex. Brown's engagement hereunder. Any fees and/or disbursements individually or in the aggregate in excess

of $25,000.00 must be approved in advance by the written consent of the Company.

Termination

When drafting a broker's agreement, it is smart to look at the worst-case scenario. Say the broker does not find good leads—or fails to do any work at all on your behalf! If so, you should not be locked into an agreement. That's what the termination clause is for.

The broker will, however, want some assurance that it will be paid the partial or entire commission if the seller ultimately consummates a deal with one of the broker's prospects. Unfortunately, some sellers will engage a broker, get a lead, delay any action, and *then* do the deal after the agreement is terminated. No doubt, this is acting in bad faith, and a broker will be inclined to sue—and perhaps try to abort the transaction.

Here is how termination was handled in the Women .com deal:

> BT Alex. Brown's engagement hereunder may be terminated by either the Company or BT Alex. Brown at any time, with or without cause, upon written notice to that effect to the other party; provided, however, that BT Alex. Brown will be entitled to its full fee under Section 2 hereof in the event that (i) at any time prior to the expiration of 18 months after such termination by the Company, a Transaction is consummated with a party which contacted the Company or was contacted by the Company or BT Alex. Brown on behalf of the Company (provided such party is not an existing shareholder of the Company) during the course of this engagement pursuant to the terms of this Agreement; or (ii) the Company enters into an agreement during the term of this Agreement which contemplates a Transaction and such Transaction is consummated within 24 months after termination with

a party which contacted the Company or was contacted
by the Company or BT Alex. Brown on behalf of the Company during the course of this engagement pursuant to
the terms of this Agreement.

CORPORATE CLEANUP

Your chief overall task is to make your company as appealing a property as possible. Even if you've been slack
about aspects of operations or finances, there are numerous actions you can—and should—take during the pre-
selling phase to enhance your company's value.

When a house owner prepares to sell his property,
there's often a flurry of long-deferred activities—founda-
tion cracks get fixed, fences painted, garages cleaned,
and so forth. The same type of situation applies to businesses. The preparatory steps can take countless forms.
Sometimes it entails correcting problems—say, if there
are some "messes" to clean up, such as lingering lawsuits or personnel conflicts. Or they might include the
active pursuit of improvements—such as running a marketing campaign designed to boost quarterly revenues.

What you must do is anticipate all the things that
prospective buyers will assess and investigate. And remember: No matter what, there's always something
wrong with the business, and a good buyer will try to
find and exploit that. Meanwhile, a smart seller minimizes the number and severity of problems *before* a
buyer comes along to point them out.

As I've stressed before, it is critical to start the remedial process as early as possible. In fact, even if you
are not currently interested in selling the company, it is
a good idea to prepare your company as if you are looking to sell as soon as possible. Markets can change
quickly. If another company offers you a deal you "can't
refuse," you will be in a good position to negotiate.

However, cleanup often doesn't begin in earnest until after the seller has hired a broker. In such cases, the first stage of working together will involve the broker diagnosing a company's weak spots and prescribing the necessary remedial measures. The broker will make his recommendations and agree to return in a couple of months to follow up and assess the situation. In fact, it's not uncommon for a good broker to slam on the brakes until problems are cleared up; the seller thought the company was good to go, but the broker thought otherwise.

Informality

For public companies, corporate cleanup typically is not much of a problem. Because they are required by the SEC to make quarterly and annual reports to shareholders, they must have documentation in place to ensure that the company is properly running the operations. However, this is not so with privately held companies, which may be run a little too "informally." For instance, the founder may be using the corporate cash account for personal reasons or failing to record certain types of contracts. Problems such as those can literally scare away buyers.

If your company has been run informally for a long time (say, more than five years), it could require a lot of time and expense to correct the situation. And the decisions can be wrenching: You might need to lay off people or remove a loved one from the board of directors. Despite the psychological fallout such steps likely will produce, they may be required to ensure you do the right thing for your company.

Two Key Focus Areas

While all the facets of cleanup described in the following are important, the single area I would most emphasize is financials. Analysis of the target company's financial records constitutes a very large part of due diligence, so it's crucial that the seller has paid close attention to the books. If you don't already work with a good accounting firm, this is the time to go find one. That should be your highest priority. Be sure your accountants adhere to strict, rigorous principles.

The other element I would emphasize is legal. This is the most commonly overlooked area, with painful or even disastrous consequences. One category of legal hang-up involves liability. Obviously, if there are any outstanding lawsuits pending that involve your business, it would be far better to resolve these before you sell the company.

But more typically, the source of legal problems is contractual: A seller will have a number of binding contracts in force that effectively "give away the store." That is, these legal covenants freeze key assets. For example, one customer might have exclusive rights to a product line of yours. If such a contractual limitation surfaces during the buyer's due diligence, that is a huge problem. Not only do you have to resolve the specific situation—say, to pay the customer to release the contractual hold—but you've also created a serious credibility problem. Many a deal has been scuttled this way.

Action List

The corporate cleanup areas to focus on, and specific steps to take, are described below. While it is unlikely you will need to address every category, it's worth taking a fresh look at each one.

BUSINESS PLAN. Update your company's internal business plan to specify your forecast for at least the next three years. The forecast should be consistent with the company's past performance, not based on best-case scenarios (unless you can support your case).

COMPENSATION. A company's workforce usually constitutes a substantial part of its overall value. Thus, it is important to establish compensation arrangements to retain key employees—for example, employee stock option plans, bonuses, and employment agreements.

VALUE DRIVERS. Determine what are the elements that give your company value and try to fortify, enhance, and protect these. If market penetration is your company's strongest suit, for example, you would want to apply a large percentage of your marketing resources in coming months to bolster your lead. Here are two more examples of value drivers:

- **Customer base.** Let's say your company has a loyal customer base in a niche part of the real estate industry where you have 80% of the market. This took 10 years to develop and would be prohibitively expensive for another company to capture. Since this is a key to your business, you would want to try to capture the rest of the market.

- **Intellectual property.** Though your high-tech company produces three different technologies, only one of them is truly cutting edge. With that one, you have at least a year lead on the competition. While you don't want to neglect your other lines, you should focus extra resources on that key product to enhance your lead.

FINANCIAL STATEMENTS. At minimum, you should have a qualified CPA maintaining your financial statements on a regular basis. And if you have the statements audited by a CPA firm, that would be a great way to enhance your credibility with potential buyers. In many cases, a buyer will demand an audit anyway. If you have one conducted on your own, that would allow you to solve any potential problems that are uncovered.

Another crucial point: Private companies often maintain two sets of accounting books—those used to show investors how profitable it is and those to show to the IRS that are geared to minimize tax payments. This is known as recasting the books. When selling your business, you should show both types of financial statements.

BOARD MINUTES. Make sure all board meetings are recorded. If they're not you could lose your limited liability protection and the IRS might disallow certain tax advantages.

BOARD OF DIRECTORS. A strong board of directors serves to bolster a company's long-term growth. This is a good time to rally its members and solicit strategic feedback.

FAVORITISM/NEPOTISM. Look for any potential red flags. For example, is a family member being employed at the company for no good reason? Or did a family member get a loan with no interest payments? You need to have a standard policy for wages and perks. An independent compensation committee of the board can deal with these issues.

COMPENSATION. A business can deduct "reasonable" salaries, but some business owners stretch this definition to the limit. If the IRS deems the compensation unreasonable, the excess amount could be taxed as a dividend. Bearing this in mind, wage-scale adjustments might be in order.

INDEPENDENT CONTRACTORS. There are many well-known advantages to using independent contractors, such as not having to pay for the person's benefits or to withhold taxes. But in recent years the IRS has pursued a more aggressive policy on how to classify independent contractors, with a 20-factor checklist used to discern the difference between employees and contractors. Quarrels between companies and the IRS over this issue are common, and when a company is found at fault, it could be hit with back taxes and penalties. So this is an area to examine closely, making sure you have applied strict definitions.

PROFESSIONALISM. For starters, it is essential to ensure your company's premises are always clean. And if you own a family business, avoid such forms of address as "Dad" during work hours. If there are personal family disputes, they should be handled away from the other employees.

ENVIRONMENT. Make sure you comply thoroughly with current environmental and OSHA regulations. Any potential environmental liability exposure is likely to scare away a potential buyer.

CORPORATE STRUCTURE. Is your balance of debt load and cash flow healthy? Or is your company's debt too high for existing cash flows to retire in several years? Remember that in many (if not most) cases, a buyout will require the buyer to borrow money. Therefore, it is a good idea to take steps to structure your company's current debt to make an acquisition easier on the buyer. It's a good exercise to look at how much more debt your company can take on if there was an acquisition. If the margin is slim, then it is probably smart to look at ways to reduce debt. (Your broker should be very helpful here.) Of course, every industry is different. The cable industry, for example, generates both massive debt loads and gushing cash flows.

Good Housekeeping

While the following three elements don't necessarily fall under corporate cleanup per se, they are all indicators of sound business practice. A potential buyer—especially a savvy one—will take you more seriously if you have these pieces in place. They demonstrate that you have done your homework, work with competent advisers, and are forward looking.

Succession Plan

It is critical to build a management team within the company that will allow for an orderly transfer of power if and when the founder leaves. Especially with smaller companies, the danger is that when the founder leaves, the business founders. This is why smart buyers often arrange to ensure the owner stays involved in the company's management after the transaction—and often has a financial stake in the company's continued success.

Business succession is a touchy subject because owners often shy from considering the inevitable time when they will no longer run their business. Owners find it all too easy to *not* have a plan. In fact, according to a study by Deloitte & Touche, only about 28% of family-owned businesses have a succession plan in place. Such is the effect of the entrepreneurial ego. (And this is why some business owners can't even get away for a brief vacation—"My company would fall apart without me.")

The existence of a sound succession plan goes a long way in instilling confidence in a potential buyer. It also adds an incredible amount of value to your company. Remember: Indispensability loses you valuation points. If you plan to sell your business some day, it is utterly essential that you build your team as the company grows so you're not absolutely indispensable.

The plan—which, like a business plan, must be updated regularly—should have the following elements:

OWNER'S GOALS. The owner defines what he wants: dividend income, for example, or the sale of all his interest. If he wants to remain on the board of directors, that should be specified.

SUCCESSOR. Who will lead the business after the owner? If this person or people do not already have the necessary managerial abilities, a training regimen is imperative.

ESTATE PLAN. For the owner's sake, there should be an estate plan to minimize taxes.

DISABILITY CONTINGENCY. There must be a plan of action in case the founder is disabled. There also should be a key person insurance policy. (See the next section.)

BUY-SELL AGREEMENT. This is another key element to eliminate confusion or conflicts. (See the following.)

Key Person Insurance

This policy determines what happens if a key person dies. Such a life insurance policy specifies the corporation as the beneficiary if the key person dies. Though the premium payments are not tax deductible, if the policy is activated, the distribution to the corporation is tax free.

The distribution helps a company navigate a transition, such as finding a replacement and paying the salary. Also, the insurance can compensate for the potential reduction in revenues due to the departure. The rule of thumb is that coverage should be at least five times the salary of the key person. The amounts tend to range from $1 million to $10 million and is usually for a term of two to 10 years.

To illustrate, when Martha Stewart Living Omnimedia filed to go public in July 2000, the prospectus filed with the SEC had a risk factor titled "The loss of the services of Martha Stewart or other key employees would materially adversely affect our business." Because Martha Stewart is the personification of most of the company's brands and also a highly active senior executive officer, two steps were necessary to protect the company. First, Martha signed a five-year employment agreement. And second, the company purchased a key person life insurance policy with a minimum amount of $10 million.

From a buyer's perspective, the existence of such a policy (or policies) may prove invaluable. For example, deals often go on for several months before they're finalized. What happens if the principal dies during that period? Also, there are other critical, perhaps even indispensable, people other than the founder—perhaps the chief technology officer, operations vice president, or even a key project manager. The disability or death of key persons could spell disaster for a potential sale. But with a key person policy in effect, the deal could probably survive, and negotiations won't have to begin from scratch.

Buy-Sell Agreements

A buy-sell agreement is a binding contract among owners of a business that specifies who will buy a departing owner's equity share as well as the price per share. You could see it as a kind of corporate prenuptial agreement.

For example, let's take one common scenario: A company is co-owned by two partners, one of whom suddenly dies, leaving his share to his spouse. The other partner and the dead owner's wife have never gotten along, and both know it wouldn't fly to try to run the business together. So one has to buy the other out. That's where having a buy-sell agreement makes all the difference.

There are different approaches to structuring a buy-sell agreement:

Cross-purchase agreement. This is a contract between the owners.

Stock redemption agreement. This is a contract between the company and the owners.

Third-party buyout. This is a contract between the owners and key outside people.

In order to avoid disputes and litigation, it is crucial that the buy-sell agreement has a method for determining the price of the shares. This is a notoriously difficult exercise, and the best approach usually is to hire an independent financial appraiser.

Chapter 2

Acquiring a Business

Buying a business should be a thrilling experience, and, for many an entrepreneur, an acquired company becomes a source of wealth and personal satisfaction. Countless corporations of all sizes have wielded this method to further their development and growth.

At the same time, purchasing a company is a very tricky, high-risk matter that must be handled extremely carefully if the buyer is to avoid catastrophe. Captains of industry have gone down in flames because of disastrous buying decisions. Jill Barad of Mattel comes to mind, for example. When her 1998 decision to acquire The Learning Company turned out to be a financial debacle, Barad—a highly admired businesswoman who'd risen to CEO of a world-class corporation at the age of 40—got the boot.

In this chapter, I'll provide an overview of the buying process, explain what motivates different types of buyers, offer criteria for choosing an acquisition target, and provide guidance on how to work with advisers.

REASONS FOR CATASTROPHIC OUTCOMES

Hundreds of factors can cause a deal to buckle—personality problems between buyer and seller, inability to negotiate key points, discovery of unexpected problems during due diligence, and so on. But when a deal goes through and the outcome turns out to be catastrophic for the buyer, it's virtually always the result of a big mistake. Most of these errors involve poor due diligence or inadequate planning for post-merger integration problems. I'll explore these issues in great depth in later chapters, but in the meantime, these are some points to keep in mind:

Bad due diligence. Sometimes the buyer doesn't pick up on a seller's fraudulent or other criminal activities. A classic case is Cendant Corp., Henry Silverman's merger of Hospitality Franchise Systems with CUC International. (See chapter 6 for the full story.) More often it's a failure to look closely enough at trends in the financials. Another big problem area is legal issues, where some sellers have ceded their intellectual property rights. Also, sometimes paperwork is dicey—the seller seems to have strong contractual bonds with customers, but when you look at the small print, you find the documents are dicey.

Information technology integration. Buyers often tend to underestimate the costs of making disparate technology systems work together. Accounting and information systems are two especially tough areas.

Blind spots. Many buyers tend to look at the benefits, not the warning signs. This applies not only to due diligence but also to the entire buying process.

Culture clash. Sometimes the two companies find they just can't get along. To take a classic dichotomy, perhaps it's a difference between East Coast and West Coast ways of doing things. This problem source is notoriously tough to detect until after the deal is done. Cultural differences actually can be a good thing, but they need to be recognized and analyzed.

Power struggles. When the acquired company's founder comes along as part of the deal, trouble is quite likely. The buyer usually wants the sold company's ex-owner or chief executive to be involved but to "know his place"—which doesn't always sit well with the seller.

Overextension. Sometimes the purchaser devotes too much time and resources to an acquisition and thus ignores its existing, core business.

Along the way, I'll spell out the most common pitfalls to help you steer clear of learning them "the hard way."

Those seeking to acquire a business have two main concerns: (1) to make sure the company they purchase is viable, that is, that it can continue to make money without requiring a massive overhaul, and (2) to not overpay. It's all too easy, when you're fired up by enthusiasm over a pending acquisition, to agree to shell out more than a company is worth and then find yourself cash strapped and tactically hobbled afterward, bemoaning your error. But as bad a mistake as that can be, a far uglier scenario is to buy a company and *then* discover that it had been cooking the books and is verging on insolvency, that it had given away all its intellectual property through previous contracts, or that you're holding the liability bag for unresolved legal wrangles. In such cases, the purchase could be your ruination.

This is why savvy, successful buyers spend a tremendous amount of time researching the marketplace. They know the value of patience. In fact, they may spend a few years until they find the right candidate to purchase. (Of course, they also know how to pounce when market conditions or other factors create sterling opportunities.)

And smart buyers, who also know the value of teamwork, rarely work alone. Rather, they build relationships with a variety of advisers, such as investment bankers, brokers, attorneys, and CPAs.

One more point: Wise buyers try to understand how sellers think and operate. That insight will make you a more effective negotiator and collaborator. (See chapter 1 to become familiar with "how the other side lives.")

Buyers of companies fall into three main types, each with its own buying criteria:

Entrepreneurial buyer. A person who wants to run his or her own business.

Strategic buyer. A company that buys another company for long-term reasons—for example, to acquire new technology, obtain talented workers, or expand its customer base.

Financial buyer. A firm that manages pools of capital to buy other companies and generate high rates of return. This type of buyer emerged relatively recently, in the mid-1970s.

Within these categories, of course, each individual buyer has particular criteria, depending on its needs and capacities. Despite these complex variables, however, the buying process should be essentially the same for all three groups. In this chapter, I explain the buying process in terms of how it applies to the three main types of buyers.

BUYER PSYCHOLOGY

Just as many sellers undermine themselves through psychological blind spots, delusions, or biases (see chapter 1), prospective buyers need to be on the lookout for their own foibles. Fortunately, buyers aren't as prone to such problems; after all, you're not selling your "baby," so the emotional stakes are generally not as high.

The most common mental obstacle I've encountered among buyers—*especially* first-timers—is overoptimism and impatience. Those who don't know the ways of M&A tend to be a little more optimistic than experienced players, who realize that in anything as complex as an M&A transaction, nothing goes exactly as planned. Every deal makes you a little smarter, but every deal entails doing something wrong. (Of course, sometimes you hit a home run the first time out—but that can be *even worse*.) You need to anticipate problems so that they don't throw you.

Another common pitfall is becoming too attached to the immediate goal. Once a buyer believes, even subconsciously, that he *has to have* a particular company, that person is in grave danger of overpaying (which is the most common error). Don't fall into the trap of feeling like you're losing if you don't buy this business. Remember, if the acquisition is too pricey, you could do it on your own or find another company.

This is where having a team of seasoned M&A professionals can be your safety net.

ORDER OF OPERATIONS

The same caveats apply to buyers as to sellers concerning the "normal" sequence of an M&A deal: There is no one-size-fits-all process. For starters, each deal is unique. And M&A deals are notoriously complicated and often drawn out. The play of numerous variables can affect the pace of the process and even the order of operations within it. For example, if you find a problem with the seller during due diligence, you might have to hit the pause button for a month or more to allow the seller to work it out (assuming the problem is not a deal killer, of course). So applying a rigid structure of expectations is liable to lead to frustration.

But still, most M&A deals do unfold along similar lines. A buyer would be foolish to start searching out a company to acquire before he knows what his criteria are, for example. Roughly, the buying process is as follows:

ASSESS YOUR MOTIVATION FOR BUYING A COMPANY. Anyone considering the purchase of another company should have clear reasons, and this will determine the game plan. If, for example, you're looking to snatch up a particular company before one of your competitors does, you will proceed differently than if you're looking to gradually diversify your product lines.

DEFINE SCREENING CRITERIA. These criteria will be crucial in guiding your search for suitable acquisition targets, so formulate them carefully. If the search drags on longer than you'd anticipated—as it often does—it's important you hold fast to your conditions rather than yielding to "flexibility" and settling for an imperfect buy.

LOOK FOR DEALS BASED ON YOUR CRITERIA. This phase might be brief or prolonged, depending on a panoply of factors, many beyond your control. Many purchasers engage the services of a broker or other professionals to assist them. In other words, the following step often precedes this one.

HIRE ADVISERS. Some buyers wait until they've found a suitable acquisition target, but I recommend you gather yours earlier.

START PRELIMINARY NEGOTIATIONS (SEE CHAPTER 4). This is when you start to get to know the seller and his company and establish a mutual relationship. Since most M&As involve extensive contact between the two sides after the deal is actualized, you want to be sure you, the seller, and your respective companies are compatible. Once you're sure of your interest in a given company, you will sign a letter of intent (LOI). (See chapter 1 for a full discussion of this document.) Negotiations will continue until the merger agreement is signed (see chapter 7).

VALUATE THE COMPANY (SEE CHAPTER 10). Before you make an offer, you want to calculate what a reasonable price is. Not every buyer will treat this as a separate step, though; in some cases, due diligence will affect your offer amount.

CONDUCT DUE DILIGENCE (SEE CHAPTER 6). It is impossible to overemphasize the importance of this process. Performing due diligence is a make-or-break matter; the majority of bad deals—that is, where the buyer got burned—could have been averted if due diligence had been more thorough or careful.

INTEGRATE THE ACQUIRED RESOURCES (SEE CHAPTER 8). Make sure to allocate substantial time, personnel, and material resources to this critical stage. Integrating an acquired company and its employees into your business is a sensitive, tricky business, and I've seen many buyers damage their prospects by focusing too little on this part of the M&A process.

REASONS FOR BUYING

"Why buy?" is a daunting question, and unfortunately some buyers fail to look deeply enough at their drive to acquire another company. Some motivations for purchasing make more sense than others. Your reasoning should be watertight because once you've bought a company, you're stuck with it. In this section, I'll provide advice for answering this question for each type of buyer.

Entrepreneurial Buyer

Sometimes individuals want to leave the "rat race" of corporate America to start their own business. With your own company, you have more control and freedom for your creativity. Business ownership also can be a status symbol. And of course, there's the potential for making lots of money.

However, starting a new business is not easy and is filled with risk. According to the Small Business Administration (SBA), there is an 85% failure rate for those businesses in which the founder spent less than six months planning the new venture.

But by buying an existing business, according to this line of reasoning, the risk is reduced. In most cases, you'll have a built-in product line and a clientele that can be leveraged.

But buying a going concern is hardly low risk. Remember that when you adopt a company's preexisting strengths, you also inherit its weaknesses.

The things that can go wrong when you buy a company include the following:

- A competitor can take advantage of the changeover to encroach on your business.

- You may have trouble with the employees.

- A top customer may leave, or relationships with suppliers can change for the worse.

- You might be cash starved as a result of the acquisition, which can easily cost tens or even hundreds of thousands of dollars. This money will be illiquid for a while.

- What's more, you'll likely have to borrow money. If you provide a personal guarantee for the money, you will need to pay back the loans if the company fails.

So consider carefully if you believe you control your risk exposure when you purchase an existing business.

Entrepreneurial buyers are prone to another sort of danger: Such buyers are often driven to buy a company on the basis of emotional reasons. That is, he or she desperately wants to own a business and will rush to do so. Of course, this usually means the buyer overpays and fails to negotiate key terms.

Ultimately, the wisest course for an entrepreneurial buyer is to look at a company purchase from an investment standpoint. That is, you need to make a profit based on the price you pay. The best approach is to use the discounted cash flow method (which is explained in detail in chapter 10). Basically, you estimate the cash flows from the business and then discount them to their present value. If this is higher than the purchase price, then the deal is expected to be profitable.

A critical factor for an entrepreneurial buyer is experience. If you have worked in an industry for several years, this certainly provides you perspective. This should help you spot trends, good values, and danger signs. You will also have contacts in the industry. However, I'm not implying you should shun all businesses for which you lack industry experience. If after much homework you think you can make money from the acquisition, then go for it.

An example of someone who leveraged his industry experience into an effective buyout is famed entrepreneur Gordon Cain. By 1987, the 75-year-old Cain had more than 50 years' experience in the chemical industry. Starting out as an engineer in 1933, he'd ascended to executive-level positions for such companies as Standard Perlite, Westaco Mineral, Petro-Tex, and Sterling Chemical (where he was chairman of the board until 1987).

In 1987, the ethylene industry had been in a major, prolonged downturn. But Cain thought it was on the cusp of reviving. So he arranged financing from investment banks to purchase seven plants from four different companies, which he got at fire-sale prices. His personal outlay was $2.3 million—or about 2% of the purchase price.

Cain quickly cut overhead costs and also instituted an employee ownership plan. (He believes strongly in the use of equity to motivate managers). Within a year, the ethylene industry made a comeback, and Cain sold his company to Occidental Petroleum. His $2.3 million equity investment turned into about a $100 million profit.

In addition to profit, entrepreneurial buyers are often motivated by creative challenge. Indeed, some have proven to be among the shrewdest businesspeople, able to recognize opportunity where others would see only a losing proposition.

A classic example of noticing a "diamond in the rough" was Ronald Perelman's experience with Technicolor. Perelman achieved his greatest renown as a flamboyant corporate raider in the 1980s, famous for his $1.8 billion purchase of Revlon in 1985. But perhaps his greatest business triumph came in the 1970s, when Perelman started to pay close attention to a company called Technicolor.

The company, an innovator in color technology, had undertaken a diversification campaign that apparently was dragging down the performance of the company. Sensing an undiscovered gold mine, Perelman put up $2

SKILL SET FOR ENTREPRENEURIAL BUYERS

Buying a company is not for everyone. It often demands incredibly hard work to turn a buyout into a big-time success. And certain personality traits can be invaluable.

To succeed, you should have the ability to do the following:

- Make tough decisions. (Perhaps you'll need to lay off people or sell off divisions.)

- Generate new business. (You have either a gift for sales or the know-how to hire others that do.)

- Live with big risks. (At any time, a business can fail.)

- Cope with strain on personal life. (Long hours and irregular hours can make it difficult to have a normal family life.)

- Deal with crisis. (Crisis is inevitable, and you need to be prepared for just about anything.)

---

million of his own money and borrowed $118 million to purchase Technicolor. With control of the company, Perelman took swift action, selling off five divisions and much real estate, thereby cutting the debt by $68 million.

He then was free to focus exclusively on the film processing business. In meetings with all the major studios, Perelman was tenacious in convincing them to use the Technicolor systems. It was particularly timely since the film industry was undergoing a major change—moving toward multiplex theaters. As a result, there was a boom for film processors.

In 1988, Perelman sold Technicolor to Carlton Communications, pocketing a cool $780 million.

Strategic Buyers

Of the millions of companies in America, most are small businesses—say, with fewer than 100 employees. For the relatively few businesses that grow into midsize or large corporations, M&A is often a key catalyst. (Which isn't to downplay the roles of talented management, top-notch products, dedicated workers, and so on.)

Yet, oddly enough, more companies than not still ignore the benefits of M&A for generating growth. This is a serious oversight, a mistake I hope you don't make.

Let's take a thumbnail example. Suppose your company has sales of $5 million and a 20% annual growth rate. Thus, at this rate, it will take several years to double your sales. Now, suppose you buy a competitor that also has $5 million in sales. Now, you've instantly doubled the size of your company. What's more, there is duplication with both companies, in terms of the sales force, administration, and executive officers. As a result, you are able to realize cost savings of $1 million, thus making the combined company more profitable.

There are many excellent reasons for making a strategic acquisition. The following sections cover the primary ones, but there are literally dozens of other perfectly sound rationales for acquiring another business. Bear in mind that these motivations can apply to companies of every size and type, from small, family-run businesses to megacorporations.

Product Line Expansion

As this implies, this type of acquisition will provide your company with new products or services to sell.

Advantages include the following:

• You avoid the need for R&D investment (time, money, and personnel).

- Your broader product line might attract new customers looking for a complete solution.

- Sales of new products to existing customer base help boost overall growth rate.

- You eliminate a potential competitor (depending, of course, on the degree of similarity among the existing and new product lines).

- You expand your sales channels for existing products as well.

Disadvantages include the following:

- It could be difficult to cross-sell new lines of products. For example, your existing sales force may not have the necessary skills to sell the product effectively. Or your current customer base may not be interested in the new products.

- The acquired company's products could be shoddier than you thought, and you could face serious customer-support problems. (In many cases, it's more effective to start with a joint venture or a strategic alliance to sell new products. This is discussed in more detail in chapter 10.)

Example: Through both internal development and acquisitions (10 since 1985), Macromedia has built an impressive product line of Web tools. One of its products, Flash, is a standard for Web animation. (Flash was the result of the December 1996 acquisition of FutureWave). Macromedia's principal strength was in developing Web tools that make sites look professional and even, well, snazzy. But it lacked tools for enabling high-end performance, such as e-commerce. Meanwhile, a company called Allaire specialized in such types of products, such as ColdFusion, Spectra, Homesite, and JRun. When Allaire went public in September 1999, it raised $52.3 million. By one year later, though, it was suffering growing pains, and its depressed stock price reflected that.

Macromedia—which already had a strong relationship with Allaire, integrating their products—decided to take advantage of the company's reduced valuation. In January 2001, Macromedia agreed to purchase the company for $360 million. The terms: Macromedia will exchange 0.2 shares of its stock and $3 in cash for each Allaire share. Allaire closed up 56 cents to $8.50.

Consolidation / Market Share

This is when you buy a competitor to increase your company's market share.

Advantages include the following:

- You can quickly expand shares without investing in R&D or marketing.
- You eliminate a competitor.
- There is often plentiful opportunity to cut costs, by consolidating staff, facilities, advertising expenses, and so on.
- Because the buyer already understands the target's business, management can fairly easily integrate the acquisition or spot any danger signs should they crop up.

Disadvantages include the following:

- Other competitors of yours could start bidding wars that ultimately will hike up the price tag for acquisitions.
- Employees from two ex-competitors sometimes find it hard to cooperate.

Example: One acknowledged master in building market share is Wayne Huizenga. This high school dropout bought a garbage truck when he was 25 and proceeded to grow the business aggressively by buying out other garbage companies and eventually went public. Realizing that the trash industry was highly fragmented,

Huizenga used his public stock to go on a spending spree, acquiring heaps of other garbage companies. By the time he reached his mid-30s, he'd created Waste Management—the country's largest garbage company.

Huizenga is also known for parlaying the $18 million Blockbuster video rental company into an $8.4 billion empire, which he sold to Viacom in 1994. With his latest venture, AutoNation, he is attempting to consolidate the $1 trillion car-sales market.

Geographic Reach

This is when you buy a company that makes the same or similar products but sells them in different geographic markets.

Advantages include the following:

- You can rapidly penetrate new markets without new investments.
- There are potential cost savings, in terms of consolidating facilities, staff, and advertising expenses.
- Management already has experience in the industry of the target.
- The acquisition results in the elimination of a competitor.
- The new, larger company might gain volume discounts on supplies.

Disadvantages include the following:

- It may be difficult and expensive to manage companies in two (or more) locations, especially if they're far apart, such as transcontinental or transglobal.
- This is a relatively high-risk approach; a better first step might be to engage in a strategic alliance or joint venture.

Example: Smithfield Foods purchased Moyer Packing in April 2001 (for an undisclosed amount). Though Moyer was a relatively small company in the beef processing industry (with about 1.3% of the U.S. market), it had a strong presence in the Northeast—a region in which Smithfield was weak.

Vertical Integration

This is when you buy a company that is not a direct competitor but rather a constituent in your supply chain—such as a supplier or wholesaler or a retailer of your products or services. For Ford Motors, examples of vertical integration targets would be a car dealership or windshield-wiper supplier.

Advantages include the following:

- In some cases, this guarantees a market for your products.
- In some cases, this ensures your access to supplies or materials.
- By securing a reliable supply source, you can respond faster to market forces. Also, you can reduce the availability of supplies for your competitors.

Disadvantages include the following:

- Trying to run two types of companies can prove to be a difficult managerial task.
- Different types of companies often have divergent corporate cultures, which can hinder integration.
- You're locked into procuring supplies from your acquired company even though one of its competitors rolls out superior products.

Example: In vertical integration, a buyer doesn't necessarily have to purchase the whole company. Rather, it could buy a minority interest. This is what MGM did in

February 2001, when it paid $825 million for a 20% share of Rainbow Media, which owns four cable channels: American Movie Classics, Bravo, Independent Film Channel, and We: Women's Entertainment. The deal allows MGM to better distribute its 4,000-plus films to the cable industry.

Diversification

This is when you buy a company in a market sector unrelated to your own.

Advantages include the following:

- It gives you the opportunity to enter an industry that offers better growth prospects than your own.
- You can balance cash flows. For example, a manufacturer of auto parts (which tends to be a very cyclical industry sector) might choose to buy a company in the healthcare field (which is a steady-state growth sector) to offset periodic slackening in auto-part demand.

Disadvantages include the following:

- It can be difficult to manage two different types of businesses.
- Historically, diversification has generally proved to be a failure. During the 1960s, the U.S industry underwent a massive diversification spree. But during the 1970s, these companies suffered.

Example: Tyco International's CEO, Dennis Kozlowski, has pursued a successful conglomerate strategy ever since Tyco hired him in 1976. Since then, he's purchased more than 200 companies and seen the company's earnings increase more than 40-fold. Kozlowski focuses on four, mostly unrelated, industries: fire alarms and security systems, flow control (such as valves), medical products, and semiconductors and fiberoptics. Tyco's successful strategy has been to purchase companies that will be immediately profitable, usually as a result of cost reductions and product synergies. Another element of its M&A success is the company's culture. Steeped in M&A experience, Tyco authorizes thousands of its employees to do an M&A deal. Before any deal is done, an operational person must be in agreement. Moreover, Tyco is constantly looking for acquisition opportunities. One employee spends all his time tracking the 10 best companies in each of Tyco's core business segments. He will also periodically call these companies and indicate that, if they are interested to sell, they should contact Tyco.

Financial Buyers

A financial buyer is usually a small group of seasoned financiers that have much experience in the M&A process. For example, one of the best-known financial buyers, Kohlberg, Kravis & Roberts (KKR), has 14 members.

A typical financial buyer has two types of members:

ANALYSTS. These professionals will research different industries and track a variety of companies that may be possible buyout opportunities.

PARTNERS/ASSOCIATES. These are the deal makers who use the analysts' information to pursue, negotiate, close, and manage buyout deals. Associates' compensation includes salary and bonuses. But partner compensation usually is salary plus 20% of the appreciation of the deals under management.

In addition, most financial buyers work with outside advisers, such as attorneys, CPAs, and investment bankers.

And the main reason for buying? It is to make money for the investors who put money in the buyout fund. Typical investors include state and corporate pension funds, banks, insurance companies, and university endowments. To provide some degree of diversification for their investors, financial buyers typically manage a variety of deals at all times.

Here's a look at the KKR mission statement:

> KKR's business is making equity investments for long-term appreciation, either through controlling ownership of a company or strategic minority positions. As the general partner of the KKR Funds, we make our money just as our investors do, by the increased value over time of our stake in the Funds' investments. Our business is not selling securities to the public or generating fees by providing merger and acquisition advice. Rather, we have a significant portion of our personal assets committed to these investments, and we share the risks of ownership.

KKR's average holding period for owning a company is about eight years. The firm eschews a dogged focus on short-term quarterly results. Instead, KKR is intent on developing the company's long-term prospects, through improving the product line, investing in R&D, seeking efficiencies, and even buying other companies with strategic fits.

Moreover, financial buyers generally don't run a company's day-to-day operations. Rather, they offer the company's managers equity incentives to meet performance targets. The financial buyer usually occupies several seats on a company's board. But they are hardly passive bystanders. In fact, they sometimes become highly involved directing company strategy and tactics—especially for those in trouble. Reputation is vitally important to financial buyers.

Example: Ted Forstmann is one of the original financial buyers. Since he started his firm in 1978, Forstmann has invested more than $15 billion in 27 deals, including such big names as Ziff-Davis Publishing, Dr. Pepper, Topps, and McLeodUSA. Perhaps his most memorable deal was acquiring Gulfstream, a company that was founded in 1958 to build luxury private aircraft and that has passed through a string of owners. In 1978, the well-known airline entrepreneur Allen Paulson bought Gulfstream from aerospace giant Grumman for $52 million. In 1985, he sold the company to Chrysler for a whopping $637 million. In 1990, Forstman arranged with Chrysler CEO Lee Iacocca to buy the company for $850 million. When the economy hit the skids in the early 1990s, Gulfstream went into a tailspin, and by 1993 it was nearly out of cash. Forstmann became de facto CEO. He cut costs, instituted budgeting, and set sales goals. In his most ingenious move, Forstmann decided to buck the decades-old tradition of pitching sales to corporate airline pilots and started to sell directly to CEOs— Gulfstream's true customers. That did the trick, and by 1994 the company was profitable again. When Forstmann took Gulfstream public a few years later, the original investors made 13 times their starting outlay. When General Dynamics bought the company in 1999, Gulfstream had captured more than 50% of the market and had a $4 billion backlog of orders. Profits were about $225 million.

SCREENING CRITERIA

Every prospective buyer needs a fairly precise set of screening criteria to help select buyout prospects. They allow you to move quickly when you find what you want and to winnow out any unsuitable prospects. In a sense, these criteria constitute your buying philosophy, so formulate them carefully.

For example, a Monterrey, California–based restaurant developer might want to focus on the following:

Chinese restaurants based in California . . .

That have gross revenues of at least $1 million per restaurant . . .

And which cost no more than $2 million per restaurant.

To prevent your criteria from becoming a straitjacket, you should look at them periodically and assess whether they still reflect your needs—and whether the underlying performance/earnings measurements still hold up. To continue the example, perhaps you've refined your calculations and now realize that you can make strong profits even if you shell out $2.5 million for a restaurant.

What to Include

Your list of screening criteria can comprise a mere five items, or it can run on for 30 pages. Somewhere in between is sensible—say, no more than several pages. Less than that is likely to be too sketchy and more than that too narrow and confusing. The following example doesn't include all the key criteria, but it covers the main ones (in abbreviated form).

You should also classify each element in terms of whether it's a "deal killer" versus a "non–deal killer." In the example below, the CEO clearly would consider the presence of a union to be a deal killer, whereas it would still be possible to buy a company that is involved with client litigation.

Example: You are the CEO of a Michigan-based advertising agency that focuses on consumer products. Company sales are currently $50 million per year, and the growth rate is 25%. This is a reasonable set of criteria for acquisition target:

INDUSTRY FOCUS. You want to purchase advertising agencies, especially those that focus on consumer products.

PRICE RANGE. You will not pay more than two times estimated sales for the next 12 months.

TYPE OF CONSIDERATION. You have about $10 million in the bank and are willing to use some cash for the acquisitions but want to use stock as most of the consideration. You are also willing to borrow about $10 million more.

SIZE. You want to focus on those companies with at least $5 million in sales.

FINANCIAL METRICS. You want to buy companies that are growing sales and profits by at least 20% each year.

LITIGATION. You want to be careful if a company is involved with litigation with clients. This must be investigated thoroughly.

UNIONS. There must not be any unions.

STRONG MANAGEMENT TEAM. Senior managers must have at least five years' experience in the industry.

The most common error in formulating buying criteria is being unrealistic. For example, if a buyer stipulates that it's looking for companies with revenue growth of 100% per year yet doesn't want to spend more than $1 million, that buyer's search is likely to be prolonged indeed. This is why it's critical to enlist a range of key constituents in the criteria-defining process.

Once again, each category will approach this step somewhat differently:

Entrepreneurial Buyer

First, you need to decide what industry or industries to focus on. Again, it is probably a good idea to focus on the sector(s) in which you have the most experience. But even if you have a wealth of experience in an industry, don't assume you know all you need to. Rather, conduct extensive and intensive research, through the Internet at the library, and by talking to industry contacts.

I recommend you spend at least several months on this type of research. Next, you might want to hire a broker or consultant with experience in the industry to gather advice and collaborate in formulating your buying criteria. You might want to spend 10 to 20 hours with this adviser.

Strategic Buyer

While the CEO should lead the effort to develop the company's screening criteria, he or she should involve other senior managers, such as the chief financial officer, chief counsel, chief technology officer, and the vice presidents of sales, marketing, and distribution. It's also smart to hire an industry consultant or broker to help. As with an entrepreneurial buyer, a strategic buyer should hire these outside advisers for 10 to 20 hours.

If your company can afford an investment banker, it is the best way to go. In fact, it is quite common—especially for public companies—to have an investment bank on retainer at all times. In addition to helping you define screening criteria, the bank will be constantly looking for buyout opportunities. For such services, a retainer's payment is dependent on the amount of services required. For small deals (companies with revenues below $10 million), the retainer can range from $5,000 to $10,000. For bigger deals, the retainer can be $10,000 to $50,000. And if an investment bank locates a buyout opportunity and a sale is eventually closed, the fees can be more than $1 million. (See the section "Investment Bankers" for a fuller explanation of investment bankers.)

If M&A is to play an ongoing, critical role at your company, you should seriously consider creating a position—say, senior vice president of business development—to be filled by someone with extensive M&A experience. This can be invaluable.

Finally, you need to involve your board of directors, soliciting their input on screening criteria. It's the CEO's role to keep the board informed—throughout all stages of the M&A process. He or she should plan on having regular meetings—perhaps monthly. Board members should have timely access to key financial reports to prepare for such meetings. Traditionally, boards of directors played a negligible role in most M&A deliberations. That has changed drastically over the years. By the 1980s, boards of directors were becoming more active. For example, in late 2000, the board of directors at Coca-Cola played the decisive role in preventing the acquisition of Quaker Oats.

If your company has a board of advisers, this group obviously should be consulted. Though they have no legal decision-making authority, these advisers can be a source of valuable guidance and information. In fact, when making new nominations for the directory and advisory boards, look for candidates with M&A experience.

Financial Buyers

Typically, partners and associates spend several months researching various industries to target. They also will hire an investment bank, broker, or industry consultant. Moreover, several of the in-house analysts probably have the background to formulate screening criteria.

LOOKING FOR DEALS

Now that you've established your screening criteria, you can start to hunt for deals. For buyers of all categories, it is good to look at as many companies as possible before you make a purchase. Of course, some large companies—such as Cisco and Tyco—have full-time M&A teams constantly on the prowl for buyout opportunities. But this is likely not practical for entrepreneurial buyers and small to midsize companies.

Even corporations with their own M&A teams employ some combination of the following methods to find prospective buyout opportunities:

PROFESSIONAL HELP. This includes brokers and investment bankers. Such professionals can be expensive, but they're often worth it. In fact, this is the most common way to find acquisition targets. But, as you learned in chapter 1, a broker traditionally represents the seller, not the buyer. So if you use a broker to help find deals or craft a screening criteria list, make sure your contract specifies that the broker represents your interests at all times.

NETWORK OF CONTACTS. Try every possible way to network with industry professionals, such as attorneys, CPAs, management consultants, and investment bankers.

INFORMATION SOURCES. There is an incredible amount of information for buyers to use to locate buyout candidates. Examples include the following:

- Databases. Top electronic databases include Lexis-Nexus, Bloomberg, Dialog, InfoTrac, One-Source, Securities Data, Predicasts, Hoover's, and Dun & Bradstreet.

- *Trade publications.* Leading trade publishers include Penton (*Restaurant Hospitality, Gases & Welding Distributor, Energy & Environmental Management, Material Handling Business*) and Primemedia (*Soybean Digest, American Printer, Concrete Products, Shopping Center World, Refrigerated Transporter*).

CUSTOMERS. If your customers want a new product, perhaps this is an opportunity to buy the company offering the product.

WEB SITE. If you have a site, include the name of the contact for prospective sellers. Also, you could describe your criteria and what type of initial information you are looking for (revenues, profits, industry, and so on).

INCENTIVES. There should be a reward for any employee in your organization who brings a good deal to you. Perhaps you can set up a companywide referral fee program.

PUBLIC SPEAKING. Buyout prospects will likely attend conferences and association events. In addition to attending such events, you can also sponsor them. This may also lead to a speaking opportunity.

HIRING ADVISERS

Hiring advisers is one of the most crucial factors in successful M&A. Here's a look at what to do.

Investment Bankers

In an M&A transaction, you will deal with a mind-numbing array of accounting issues, SEC rules, taxes, valuation, and so on. Unless you have a tremendous capacity to learn such things, you risk many potential problems with a transaction. Also, it is difficult for most companies, which are focused on running business as usual, to conduct proper target searches and due diligence. Because of all this, many companies rely on the services of M&A firms—called investment banks.

In the investment banking world—which is actually quite small—there are two basic levels:

BULGE-BRACKET FIRMS. These are the megafirms that provide one-stop services—everything from private client management to IPOs and M&A. They include the following:

- Morgan Stanley
- Goldman Sachs

- Merrill Lynch
- Citigroup Salomon Smith Barney
- CS First Boston

BOUTIQUE FIRMS. These smaller, specialized firms include the following:

- Thomas Weisel Partners
- Alliant Partners
- WR Hambrecht
- Broadview International

Fees

The fee structure is negotiable and depends on the size and complexity of the deal. And need I mention that the premier investment bankers charge top dollar for their services?

One of the most prominent M&A investment bankers is George Boutros, who works for Credit Suisse First Boston. His reputation for being a hard-nosed bargainer is such that his nickname is "Nikita Khrushchev" because he *will* pound his shoe on the table. In his 15 years in the business, he has been involved in over 300 mergers—most of them in high tech. And he does not come cheap. His typical fee is about $10 million. However, if the deal is large and complex, the fee can escalate. In 1999, he handled the merger between Ascend and Lucent and bagged $40 million.

Deal Attorneys

Besides dealing with investment bankers, you will also spend a considerable amount of time with attorneys. An M&A transaction involves many types of legal documents: letters of intent, merger agreements, confidentiality agreements, and so on. And you also want to ensure that you comply with federal and state regulations. If not, the deal could explode. And there could be shareholder lawsuits.

M&A is a specialized field and requires lots of expertise, so select an attorney who specializes in M&A. This might sound obvious, but too commonly companies use their regular corporate attorney for M&A work—a big mistake.

Some top deal firms include the following:

- Skadden, Arps, Slate Meagher & Flom
- Morgan, Lewis & Bockius
- Latham & Watkins
- Gibson, Dunn & Crutcher
- Brobeck, Phleger & Harrison

If the deal is small—say, under $50 million—you don't necessarily need a top-of-the-line firm. Actually, it may be cost prohibitive, and besides, top firms usually stay away from small deals. Also, a large firm is very unlikely to put a top partner on a smaller deal. Rather, junior or associate attorneys will probably deal with you. With a good small firm, you are likely to get more attention.

But do not select the first one you find. Interview many—say, seven or more. One way to find a good firm is to research the M&A deals in your industry. Then call the companies involved and see what attorneys they used. Were they satisfied with the services?

At all stages, you need to be up front with your attorneys. They assume you are providing all material information required for the merger. They will then implement the information in the legal documents. If the information turns out to be false, it could result in substantial liability—and unnecessary legal fees.

Fees

Even if you use a small firm, the costs will be high. Many firms want an up-front retainer: The firm will estimate the cost of the work and perhaps require several months up front. From this amount, the firm will pay for its legal fees, which range from $100 to $600 per hour.

Some cutting-edge law firms will take alternative forms of compensation. For example, a firm may take a part of its fee as equity in the company. In fact, this may provide an incentive for the attorney to make the deal work smoothly. But this potentially poses a conflict-of-interest problem. Is the advice the attorney providing for his short-term self-interest or for the long-term interests of the firm?

Deal CPAs

A deal CPA is likely be integral to your acquisition. A CPA will help with due diligence (by analyzing financial statements and internal controls), tax structures, financial terms, valuations, and audits. Both the buyer and the seller should have their own CPA firms. If a firm were to represent both sides, that would constitute a major conflict of interest and could expose the deal to potential litigation.

The Big Five accounting firms have the depth to offer all services regarding an acquisition. Of course, the prices are high. And, like a top law firm, you may not get the best people working on your project. But there are definitely strong regional accounting firms that can provide the necessary services to make your deal work.

If a CPA firm makes a mistake, the liability can be huge. In fact, several have gone bust. So before selecting a firm, see if there are any outstanding lawsuits. Just as with attorneys, allocate plenty of time to find a good CPA firm (assuming that your current CPA is not experienced with M&A work). It's a good idea to call companies comparable to yours to find out what firms they used in their M&A deals.

Fees

Fees can range from $100 to $500 per hour. Ethically, the CPA firm is not allowed to take equity in the deal because that could pose neutrality problems, especially with audits.

Interviewing Deal Advisers

Before selecting a deal professional, review a variety of firms and then conduct extensive interviews. Be patient. After all, you will probably rely heavily on outside advisers for your buyout deal. Although talented professionals don't come cheap, always remember this: It's more expensive if a deal fails.

The interview itself should be free. It should make clear whether you and the adviser have personal chemistry. You want a person who is easy to talk to and with whom you could work for many hours. At the same time, you don't want a pushover. You want someone who will persuasively pursue your interests and get you the best possible deal. In other words, someone who seems to have good sales abilities.

Here are some things to ask when you interview CPAs, attorneys, or investment bankers:

HOW ARE YOU COMPENSATED? CAN YOU ESTIMATE THE COSTS OF THIS TRANSACTION? As stated above, investment bankers get monthly fees plus a percentage of the closed deal. Attorneys usually get hourly fees and sometimes equity participation. CPAs can get only hourly fees. When asking each professional about the cost estimate, also get an outline—on a month-by-month basis—that shows what types of services will be performed and roughly how long it will take.

WILL YOU BE THE ONE HANDLING THE CASE, OR WILL IT BE A TEAM? IF SO, WHO WOULD BE INVOLVED, AND

CAN I INTERVIEW THEM, TOO? Make sure you talk to the person who will spend the most time on your deal.

WHEN WAS THE LAST TIME YOU HANDLED A DEAL LIKE THIS? DO YOU FOCUS ON SIMILAR TYPES OF DEALS? WHAT ARE SOME EXAMPLES OF PAST DEALS? Make sure the professionals have done a deal in the past month and at least three over the past year. It is important that these deals be in your industry. Each industry has its own unique aspects—in terms of valuation, regulations, and standards. You are paying lots of money for professional services, and you do not deserve a rookie. You should demand experienced professionals.

IF YOU DO NOT HANDLE THESE TYPES OF DEALS, DO YOU KNOW OTHERS WHO DO? This can provide some good leads. But again, research these leads by interviews.

HAVE YOU HAD ANY DISCIPLINARY ACTIONS BROUGHT AGAINST YOU? IF SO, FOR WHAT? Stay away from professionals who have any infractions. You do not want your deal to be complicated by an adviser who's lacking in ethics.

CAN YOU PROVIDE ANY CLIENT REFERENCES? Get at least three references. And they should be in your industry. Ask the former client, Would you use this adviser again? What were their strengths/weaknesses? Do they understand the industry? Do you think you got a good deal? How responsive were they?

CHAPTER 3

VALUATION

All M&A transactions require some type of valuation. In fact, by definition, the final price is the de facto valuation. But some bargaining is virtually always required before the two sides can settle on a mutually acceptable number. The reason is that the "value" of a company—or anything else, for that matter—is fluid. Depending on your perspective, valuation methods employed, market conditions, and countless other variables, the value can range all over the map. (As I've mentioned before, this is especially true of private companies.)

Unfortunately, a buyer or seller sometimes stints on the valuation process and as a result either pays too much or receives too little for the company. Make sure you don't fall into this trap. Even in the simplest M&A deals, valuation is tricky—indeed, as much art as science is involved. If your valuator is a spreadsheet jockey and nothing more, the end result won't be optimal. So not only is it imperative to *do* a valuation, it's crucial that it be done *well.*

In this chapter, we'll discuss how to properly value a company, either your own or an acquisition target. One topic is how to hire a valuator—yes, I'm talking about yet *another* paid adviser, but one that's well worth the outlay. I'll explain the three main valuation methods, provide step-by-step demonstrations of their application, and discuss their pros and cons. We'll also look at a few related aspects, such as potential value, Wall Street's role, and a "collar" in the contract to protect yourself from losing money because of market fluctuations.

But first, here are a few key principles and tips for you to keep in mind:

- There is no "correct" method of valuation. It's a good idea to use all methods to see which one makes the most sense for your company.

- If possible, the seller should valuate his company *before* contacting potential buyers. (In fact, it's smart to have the company valuated on a regular basis, such as every several years. This helps when it's time to sell, and it's also a good move for estate purposes.)

- Pay for a top-notch, third-party valuator. These professionals' services don't come cheap, but you get what you pay for. I've seen too many sellers (and buyers) cut corners on the valuation expense and regret it later. (In some cases, I've seen reports that were filled with spelling errors.)

- Be prepared to negotiate extensively about this issue. Many factors can be brought into play that affect how the parties interpret a company's underlying value.

- Sellers should resist the very common tendency to overvaluate their companies. If their expectations are unrealistic, a compromise might not be attainable. This is one of the main reasons to use a third-party professional.

THE HIGH PRIEST OF VALUE

One guy who really understands the workings of valuation is Warren Buffett. His inspiration and guiding light was Benjamin Graham, whose *The Intelligent Investor* is the definitive guide to value investing. In 1962, Buffett purchased a textile mill called Berkshire Hathaway, a dying business that nonetheless had nice cash flow. He used that money stream to buy other companies, generally in the insurance industry at first and gradually branching out.

Buffett's conservative and seemingly slow-paced approach to investing certainly has worked. A $10,000 investment in Berkshire Hathaway in 1965 would be worth about $50 million today. As for Buffett himself, he's worth about $30 billion.

The Graham/Buffett philosophy is straightforward: The way to make money when buying companies or investing in general is to find undervalued properties. If the fundamentals are sound, the market will eventually come around again, and the price will reflect this. In other words, it's a long-haul approach. As Buffett puts it, "Price is what you pay. Value is what you get."

Of course, the value approach to investing is hardly the only way to go. Another, equally well-recognized and often successful path is "growth" investing. In this method, the buyer seeks out companies—often with high asking prices—that offer tremendous growth opportunities. This exciting, fast-in–fast-out style was very much in favor during the technology boom years, but after that market toppled, Buffett seems to be the tortoise chuckling at the hare. For the most part, buyers are looking to find a company that can add value and get it at a reasonable price.

- The value of a company may depend on who the buyer is. Take, for example, a small company with a great technology but no distribution capacity. Its value may be quite modest, but if Microsoft is looking to buy the operation, then the value would skyrocket. If the identity or nature of the buyer might have a significant impact on the valuation, the seller should return to the valuator to have the numbers adjusted.

- In many situations, the trickiest part is putting a value on intellectual property or other forms of proprietary ownership. When the seller is in a cutting-edge sector of high tech, this problem is paramount. But it applies to a host of other types of companies, too. Sellers should be attentive to this component of their valuation, which isn't necessarily handled well in *any* standard valuation methodology.

- M&A deals take a number of months to complete, during which time valuations can fluctuate substantially. Stock-price gyrations alone can result in significant losses. Unless it's a cash-only deal, it's smart to protect against such swings—for example, by using a "collar."

Before we proceed, let's take a look at two companies, General Motors and Microsoft, to illustrate the enormous discrepancies different approaches to valuation can yield.

No question, GM is an old-line company, with real assets, such as cash, inventories (lots of cars), plant, and equipment. See table 3.1.

Now, let's take a look at Microsoft, which could be seen as GM's equivalent in the "new" economy. See table 3.2.

GM has $303.1 billion in assets, but you'd be surprised at how Wall Street values the company, only $29 billion, whereas Microsoft, with only $52.1 billion in assets, garners a Wall Street valuation to the tune of $333 billion.

A VALUATION LIBRARY

In addition to the Graham book mentioned in this chapter, the following books are solid resources for anyone who wants to delve into valuation methodology. Be forewarned, though: Some of these cost a pretty penny. The undiscounted price of the Pratt text, for example, is $95 (though you can get it for a lot less online and elsewhere).

Valuing a Business, 4th edition, by Shannon P. Pratt, Robert F. Reilly, and Robert P. Schweihs (McGraw-Hill Professional Publishing, 2000)

Valuation for M&A: Building Value in Private Companies, by Frank C. Evans and David M. Bishop (John Wiley & Sons, 2001)

The Small Business Valuation Book, by Lawrence W. Tuller (Adams Media Corporation, 1998)

The Valuation of Information Technology: A Guide for Strategy Development, Valuation, and Financial Planning, by Christopher Gardner and Chris Gardner (John Wiley & Sons, 2000)

Why the big discrepancy? Primarily because traditional accounting measures tend to understate modern types of assets, such as intellectual property. In the case of Microsoft, it has a tremendous amount of technology assets that produce high-margin profits. As for GM, it has many fixed costs and much lower margins.

Clearly, multiple approaches to determining value are necessary to suit the demands of different situations. In the case with GM, Wall Street is not looking at asset value. A big reason is that it would take a huge amount of capital to take over the company. Rather, Wall Street has seemed to focus on the company's earnings stream to determine the ultimate value of the company.

TABLE 3.1.
GM's BALANCE SHEET, 2000

Current Assets

Cash and equivalents	$ 10,284.00
Receivables	$135,002.00
Inventories	$ 10,945.00
Other current assets	$ 52,689.00
Total current assets	$208,920.00

Noncurrent Assets

Property, plant, and equipment	$ 66,852.00
Accumulated depreciation	$ 32,875.00
Intangibles	$ 7,622.00
Other noncurrent assets	$ 52,581.00
Total noncurrent assets	$ 94,180.00
Total assets	**$303,100.00**

TABLE 3.2.
MICROSOFT'S BALANCE SHEET, 2000

Current Assets

Cash and equivalents	$ 4,846.00
Receivables	$ 3,250.00
Inventories	$ 0.00
Other current assets	$22,212.00
Total current assets	$30,308.00

Noncurrent Assets

Property, plant, and equipment	$ 4,314.00
Accumulated depreciation	$ 2,411.00
Intangibles	$ 0.00
Other noncurrent assets	$19,939.00
Total noncurrent assets	$21,842.00
Total assets	**$52,150.00**

LOOK TO WALL STREET

Technical valuations and Wall Street verdicts don't always correspond. When an acquisition is announced, Wall Street's response can be hard to predict. For example, if Wall Street thinks the acquirer paid too steeply, the stock will fall. So when valuating a prospective acquisition, investment bankers try to gauge Wall Street's reaction, and their final figures are affected by such considerations. The best IBs have the experience and intuition to be accurate more often than not.

Wall Street likes to see synergies and money-generating deals. One way to look at it is whether an acquisition is accretive or dilutive to the buyer. For a public company, an accretive merger means that the transaction will result in an increase in earnings per share (EPS). A dilutive transaction results in the opposite. From this perspective, there are a lot of bad acquisitions.

Example: Citrix Systems, a company that develops networking software, was flush with $400 million in cash in early 2001. Wanting to take advantage of low valuations in the tech sector, Citrix decided to purchase Sequoia Software, which develops portal applications. It was an all-cash offer of $184.6 million, which amounted to $5.64 per share, a 13% premium over the current market value.

In 2000, Citrix had revenues of $470.4 million and net income of $94.5 million. Sequoia had revenues of $6.1 million and a net loss of $6.23 million. In the first year of the acquisition, Citrix forecast about 5 cents to 7 cents in earnings per diluted share. But by 2002, Citrix expects to realize the synergies of the deal, and the acquisition should become accretive.

But Wall Street was skeptical. On the news, the stock price of Citrix fell 81 cents to $19.81. Then, in June 2001, when Citrix announced that the integration of the acquisition was proceeding smoothly and the results would meet expectations, the stock price surged $4.25, to $27.96.

HIRING AN APPRAISER

As I stressed earlier, it's very smart to hire an expert to valuate a company that's up for sale. Keep in mind that even pros such as Buffett choose to employ outside advisers—investment bankers, brokers, CPAs, or appraisers—who can provide a neutral, third-party valuation of a company. Doing it yourself isn't the way to go: As a buyer or seller, you are biased and may not see important factors that can have a substantial impact on the overall valuation of an M&A transaction.

No question, having your own broker or investment banker perform the valuation is highly dubious. Since these advisers' fees are tagged to the ultimate selling price, there's clearly a potential conflict of interest. And as for having your current CPA do it, the downside is that valuating companies is probably not their line of business.

By going with a good-quality valuation firm, you can be ensured of a thorough, professional job, one that incorporates all the valuation methods. The final "product" will be a very fine-looking professional report—nicely bound, printed on good paper, well written, and well presented. If you're a seller, presenting such a document to a potential buyer goes a long way to demonstrate that you're not messing around. It contributes to a better negotiating position.

Now, the bad news is that high-quality valuations usually run from $25,000 to $50,000. Consider closely before you decide you can't afford that much; ultimately, you might not be able to afford to *not* pay that much.

There is a relatively small group of top-notch specialists. The four best-known ones are the following:

- Houlihan Lokey
- Houlihan Smith
- Geneva
- Equico

But this is just the top tier. There are numerous other appraisers out there, and many provide superb service. But just like brokers, small-business appraisers are unregulated. Just about anyone can claim to be an "expert" and set up his or her own operation. So you'll need to do a good amount of research before selecting an appraiser. Here are some tips:

- A good starting place is to contact the National Association of Certified Valuation Analysts *(www .cacva.com)*.

- Another excellent source is the American Institute of Certified Public Accountants *(www.aicpa .org)*. You want to hire a business appraiser who is also a CPA, as many of them are. CPA training and certifications are strenuous. Also, it is even better if you can find a CPA that can provide a broad range of M&A services, such as due diligence, financial projections, and valuation.

- Interview at least several small-business appraisers. If you're going with the high-powered firms listed above, you could interview all of them. But if you're opting for a smaller firm, approach the decision process with some healthy skepticism. Certainly, they should charge less than the big players, but make sure to get several samples of their work, ask to call their clients, and be proactive in your questioning. In addition to the questions below, find out how many of their clients actually get bought, for example.

- Questions to ask include:

  "What do you charge?" Try to get an estimate of the whole project. A business appraiser will typically charge on an hourly basis—ranging from $100 to $500 per hour. Obviously, don't allow the fee to be based on the value of the transaction.

**"What industry do you specialize in?" and
"On what size businesses do you focus?"**
Make sure the appraiser has done at least five
deals of your company's size and industry during
the past year.
"What valuation methods will you use?"
Make sure he or she uses the three main methods
(as described below).

MOVING TARGET

Since deals often involve months of negotiation, the relative valuation is likely to change—especially if the deal
involves stock as payment. Sometimes the valuation can
change radically. This happened to a variety of deals
during the bear market of 2000–2001.

Example: In January 2001, NetIQ agreed to purchase
WebTrends. In the deal, NetIQ agreed to exchange 0.48 of
common shares for each share of WebTrends, which put a
$1 billion valuation on WebTrends.

But from January to April, NetIQ's stock price
plunged from $75 to $21. And, since WebTrends' value was
tied to NetIQ, its own stock price plunged by an equal
amount. In fact, several days before the deal closed, NetIQ
announced a third-quarter profit warning. When the deal
closed, the value of WebTrends was about $250 million.
That's a 75% fall! Had WebTrends had the foresight to set
their value in stone while the deal was negotiated, they
would not have missed out on hundreds of millions of dollars. The way to peg a valuation is called "putting a collar"
in the merger agreement.

Example: In February 2001, Motorola agreed to buy
Blue Wave Systems, a telecom software developer, for an
all-stock purchase totaling around $165 million—that is,
approximately 7 million shares, which were trading at
$23 at the time of the deal. The deal had a collar. That

is, there was a minimum stock price of $20.77 and a cap of $25.38. If the stock fell below $20.77, more shares would have to be issued to bring the deal price back up. And if the stock price exceeded $25.38, then the number of shares would be reduced. So the deal has to be worth between $155 million and $175 million. This protected both sides.

Another approach is for the buyer to offer some cash—say, between 10% and 20%—as a part of the purchase price. This helps reduce valuation problems when markets are volatile, and such extra stability may make the seller more comfortable.

DISCOUNTED CASH FLOW METHOD

Now we'll work our way through the three principal valuation methods—discounted cash flow, comparative analysis, and net asset value. Discounted cash flow (DCF) is what they teach you in business school; academically, this is the method. And in fact, DCF is the most widely used in M&A transactions.

However, DCF doesn't always give you what you need because cash flows are sometimes all over the map and very difficult to estimate.

Essentially, DCF looks at an acquisition as a pure financial investment. The buyer will estimate future cash flows and discount these into present values. Why is future cash flow discounted? The reason is that a dollar in the future is at risk of being worth less than a dollar now. Of course, there's inflation—but that component is incorporated in the base federal discount rate. The real risks are business based: For example, suppose the acquired company loses a contract, a new competitor enters the picture, or an adverse regulation is passed. These are the probabilities you need to protect yourself against by discounting cash flows.

As with anything, the higher the potential risk, the more you should be compensated. For example, if you put $100,000 in the bank, your rate of return will be relatively low because there is really no risk. Regardless of what happens to the bank, the federal government will guarantee you will get your money back. But suppose you buy stock in a high-tech company. Well, of course, a lot can happen, good or bad. And to reflect this riskiness, your potential rate of return should be higher than what you get from a risk-free investment.

The essence of DCF is the greater the risk, the bigger the discount.

To understand the DCF process, we'll look at Symantec's acquisition of Axent Technologies in July 2000. Symantec is a leading developer of software utilities and security applications. As of March 1999, the company had annual revenues of $592.6 million. A year later, the company had $745.7 million. Axent was a leading provider of high-end security products for major corporations. From 1998 to 1999, sales had increased from $101 million to $112.8 million. In 1998, profits were $6.4 million, but the company sustained a loss of $6.9 million a year later. For the first six months of 2000, sales were $64.3 million, which was up from $47.8 million in the same period in 1999. During this time, the company went from a loss of $8.2 million to a profit of $1.2 million.

What these numbers demonstrate is that the company's cash flows were quite erratic, which meant the discount rate would have to be fairly high.

Donaldson, Lufkin and Jenrette (DLJ) performed the DCF analysis on Axent as follows:

Step 1—Cash Flows

The buyer (or other valuator) first will estimate the future cash flows of the target company.

DLJ used information provided by Axent—financial statements, internal budgets, and projections—for the cash flows. (In the filing, Symantec did not disclose these figures, so we'll just use round hypothetical numbers below.) DLJ also talked with management to discuss assumptions, such as the expected growth rate in the company's business and the level of expenses required to maintain this growth. DLJ factored this information in its spreadsheet and generated projected cash flows.

First of all, look at a company's income statements for at least the past three years. If a company is, in fact, less than three years old, then you should be more skeptical about projections. With such a sketchy track record, it's a good idea to reduce the growth rate—say, by 20% or so.

However, net income is profit from an accounting perspective. It is not the actual cash flow of a company. To determine the cash flow, you need to adjust the net income figures. Here are the steps:

ADD ANY NONCASH ACCOUNTING EXPENSES TO NET INCOME. This would include depreciation and amortization. Such expenses are required by the accounting profession to reflect the fact that assets—such as plant and equipment—typically lose their value over time because of wear and tear and obsolescence.

ADD ANY EXCESS CASH PAID TO THE OWNER. This applies mostly to private companies, where the owner wants to minimize net income in order to lower taxes. To do so, an owner will attempt to take out cash from the company, either as added compensation or even personal expenses. But after the acquisition, the owner won't (or certainly shouldn't) be able to take these expenses.

SUBTRACT ANY PAYMENTS THAT MAY NOT BE REFLECTED ON THE BALANCE SHEET. This would include payment of principal on a loan or the purchase of long-term

assets (which will last over a year), such as plant and
equipment. A calculation is shown in table 3.3.

TABLE 3.3
ADJUSTING FOR OFF–BALANCE SHEET PAYMENTS

Net income (1998)	$500,000
Plus depreciation	$100,000
Plus amortization	$ 10,000
Total	$610,000
Purchase of new assets	$100,000
Payment of loan principal	$ 90,000
Total	$190,000
Owner personal expenses	$100,000
Current owner salary	$200,000
Reasonable owner salary	–$100,000
Total	$200,000
Total cash	$1 million

Here's a look at the (hypothetical) numbers after
making the adjustments:

1998	1999	2000
$1 million	$1.5 million	$2 million

Next, you need to determine a growth rate for these
cash flows. Here are the main approaches:

ITEM BY ITEM. This method is time consuming, but it is
definitely the recommended approach in most situations.
For each year, you will estimate the amount for each element of the cash flow forecast (depreciation, loan repay-
ments, and purchases). This will help you concentrate on

the different types of factors that will likely affect your future cash flows.

Prior growth rate. From 1998 to 2000, cash flows have increased 100% or an average of 50% per year. If you are convinced this is a reasonable growth rate for the company in the future, you might continue to use the 50%. Remember, though, that typically the growth rate of a company will begin to slow down as it matures.

Industry growth rate. Or, you might want to use the growth rate from an analyst's industry growth forecast.

Step 2—The Term

The buyer will determine how many years will be used in the analysis. A rule of thumb is to use a three- to five-year time period. As for DLJ, it used a three-year time frame. In high-tech acquisitions, a shorter period is typically used because it's difficult to estimate longer-term cash flows in highly volatile conditions. For mature industries, a term of about five years is appropriate.

Step 3—Discount Rate

Since the point of an acquisition is to receive future income, the DCF method will try to establish the present value of the future cash flows. This is accomplished with the discount rate, which is a percentage based on the inherent risk of the company. The higher the risk, the higher the discount rate.

At the base of the discount rate is the risk-free rate—generally, the rate of return on a Treasury security (on which the risk of default is essentially zero). If you are looking at a forecast for five years, for example, then you would take the Treasury bond that matures in five years.

On top of the risk-free rate, you add a premium for the risk. In his classic book on valuation—*Valuing a Business* (1989)—Shannon P. Pratt sets forth this scale for risk premiums:

6%–10%. These are for top-quality companies that have strong earnings, great management, and high predictability. Examples are Microsoft and General Electric.

11%–15%. These are also for companies with strong earnings and great management; however, there is more intense competition. Examples are Gateway computers and E*TRADE.

16%–20%. This level applies to companies with strong earnings growth but where barriers to entry are low and the competition is intense. You tend to see this in such industries as software, advertising, consulting, printing, and restaurants.

21%–25%. This is for small, closely held business that are heavily dependent on the founder. This would be a business of less than $50 million in annual sales.

26%–30%. This is for a service business with only one owner.

Keep in mind that these are estimates. A discount rate can be subject to negotiation in an M&A transaction.

As for the Axent transaction, the discount rates actually used for the calculations ranged from 17.5% to 19.5%. This resulted in an actual price range of $33 to $44. (The reason I'm not providing the discount rate formula is because it's a little scary—quite mathematically daunting, with a lot of "moving parts"—and any good spreadsheet or financial calculator will compute it for you.)

Interestingly enough, the agreed-on acquisition price was actually $32 per share, which was below the range. In other words, valuation techniques will not provide exact answers, but they do give the parties some type of basis on which to make a judgment. Ultimately, the price is based on negotiation.

Pros, Cons, and Tips for Discounted Cash Flow Method

ESTIMATES. As you can see, constructing a DCF valuation requires a variety of estimates: cash flows, discount rate, and term. A change in any of these variables can potentially have a significant impact on the valuation. Look at the Axent acquisition. A discount range of 17.5% to 19.5% resulted in a price range of $33 to $44.

PROJECTIONS. The internal projections of the target company will likely be inflated. So temper these numbers by considering worst-case scenarios.

SYNERGIES. When two companies merge, there might be synergies. For example, the combined company may have cost savings as well as increased revenues (because of cross-selling products). In the Axent transaction, these synergies were included in the cash flow forecasts. Synergies usually enhance the value of the cash flow, which benefits the overall valuation and the seller, which is why some buyers want to exclude this—but a smart seller will insist.

COMPARATIVE ANALYSIS

This method is also very common, especially with companies that don't have a lot of traditional metrics (such as earnings). DCF is impossible in some industries, such as biotech and other emerging technology companies.

To explain this method, houses provide a useful equivalent. Just as home sellers will often gauge the value of their homes by researching the recent sale prices of similar homes in their neighborhood, the same principle applies to companies. The valuation system is called comparative analysis. (Whereas DCF would be equivalent to computing the amount of rental income a property could generate.)

We'll look at the case where Microsoft purchased Great Plains Software in December 2000. Great Plains is a leading developer of business applications—such as HR, accounting, and so on—for the small-to-medium-size company market. In 2000, the company had sales of $194.9 million, which was up from $134.9 million. During this time, net income went from $13.4 million to $13.3 million.

Goldman Sachs performed the analysis as follows:

Step 1—Defining the Industry

This is often harder than it sounds. Some companies have products or services that span several industries. In the case of Great Plains, however, its software had a definable focus: small-to-medium-size business applications.

Goldman Sachs focused not only on small to midsize players but also included major players, such as Oracle and IBM. While these companies are not necessarily great fits, it can still be helpful to see how big companies compare to smaller companies. For example, in the Great Plains example, there is a significant gap in valuation between small/midsize players and the majors.

Goldman Sachs also opted to analyze international companies. While this is not always included as a matter of course, it can be a highly useful comparison.

Goldman Sachs looked at only those companies that were public (and thus had a market value) or companies that have been sold within the past year. Here's the list:

Enterprise Applications Companies

- International Business Machines
- JD Edwards Company
- Microsoft
- Oracle
- PeopleSoft
- SAP
- Siebel Systems

Domestic Midmarket Companies

- Citrix Software
- Epicor Software
- Hyperion Solutions
- Interact Commerce
- Made2Manage Systems
- Mapics
- Onyx Software
- Pivotal
- QAD
- Symix

International Companies

- Damgaard A/S
- Exact Holding NV
- Navision Software A/S
- Sage Group PLC

Goldman Sachs has access to world-class financial databases, but this does not mean you are at a disadvantage. In fact, the above information could have been obtained by doing industry searches on such Web sites as MSN Investor *(investor.msn.com)* and Hoover's *(www.hoovers .com).* As for finding information on companies—even private firms—that have been sold recently, this is available from Mergerstat *(www.mergerstat.com).*

Step 2—Financial Ratios

Goldman Sachs compiled financial information on all the companies (again, this is available from MSN Investor or Hoover's) and then computed ratios for the three industry segments (these are expressed as an average and a median). The following percentages are based on numbers not included above:

Closing Share Price as a Percentage of the 52-Week High Share Price (Average/Median)

Great Plains	42.6%
Enterprise Applications	53.1%/50.1%
Midsize	27.7%/28.0%
International	25.9%/21.7%

On the day before the acquisition, Great Plains was selling at 42.6% of its 52-week high. Major enterprise software companies were selling for about 50% of their highs. So they had fallen by less than the rest of the industry, as indicated by the low percentages for midsize (and international) companies. Thus, on average, the shareholders of Great Plains were getting a valuation that was a premium to the midsize companies:

Equity Market Capitalization (in Millions) (Average/Median)

Great Plains	$724.9 million
Enterprise Applications	$88,630.8/$40,241.3
Midsize	$1,806.7/$609.7
International	$576.4/$104.1

Based on market capitalization, the valuations of the enterprise application companies are not good comparables since the difference in value is very large. Great Plains does, however, fall within the valuation range of midsize companies and is on the high side for international companies:

Enterprise Value (in Millions) (Average/Median)

Great Plains	$673.0
Enterprise Applications	$87,856.6/$39,483.3
Midsize	$1,768.6/$557.2
International	$530.3/$137.5

Enterprise value is calculated as market capitalization plus cash minus debt. We saw above that Great Plains has more cash than debt, so its market capitalization is larger than its enterprise value. Cash is subtracted because in an acquisition the acquirer gets all the cash, which can then be used to immediately pay down debt. By using enterprise value, there is little difference between the analysis of looking at the companies on the basis of market capitalization or enterprise value:

Multiple of Enterprise Value to Revenues for 2000 (Average/Median)

Great Plains	4.0x
Enterprise Applications	8.3x/6.3x
Midsize	4.7x/3.7x
International	3.4x/1.4x

The current valuation of Great Plains is within the parameters for midsize companies and higher than international firms. Why the gap with international firms? There are many possible reasons: The overseas markets may be growing slowly. Or the United States may have a more competitive software industry. Also, the financial markets in the United States are larger and have more buying power to create higher valuations:

**Multiple of Enterprise Value to Revenues for 2001
(Average/Median)**

Great Plains	2.6x
Enterprise Applications	6.6x/5.1x
Midsize	3.7x/2.9x
International	2.4x/0.8x

Goldman Sachs used the Institutional Brokers Estimate System (IBES) for all the revenues estimates for 2001. This chart is very useful to Great Plains. The 2.6x multiple is below the range for midsize companies. This means that Great Plains is expected to grow faster than its peer group and deserves a higher valuation than its current one:

**Price-to-Earnings Multiple for Calendar Year 2000
(Average/Median)**

Great Plains	37.6x
Enterprise Applications	33.6x/23.2x
Midsize	51.8x/45.4x
International	24.1x/20.7x

Based on the PE ratio, Great Plains appears to be undervalued compared to its peers. This is further evidence for Great Plains to get a higher valuation:

**Price-to-Earnings Multiple for Calendar Year 2001
(Average/Median)**

Great Plains	27.6x
Enterprise Applications	45.6x/43.2x
Midsize	30.4x/30.6x
International	18.0x/17.7x

Great Plains is undervalued on the basis of year 2001 PE ratios, too.

Step 3—Negotiation

In the first half of November 2000, Great Plains and Microsoft held preliminary negotiations for a buyout. After both sides approved a nonbinding list of acquisition terms, due diligence ensued. By December 20, the parties had an agreement: Microsoft would purchase Great Plains for about $1.1 billion, which represented a 29.3% premium over its current stock price.

Pros, Cons, and Tips for the Comparative Method

AVAILABLE DATA. Some industries have a dearth of public companies or recent purchases. As a rule of thumb, there should be at least 20 comparables that are public or sold within the past year.

SELECTIVITY. If you happen to omit some companies in your analysis that have relatively lower valuations, this would skew the results upward. In fact, this is often done intentionally to predetermine a better result. But don't be tempted. This is fraud and can result in a lawsuit—another good reason to find an outside adviser to do the valuation.

RANGE. If your company has been consistently outperforming the competition, you have a much stronger argument for the top part of the valuation range. This was the case with Great Plains.

MARKET DROP. Suppose the market collapses. Even if your company is still performing well, Wall Street will punish all companies in your industry. In such circumstances, the comparative method may be a poorer choice than DCF, which is based on the earnings of your company.

NET ASSET VALUE METHOD

Of the three main methods, net asset value is a distant third in popularity. Actually, it's considered more of a verifier than a primary valuation approach. The attitude is "Let's try this one out and see if we're in the same neighborhood."

But for some companies with a large amount of high-priced assets, NAV might be a useful gauge. A buyer is unlikely to buy a company if he or she can find the same types of assets for a lower price. This technique was popular during the 1980s, when investment bankers would often look at the breakup value of a company. That is, how much would you receive if the assets were sold off?

The types of businesses that would likely be rich in assets would include the following:

- Energy
- Real estate
- Natural resources
- Manufacturing
- Transportation

When estimating the asset value, these are the main types of areas to look for:

- Cash
- Real estate
- Equipment
- Leases
- Leasehold improvements
- Mineral rights
- Accounts receivables
- Inventory
- Customer list

- Investments
- Patents/copyrights/licenses

Example: ABC is a trucking company that owns five vehicles and its real estate: its land and office building. It also has outstanding accounts receivables and cash in the bank. You hire an appraiser to estimate the value of the assets. The accounts receivables and cash balance are straightforward, of course, but the rest requires more analysis. For example, the land was purchased 10 years ago for $300,000, but real estate values have soared since then. So the appraiser needs to estimate the land's current fair market value, which means looking at comparable sales of land in the last year or so. As for the trucks, the appraiser will probably use the Kelly Blue Book and then adjust the prices on the basis of their condition. Furniture and improvements will probably have lost some value, and the appraiser will adjust the value accordingly:

- Five trucks: $300,000 (this is after the loans are paid off)
- Land and building: $1 million
- Furniture/improvements to the building: $100,000
- Bank account: $100,000
- Accounts receivables: $150,000

From the value of total net assets—$1,650,000—the appraiser will subtract outstanding liabilities. The result will be the net asset value of the company.

Pros, Cons, and Tips for the Net Asset Value Method

SHIFTING VALUES. Some asset values fluctuate widely. For example, suppose you value a company's inventory at $500,000. But a new competitor comes on the scene and renders the company's product basically obsolete, making it impossible to sell any of your inventory. This asset suddenly becomes zero.

TIME TO LIQUIDATION. When computing the asset values, it can give you a false sense of timing. Inventory and accounts receivable can be converted into cash quickly, but that's not so of real estate, leases, equipment, and customer lists. These assets may take quite some time to sell—perhaps more than a year. And during this time, the values could be falling.

UNDERESTIMATE OR OVERESTIMATE VALUE. The net asset valuation method can underestimate—or even overestimate—the value of your business. Let's continue with the ABC example from above. Based on the asset method, the company is worth roughly $1,650,000. Now, suppose that the company generates $500,000 in profits each year. However, it's normal for a trucking company to sell at five times its profits, which would value ABC at $2.5 million. If the net asset value were used for the sale, it would mean the seller would forgo nearly a million bucks.

POTENTIAL VALUE

If a company has no revenues, how can a reasonable value be determined? Through traditional methods, the value is close to zero. But in the high-tech world, the value could, in some cases, be billions. Because of this, some acquisitions seem very strange on the surface. But some of these buys are actually quite savvy. The buyer is looking at the potential value of a seller.

Suppose a seller is developing a cutting-edge technology that will be a full year ahead of the competition, and you're sure you could roll it out within six months. If you buy this company, you can offer the product to your customers and generate about $200 million in revenues for the first year, $400 million in the second year, and so on.

With these estimates, you can do a DCF analysis. You can also perform a comparable method analysis, providing that similar types of companies are either public or have been sold in the past year. But the net asset value method has very little use because the vast majority of the tech company's assets are intangibles, such as patents and valuable employees.

One example is Ciena's purchase of Cyras Systems, which had no revenues, for a stunning $2.6 billion in December 2000.

Ciena itself had experienced rapid growth from 1997 to 2000, with sales surging from $373.8 million in 1997 to $858.8 million in 2000. It was aggressively looking for ways to expand its technology's bandwidth—and to cut costs.

Meanwhile, Cyras had developed a key bandwidth management product. Ciena management considered Cyras to be a good strategic fit. It would provide a broader product line that meets the needs of next-generation technologies. And due diligence showed that prospective customers were very interested in Cyras solutions. Beyond this, Ciena saw Cyras as having an entrepreneurial vision—one that meshed well with Ciena's.

Credit Suisse First Boston conducted the valuation analysis. In all, CS First Boston looked at 30 publicly traded companies in the communications industry. One comparable that likely had a big influence was Cisco's purchase of Cerent for $6.7 billion. At that time, Cerent had zero revenues but a year later contributed about $700 million in revenues. Interestingly enough, CS First Boston did not perform a DCF analysis. The main reason was the difficulty in coming up with projections for future cash flows.

Initially, Wall Street was very skeptical of the deal, and Ciena's stock immediately plunged $23 to $73.19, followed the day after by another $9.38 nosedive.

Interestingly enough, in late 2001, Ciena admitted that it paid too much for Cyras and took a whooping $1.72 billion write-off.

CHAPTER 4

PRELIMINARY NEGOTIATIONS

Negotiation is an integral part of selling or purchasing companies. As such, it should not be dreaded but seen as an opportunity to get the best deal possible and also to become familiar with the other side. The end result is not only mutual agreement on terms both parties can live with—a set of acceptable compromises—but also a working relationship.

Any deal should be a "win-win." A lopsided victory causes ill will and can ultimately damage the acquisition. After all, the buyer and seller often must live with each other after the transaction. So always be honest and reasonable during deliberations. After all, your reputation encompasses more than this one transaction.

Nevertheless, it is perfectly acceptable and natural to try to get the best deal you can. As long as you don't mislead or unfairly manipulate the other side, you're permitted to play hardball. Competition is an integral element in any deal making, and a certain amount of posturing is to be expected. Sellers try to hype their companies' positive attributes to drive up the price, and buyers emphasize the faults they uncover in order to pull the price down. Some exaggeration is an expected element in this "dance."

It is essential that you do your homework *before* negotiations kick off. When it comes to negotiating, the phrase "knowledge is power" is the best motto. One sure-fire way to undermine your chances for the best deal is to head into negotiations cold.

Also, M&A negotiations are very complex matters, so unless you're a professional negotiator, this is when your adviser(s) are critical to ensure a good outcome for you. Before you meet with any prospective buyer or seller, you need to establish that all the players on your negotiating team are clear about what will and won't be acceptable.

In this chapter, we'll take a look at negotiating strategies to help maximize your position in an M&A deal—whether you're the buyer *or* the seller. As you will see, the process is very subjective, and there are different styles. Yet, there is an overall structure to all successful preliminary negotiations for M&A transactions. I will walk you through the normal sequence of meetings, describing the pace and tone with which the elements of the deal are discussed, wrangled over, and decided.

After this, I describe in detail the terms of a letter of intent (LOI); even though this document isn't completely binding, it is still very important. If the terms of the LOI aren't favorable, it is exceedingly tough to wrest a good end result. Finally, I offer you my condensed guide to effective negotiating.

Generally, the negotiation process flows as follows:

CONTACT FROM THE BUYER. The potential buyer indicates his interest in acquiring the company, and the two parties agree to a face-to-face meeting. (Sometimes it works the other way around, with the seller initiating contact. Either way, brokers are usually the intermediaries.)

You Can Work It Out

Negotiation is a complex subject, and there's a growing library of resources to help you attain mastery. For more information on negotiation, check out these books:

Getting to Yes: Negotiating Agreement Without Giving In, by Roger Fisher and William Ury. The acknowledged classic work on the subject of negotiation, this book covers all bases. It describes BATNA, which stands for the Best Alternative to a Negotiated Agreement. The key question: If the deal does *not* happen, will you be worse off?

Winning with Integrity, by Leigh Steinberg. One of the top sports agents, the author has represented superstars such as Troy Aikman and Steve Young. In fact, Steinberg was the basis for the popular movie *Jerry Maguire.* His book is jammed with great stories of how he closed major deals by strong negotiation strategies.

Smart Negotiating: How to Make Good Deals in the Real World, by James C. Freund. The author was a senior partner at one of the top M&A law firms on Wall Street—Skadden, Arps, Slate, Meagher & Flom. He was involved in such high-profile deals as TWO and Federated Stores. Freund also teaches negotiation at the Fordham University Law School.

FIRST MEETING BETWEEN BUYER AND SELLER. At least one week is allocated to prepare for this important encounter. Both sides learn about each other and try to establish rapport. Deal terms are not discussed yet.

SECOND MEETING. The parties begin to discuss specific terms. After they sign a confidentiality agreement, the seller discloses financial information so the buyer can form a valuation and bid.

THIRD MEETING. The buyer presents the valuation and bid. The parties try to negotiate a mutually satisfactory price and discuss deal terms in detail. If there is agreement, the next step will be to draft an LOI. If the parties cannot close the gap at this occasion, they set another meeting.

CONTACT FROM THE BUYER

Based on a criteria list for buyout candidates (discussed in chapter 2), a prospective buyer will locate one or more suitable companies and then initiate contact with the seller.

Sometimes the buyer's CEO makes the actual contact, but this may make the buyer seem overeager to make a purchase. Rather, you might instead have a vice president of business development or your investment banker or broker make the contact.

Buyers, in this initial conversation, do not say that they want to purchase the company. Rather, they are somewhat noncommittal, saying, "We have been following the progress for your company for some time. We think there are synergies between us. Perhaps there is even a possibility of a combination."

Bear in mind that it is common for companies to get buyout overtures. The target company may have been burned in the past and thus skeptical of any offers. Or the seller may simply not be interested in being acquired. So if the initial feedback is negative, describe your company and the synergies you envision. If you have already done several M&A transactions, mention that fact. All this indicates that you are serious.

If there is still resistance, do not push. Just say to the seller, "If you are interested in the future, give me a call any time." And then periodically—and tactfully—check back in with the company and see if the sentiment has changed.

First Meeting

Trying to buy or sell a business alone can be incredibly difficult and is likely to lead to mistakes, such as getting a bad price or poor terms. It's crucial to have a team. I strongly recommend that by the first meeting, the buyer and the seller have retained deal professionals—either a broker or an investment banker, an attorney, and a CPA—and developed strategies for handling a first meeting.

Here are some tips:

Communications. Your professionals need to have a clear idea of your positions and motivations. This will help them better construct an effective strategy as well as speak on your behalf when negotiating. The buyer should have already done this, but this is probably not the case with the seller.

Expertise. Don't micromanage your professional experts. Recognize that their expertise means they understand the intricacies of certain elements in the negotiation process better than you do; that's why you hired them. With regard to these matters, it is usually wise to give them as much negotiation leeway as possible (within the confines of your goals and expectations of course). For example, your attorney deeply understands the intricacies of possible liability exposures, including potential pitfalls you may not have considered. And the CPA will have great knowledge of tax strategies. Your investment banker will have a strong understanding of the general valuations of your industry.

It's important that these professionals follow your guidelines, of course, but it's equally important that you give them the opportunity to do what they are paid to do—negotiate. Owners and CEOs of smaller companies are especially prone to micromanage every term in the negotiation process. Your interference may make it difficult for your professionals to execute the best deal. Avoid this tendency by building strong trust and understanding among your professionals right from the start.

And naturally, there are subjects about which you will have the most understanding, such as your specific industry. The main goal should be excellent coordination among your advisers. It can be a nightmare to offer something to the other side and then talk to your attorney and realize it was a big mistake.

POSITIONS. Screening criteria are essential to buyers looking for suitable acquisition targets, but both buyers and sellers also should apply a rating system to prioritize their positions. Ideally, this should be done before the first meeting but definitely before the second. Classify your positions by rank so you know which to press hard and which are subject to compromise. I recommend the following three-tier approach.

1. **Nonnegotiable.** These are issues on which you can hardly budge, such as a minimum or maximum price for the deal. Bring your nonnegotiable positions into the negotiations from the get-go to establish their importance. And be consistent—stick to your guns. If you start to cave on core issues, you'll rapidly lose ground. If you realize at the first meeting that you and the other party are at loggerheads about your nonnegotiable positions, then you should probably

end the negotiations. Why waste time? Look for the next deal.

2. **Middle ground.** These are positions with more latitude but over which you won't give ground unless there's some quid pro quo. You must get something of value in return.

3. **Nonmaterial.** These are positions that are of little importance to you. But the other side may not know this. So, you can still use these as bargaining chips. Or you can opt to voluntarily cede a nonmaterial position if negotiations start to stall, as a sign of goodwill.

LOCATION. Meetings should take place in an area free of distractions, such as a conference room. As for whether they should be held at the buyer's or the seller's offices, you might offer a compromise: Perhaps the first meeting can be at the seller's and the next one at the buyer's or vice versa. If the seller is skeptical of the offer, it sometimes helps to conduct the meeting at the buyer's headquarters; it helps convince the seller that the buyer is a real company and offers a window to the nature of the organization.

ATTENDEES. The first meeting should include the CEOs, investment bankers or brokers, and attorneys from both companies. In fact, this set of players should attend all three meetings, augmented only if necessary for a specific reason—such as, for example, a physical plant expert if OSHA regulations prove to be a sticking point.

THE EVENT ITSELF. Now that your team is fully prepared and confident, it's time for the meeting. The most important thing to remember: Be patient! This session should not result in an offer (let alone an acceptance).

Instead, it is a way to establish a relationship between the parties, to start developing some chemistry, and to ascertain whether you can execute a fair and equitable deal with them.

Do not exchange too much information. From the seller, a summary of the company's financials and background is sufficient. From the buyer, general questions about the target company are appropriate, but nothing too detailed.

Make it absolutely clear to everyone that the negotiations must remain confidential. This serves both sides' interests: buyers, because they wouldn't want to elicit undue attention from other potential bidders, and sellers, because they wouldn't want to alarm employees or alert competitors.

POSTMORTEM. Either at the conclusion of the meeting or afterward, establish a time line in conjunction with the other party. Define the issues to be tackled at each subsequent meeting and whether there should be any additional attendees. Agree on the location(s) for follow-up sessions. Most important, clarify the lines of communications; each side must have a single point person to keep the other constituents informed. All manner of problems will develop if there are crisscrossing circuits, especially early on.

Once the seller's owner or CEO is inclined to sell, he should then notify his board of directors. (See the section "Informing Others" in chapter 1.) He should set out the reasons for the sale and get advice from the board. If the board gives the go-ahead, serious negotiations can begin.

SECOND MEETING

By holding a second meeting, both parties indicate they do indeed see a potential combination. At this session,

you want to cover any remaining potential deal break-
ers. If these can be resolved, a deal is possible.

You need to discuss what the merged company will
look like. (Of course, true "mergers" are rare; in nearly
all cases, one company is essentially buying another. But
even so, the transaction nearly always requires a blend-
ing of resources, assets, personnel, and so forth.) Will the
seller's management stay on board? Are they comfortable
with an earn-out? Is the buyer planning to allocate adequate resources to ensure that the seller's division can
keep growing properly? Will there be layoffs?

Typically, this is the point when a seller will ask
about payment amount. As the buyer, do not commit to
anything. Say, "We are prepared to offer you a fair price,
and we can back that up. There is no problem there. But
for us to come up with this price, we need to take a look
at your financials. We are willing to sign a confidentiality agreement to do this."

Sellers should know that it is highly unusual for a
buyer to commit to a bid before you have disclosed your
financials. But before doing so, you need to feel thoroughly confident that a deal makes sense with this particular buyer. If not, you should end the negotiations. As
for the buyer, it is imperative that you convince the
buyer you are a credible company that will follow
through on the deal. A couple of ways to instill such confidence are to show how the seller's business would help
compensate for weak points at your own company and to
praise the seller's company for its strengths.

After the confidentiality agreement is signed, the buyer
should ask the seller for (1) financials for the past five
years; (2) revenue, profit, and cash flow projections; and (3)
budgets. All together, this information will allow the buyer
to perform a valuation of the selling company. (See chapter
3 for a detailed explanation about conducting a valuation.)

Before adjourning, the parties should set up the
time for the next meeting, at which the buyer will present its valuation.

THIRD MEETING

This meeting is when money issues need to be hashed out. Often, when the seller first hears the buyer's bid, it seems too low; and when the buyer hears the seller's counterfigure, it sounds exorbitant. Yet, somehow, with strong negotiation, a reasonable price usually prevails—allowing for the transaction to be completed.

Some sellers are too focused on price and fail to understand that there are other valuable ways to be compensated—such as an employment agreement or consulting agreement or an earn-out. So if the buyer's proposal includes any such elements, it's important to explain the terms and to do so quickly, before the seller has a bad emotional reaction. The best way to explain the matter is with a term sheet—a one- to two-page document that describes the entire purchase price and all its components.

Also, the buyer should explain how he arrived at the purchase. Did he use comparable information? A discounted cash flow analysis? (See chapter 3 for detailed explanations of these techniques.) In other words, let the seller know the offer is based on hard data and analysis, not gut feeling. You are not making a "lowball" bid.

The buyer shouldn't expect the seller to accept the price on the spot. Some give-and-take will probably be required. Quite likely, another meeting will be needed to discuss the offer details further. But once the process has gone this far, an agreement is usually close at hand.

So now we hop on to the next step—drafting the LOI.

LETTER OF INTENT

After several meetings, a general consensus has taken shape on the basic terms of the deal. Traditionally, M&A deals involve a letter of intent (LOI) document to set the

LETTERS OF THE LAW

If you have any doubts about whether LOIs are a serious matter, this case should set you straight.

After Tyson Foods had signed an LOI to buy IBP, the target corporation hit the skids. When Tyson tried to back out of the deal, IBP sued. The judge ruled—in no uncertain terms—that the LOI was binding and ordered Tyson to follow through and purchase IBP.

This case reflects the prevailing trend in U.S. courts: If a deal's a deal, companies shouldn't always be allowed to back out.

parameters. The LOI also plays an important psychological role because it indicates a high level of mutual commitment. Once this document is signed, both sides can begin due diligence and negotiation of the merger agreement—the definitive contract specifying the binding terms of the M&A transaction. (See chapter 7 for a full discussion.)

Logically enough, the LOI is in the form of a letter, from the buyer to the seller. And as the name implies, an LOI is generally not a binding agreement; rather, it is an intent to agree. But be careful. An LOI may be partially and fully binding—depending on how it is composed. In fact, sometimes the parties hastily issue an LOI based on a boilerplate agreement that may not necessarily meet the legal needs of the situation. That can be disastrous. We will look at the famous Penzoil case below to see how these agreements can go awry.

Historically, the LOI is an integral part of an M&A transaction. It is a great starting point, and it serves to reduce problems with miscommunication—which is the most notorious downside of oral agreements. But not all deals necessarily demand an LOI. For small-dollar, simple deals, for example, it could make more sense to go straight to a merger agreement.

Traditionally, the buyer drafts the LOI and merger agreement. But if the buyer offers the task to the seller, I would urge the seller to grab the chance. Drafting these documents provides tremendous leverage. The drafter can insert language that is advantageous to him or omit clauses not to his benefit or liking. What's more, the party drafting the document controls the speed dial.

Example: In 1985, Pennzoil agreed to purchase Getty Oil and expressed this in an LOI. Then Texaco negotiated a deal with Getty and ultimately purchased the company. Pennzoil thought the LOI was binding and sued. In one of the biggest jury awards ever, the jury found for Pennzoil for $11.2 billion.

As the example illustrates, it is important to have experienced counsel when drafting an LOI—whichever side is doing it. Even after the Getty Oil case, the rules on the binding nature of LOIs are not clear-cut. A big part of the determination involves the facts of the situation. The legal question in the Pennzoil case was this: Would a reasonable person assume that both parties would consider the LOI to be binding? Some courts assume that signing an LOI implies a large element of good faith. Which is to say, a party must have good reasons for breaching the LOI.

To best understand an LOI document, let's take a real-life example. In March 2000, Halis, a medical software company, entered an LOI to purchase Health-Watch, an online healthcare site. We will use portions of this document as exhibits of the various components of a good LOI.

Here's the preface of the letter:

Gentlemen:

This letter will confirm the various discussions that we have had regarding the acquisition by HealthWatch, Inc., a Minnesota corporation (the "Purchaser"), by means of merger of Halis, Inc., a Georgia corporation (the "Seller") into Purchaser or a wholly-owned subsidiary of Purchaser (the "Subsidiary"). Subject to the preparation, execution, and performance of a definitive written agreement (the "Agreement") containing such terms, conditions, covenants, representations, and warranties as either party may in good faith require, I understand that we have agreed in principle to the following general terms:

The phrase "subject to" indicates that the LOI is not a binding agreement. In other words, there is much work to do before both parties enter a final merger agreement (termed here the "definitive written agreement").

The next section is the heart of the matter—the "basic transaction," which sets forth the fundamental terms of the deal.

Basic Transaction: On a date to be agreed upon (the "Closing Date"), Seller will merge into Purchaser or Subsidiary under the terms of which each shareholder of Seller will receive that fraction of a share of Purchaser's Common Stock, $0.05 par value, equal to $0.33 divided by the average closing price of Purchaser's Common Stock on the NASDAQ Small Cap market for the ten days preceding the Closing Date in return for cancellation of each outstanding share of Seller's Common Stock, $0.01 par value. The $0.33 value referenced in the preceding sentence reflects approximately a 50 percent premium over the average closing price of Seller's Common Stock for the ten trading days immediately preceding the date of this letter.

This sets forth the formula for computing the price per share for the acquisition. Like most LOIs, the purchase price is not necessarily fully described. For example, there may be an earn-out or other types of compensation involved. These elements will be negotiated after the LOI is signed. As the title says, this is merely the "Basic Transaction."

The clause says "Seller *will* receive. . . ." The use of the word "will" indicates the buyer is being definite. But this assertive usage does not necessarily make it legally binding. The sentence means only that this will be the price should a merger agreement be signed.

As for HealthWatch, the company is getting a 50% premium for the 10 trading days immediately preceding the date of the LOI. But what if the stock price declines substantially by the time the merger agreement is signed? Well, you might want to negotiate a collar. (This is described in much more detail in chapter 3.)

> *Representations and Warranties:* Seller will make the representations and warranties usual and customary in such a transaction, including, without limitation, the following: (a) the clear and unencumbered title of Seller to all of its assets; (b) all of the Seller's personal property in good working condition subject to ordinary wear and tear; and (c) the right and power of Seller to assign all of its license agreements and customer contracts to Purchaser.

We discuss representations and warranties in greater detail in chapter 7. In fact, drafting these types of clauses takes up quite a bit of the process of drafting a merger agreement. Because of this, the LOI will usually defer these clauses for the merger agreement (which is the case here). However, if there is a deal breaker—such as assuming the liability for environmental exposure—it may be a good idea to mention that in the LOI, indicating that it is indeed an important issue and must be dealt with in the merger agreement.

> *Access:* Seller will grant Purchaser and its representatives access to the personnel, property, contracts, books, and records of Seller and will furnish to Purchaser and its representatives such financial, operating, and other information with respect to the business and properties of Seller as Purchaser shall, from time to time, reasonably request. In connection with its examination of Seller,

with prior written notice to Seller, Purchaser and its representatives may communicate with any person having business dealings with Seller. All of such access, investigation, and communication by Purchaser and its representatives will be conducted in a manner designed not to materially interfere with the normal business of Seller.

To allow for the drafting of a merger agreement, there must be due diligence. The above clause allows the buyer to conduct due diligence. Access is broad, including not only records and access to the buyer's facilities but also the right to interview personnel and even customers.

Exclusive Dealing: In consideration for the expenditures of time, effort, and expense to be undertaken by Purchaser in connection with the preparation and execution of the Agreement and Purchaser's investigation of Seller which is a condition precedent to the execution of the Agreement, the Halis Board of Directors will not and will not cause the Seller to, between the date of the execution of this letter and the Closing Date, enter into or conduct any discussions with any other prospective purchaser of the stock or assets of Seller. In addition, the Halis Board of Directors shall use its best efforts to preserve intact the business organization and goodwill of Seller.

This is known as the "no shop" provision, in which the seller is not allowed to solicit or agree to any buyout offer from another third party. However, keep in mind that the seller is giving up a significant right. It is always a good idea to try to negotiate a (nonrefundable) fee that pays for the "Exclusive Dealing."

Suppose the seller does eliminate the clause. Well, the buyer and seller should negotiate a "breakup" fee. Think of it as a form of M&A insurance (some call these "corporate prenuptial agreements"). Basically, with a breakup fee, if a deal falls through, the party at fault will pay a fixed amount. This is negotiated by both the buyer and seller—and not only involves being reimbursed for expenses but may also include loss of business opportunity. These things are tough to calculate and should involve the help of an investment banker or broker.

In most cases, the fee is payable in cash. However, there are stock lockup fees. Here's how it works: ABC agrees to purchase XYZ for $40 per share. In the deal, ABC gets an option to buy 1 million shares at $40 per share. If a rival bidder ultimately purchases XYZ, then ABC can exercise the option at the higher price and flip the stock.

Breakups are becoming more common as mergers become much larger—especially for public companies. Why? Well, if a deal falls through, the target company does not usually want to be considered "in play." Also, complex deals take longer to complete. In other words, both companies will be expending many resources to make the deal happen. If the deal fails, this will have been a big waste of time and effort.

> *Nonsolicitation:* Purchaser agrees that during the period commencing on the date of the execution of this letter and ending on the Closing Date, or for one year after the termination of this letter, Purchaser shall not, directly or indirectly, solicit or attempt to solicit, any person who is an employee of the Seller at that time, or induce or attempt to induce any employee of the Seller to terminate his or her employment relationship with the Seller.

In the due diligence process, the buyer will learn about the abilities of the employees of the seller. If the transaction fails, the buyer may be tempted to hire some of the key employees. This clause forbids this process.

> *Disclosure:* Except as and to the extent required by law or required for the Purchaser or Seller, as the case may be, to obtain financing, due diligence, or legal and financial opinions, each party agrees that it will not release or issue any reports, statements, or releases pertaining to this letter of intent and the implementation hereof without the prior written consent of the other party hereto.

This clause indicates that there are special rules regarding disclosure for public companies. If an LOI is signed that has a material impact on the buyer, then it must be disclosed. Thus, this clause is intended to allow the buyer to make sure it complies with federal securities disclosure rules. No doubt, these laws are incredibly complex and require the assistance of a good securities attorney.

Also, an acquisition can be a PR event. It is smart for both sides to agree on how to disclose it—with a press release or, perhaps, through CNBC.

Costs: Each party will be responsible for and bear all of its own costs and expenses (including any broker's or finder's fees and the expenses of its representatives) incurred at any time in connection with pursuing or consummating the proposed merger.

This sets forth how expenses will be handled. In some cases, the seller may not have the resources to handle some of the costs, and the LOI can set forth what the buyer will be responsible for.

Conditions: The closing of the merger will be conditioned upon (i) Purchaser and Seller obtaining appropriate approval of their respective shareholders; (ii) Purchaser having raised a minimum of $5,000,000 from issuances of equity securities of Purchaser, prior to closing; and (iii) obtaining required governmental and regulatory approvals.

Both sides can set up conditions for a binding merger agreement. As indicated in this clause, these usually require new financing and regulatory approvals.

Termination: This letter will automatically terminate, unless extended by mutual consent of the parties, upon the earlier to occur of: (a) the date the Agreement is signed by all parties, or (b) two months after the date this letter is signed by the Seller. In addition, this letter may be terminated earlier upon written notice by Purchaser to Seller unilaterally, for any reason or no reason, with or without cause, at any time; provided however, that the termination hereof will have no effect on the liability of a party for a breach of any of the Binding Provisions. Upon termination of this letter, the parties shall continue to be bound by all of the Binding Provisions other than those relating to "Access" and "Exclusive Dealings," which obligations will survive any such termination in accordance with its terms for a period of six months.

The agreement will terminate if a merger agreement is signed or two months elapse—unless both parities agree to change this. Both sides can back out of the agreement as long as none of the binding clauses are not violated (these clauses are defined below).

Entire Agreement: Except as provided in paragraphs 1, 3, 4, 5, and 9 hereof, which are intended to represent binding agreements of the parties hereto ("Binding Provisions"), this letter is intended to be, and shall be construed only as, a letter of intent summarizing and evidencing the discussions between Purchaser and Seller to the date hereof. Except as otherwise provided in the preceding sentence, the respective rights and obligations of Purchaser and Seller remain to be defined in the Agreement, into which this letter and our prior discussions shall merge. The Binding Provisions constitute the entire agreement by and between the parties, supersede all prior oral or written agreements, understandings, representations, and warranties, and courses of conduct and dealing between the parties on the subject matter hereof. Except as otherwise provided in this letter, the Binding Provisions may be amended or modified only by a writing executed by each of the parties.

The binding provisions include the following: basic transaction, access, exclusive dealing, and nonsolicitation. It's a good idea to specify which clauses are binding and which are nonbonding. That will help avoid disputes if one of the parties terminates the agreement.

TOM TAULLI'S NEGOTIATING PRIMER

One attribute common to all successful M&A deal makers is negotiating skill. Some seem to have been born with a gift for it; most had to develop such skills through experience. But even if you're new to negotiating, don't let it daunt you. A little coaching can give you a hefty boost up the proverbial learning curve.

In this section, I offer a set of techniques that should enhance your negotiating abilities. These tips are purely subjective, but in addition to applying them myself, I've seen them used effectively by masterful negotiators numerous times. In short, these are the insights I wish I had known when I started out. Of course, all the advice here applies equally to either buyers or sellers. In fact, although this section is geared to M&A negotiations, everything herein can be successfully applied in virtually any important business meeting.

To reiterate a big point: Unless you're a veteran M&A negotiator, it is *highly* advisable to have a trusty adviser by your side during any and all negotiation sessions. Actually, this is where your broker or investment banker—or deal attorney or CPA—should truly earn his or her keep. And once you and your adviser establish a working rapport, you can employ this teamwork in creative ways. In many deals, I've seen the broker and seller (or buyer) employ the old good cop–bad cop dynamic. (If you take this tack, just make sure you play the good cop.)

The following two subsections contain a career's worth of learning, much of it through trial and error. Don't expect to master all of it at once. You might find it useful to bring a photocopy of this guide to negotiation

---

POWER SHIFTS

One fascinating aspect of M&A deals is the push/pull power dynamic between buyer and seller. Each new stage represents a subtle variation in the two sides' relative strength. Here's the rule of thumb among M&A pros: Up until the LOI, the seller has the superior leverage. Once the LOI is inked, the buyer holds the reins (and, if it chooses, the buggy whip). As due diligence proceeds in the background, buyers tend to dominate negotiation sessions.

But once the deal has gone through, the power pendulum swings again, along a different axis. The new buyer is on the line and often must enlist the seller's efforts to help ensure the company's success.

---

sessions and occasionally review the information to keep it fresh.

Basic Approach

BE REALISTIC. Don't let emotions prevent you from seeing the situation accurately. For example, suppose 10 buyers have put bids on your company that fall, say, within $2 million to $2.5 million. It would be unrealistic to think that your business is worth $10 million. It's not. The market tends to be fairly efficient. Fight the market, and you'll probably forgo the right deal.

Example: Let's look at PointCast. The company pioneered "push technology"—consumers could get useful information sent to their desktops 24/7. By 1997, Point-Cast was red hot, with several major firms lusting to buy it. One of these was media mogul Rupert Murdoch's News Corp., which offered to purchase PointCast for

$450 million. But management thought this was too low a bid and refused. It was about that point in time that the company's traffic started to diminish. On two occasions, PointCast attempted to go public—to no avail. By May 1999, the near-bankrupt company sold out to Idealab!, an Internet incubator, for a reported $10 million in cash and stock.

FACE PROBLEMS SQUARELY. Every deal has problems. And some aren't solvable. For example, if your industry is in decline, there is little if anything you can do about this. If you try to ignore this reality, you will look foolish. In this case, you must assume the other side knows what's going on. Both sides should openly acknowledge this and talk it through.

DON'T RUSH. A lot is at stake here, so make sure you fully analyze the situation and feel comfortable with the transaction. In fact, if you seem to be rushing matters, the other side may interpret this as a mark of desperation.

DO YOUR HOMEWORK. Negotiations are inherently imperfect because both sides must act on incomplete information. So the more you know, the greater your advantage. Before you make any move, make sure you're well prepared. Make sure you have a firm grasp of your own situation, of course—such as how much you can afford to spend or need to be paid. And be certain to look at the other side. For example, is the owner known to be a tough or easy negotiator? Scenario planning is critical. Try to envision all the possibilities: What is the best-case scenario? What is the worst? This way, you'll be prepared.

AVOID MISREPRESENTATION. Misrepresentation is misstating a material fact that induces the other party to do something it would not otherwise do. The key word here is "material," which has been subject to much legal wrangling and, as always, seems to depend on the situation. If a misstated fact is not "material," then the communication is considered "puffery." That is, you are trying to bolster your position as much as possible—but not being fraudulent. It's a fine line.

Also, if the other side finds out you've misrepresented at all, this will cause a huge loss of credibility. There's a good chance this will kill the deal. Never forget that there are legal implications to misrepresentation, including liability exposure and the rescinding of contracts.

BE POSITIVE. In negotiation, the opposing side will "pick up on your vibes." As much as possible, try to feel positive about the discussions. Transmit the impression that the deal will be a success and that both sides will win. Contrarily, if you are hostile or arrogant, this will probably put the other side on the defensive. Another quality that counts a lot is passion. Successful deal makers love the process—the whole give-and-take. If you seem lukewarm to the whole enterprise, it might come across as a lack of commitment and hinder the deal.

BE YOURSELF. Some negotiators' style is combative and unrelenting; they'll even slam their fists on a table and storm out of a room. Others take a more congenial approach, always willing to work together toward a solution. It's up to you; I've seen a lot of different personality types do M&A deals. But whatever style you adopt, make sure it comes naturally. Pretending to be someone else always comes across as phony, and it will hurt your chances.

BLUFFING. This is a common technique, and it can result in big ground gains—*but* it has risks. So before you bluff, make sure to examine the range of possible outcomes. For example, the other side may buy your bluff completely and decide to back out of the deal. You might even lose out to another party as a result. For example, suppose you offer to buy ABC for $1 million and assert the offer is final—whereas in truth you'd be willing to spend $1.2 million. ABC rejects your bid and ends up selling the company to a dangerous competitor of yours for $1.1 million.

And once you bluff, you can't necessarily back down. If you decide to own up to your ploy to try to save a deal, your credibility is severely damaged. Such a situation rarely yields a favorable outcome.

However, if you do decide to bluff, here are a couple of key pointers: Most important, the bluff should come at the *end* of negotiations. Bluffing early on in the talks can easily sink a deal. Furthermore, make sure you bluff about an issue that is very important.

If, however, the other side tries to bluff you (and you know it), how should you handle this? Do you call the bluff and threaten to walk away—in effect, a double bluff? Or do you take the offer?

Once again, there is no single simple answer. Certainly, if the bluff concerns a position that you cannot accept, then call it. Or if the ruse seems outrageous and not in accordance with any reasonable interpretation of the facts, then call the bluff. In other situations, you might ultimately gain by accepting it; the opposition might be compliant about an issue that matters more to you.

And when you call a bluff, don't ram it down the other side's throat. Be diplomatic: "This is a position I cannot accept. Although, if we can make some changes, I think we can make this work out."

BE TRUSTWORTHY. Big money is at stake with an M&A deal. As a result, it can be tempting to cut corners or even do things that are unethical. But no deal is worth compromising your values. In the M&A business, a reputation of fair dealing is of utmost importance. True, you should seek your self-interest, but do not engage in any manipulation.

MANIFEST PROFESSIONALISM. Present yourself as a consummate professional. It shows respect for the negotiating process and for the other parties involved. Self-presentation is very important. Your standing posture—an important indicator of a person's self-regard—should be straight and alert. When sitting down, do not slump in your chair. In terms of dress code, it's a good idea to be conservative and wear a suit, but not one that's flashy. A $5,000 suit could be distracting, and such ostentation might suggest to the other side that you can afford to pay through the nose. In fact, pay careful attention to presentation in all its guises. For instance, if you draw up a document about your company, make good use of graphics and charts and be sure the text is well written, free of spelling errors, and grammatically correct. (The built-in word-processor tools help a little, but for certainty run the document past a literate third party.) Make sure to carry an ample number of business cards, an extra pen, your portable calendar book, and any other accoutrements you might need.

DON'T OVERDO THE SMALL TALK. Chatting is a good way to break the ice and to establish rapport. Certainly, try to establish an initial comfort level with the other side. If you see an interesting picture on a desk, for example, you might want to ask about it. But avoid *excessive* small talk; don't use chitchat to deflect dealing with the important issues of a negotiation.

LEVERAGE. As much as possible, locate the leverage factors—for both sides. When you're clear on what these are, it is much easier to negotiate. You will know if you can play hardball or, conversely, give in to the other side.

The most common leverage factors include the following:

- **Time.** The clock might be ticking, especially for the seller. For example, he might need to sell the business in the next six months to pay off company debt or taxes. It's not always easy to tell *why* a party is hard-pressed for time, but the fact itself is usually apparent.

- **Necessity.** Perhaps you have no choice but to buy a company. Say, you've tried to build certain key products in-house, but it proved too difficult. Or your customers are demanding a new product line. Perhaps your company faces bankruptcy unless there is a sale. This was a common theme for many dot-com companies during the early part of 2000.

- **First move.** Did the buyer contact the seller or vice versa? This can be crucial information. If the seller made the first move, this could indicate an eagerness to sell—and flexibility. When a buyer makes the first move, it may be a sign of especially strong interest to purchase the company—even at a high price. (But be careful. The buyer might also be checking the competition, that is, basically doing a "fishing expedition" without any intent to buy.)

GO FOR "SEAT POWER." Think strategically about physical positioning when you meet in a conference room. One strong move is to grab the chair at the head of the table: The resulting "seat power" can help you guide the meeting. Or you might want to sit next to the white board so that you'll be the person who actually writes the structure of the deal.

DON'T INSIST, JUSTIFY. Hard negotiators constantly *demand* more, and this can start to rub the other side wrong. Rather, it is more effective to justify why you should get more. Prove it.

GET TOUGH. Sometimes being firm is the only way to handle a situation. Suppose that both parties have come

to agreement on major points but that later in the negotiation the other side reneges on the agreed-on position.
In this case, you need to stand tough. Don't be afraid to
show some anger over this unacceptable move. Make it
clear you won't tolerate this type of behavior. It's well
within your rights to indicate there will be no deal unless the other side recants.

SET DEADLINES. Time limits can be effective to move a
deal along. But they must be reasonable. Once a deadline is set, plan out your approach, making sure to allocate sufficient time to cover the issues important to you.
If the other side is imposing a forced deadline, find out
why. If the other side has compelling time issues to wrap
up the deal, that could translate into leverage for you.
Moreover, if you are approaching the deadline, resist the
temptation to give in on important points. Rather, see if
the deadline can be extended. In most cases, this should
not be a problem.

TAKE BREAKS. Prolonged negotiations can be grueling.
Sometimes it is smart to take a break, either a brief
breather or a recess until the next day. These give both
sides a chance to consider the options when they're not
as physically and psychically stressed.

POSTMORTEM. So much information is involved in a
negotiation that it's easy to forget the details—such as
how you arrived at the final outcome. So, as soon as possible after each meeting, conduct a postmortem with
your team.

Communication

BE AN OPEN COMMUNICATOR. Communication, in all
its varieties, is the soul of negotiating, so you want to be
as reliable a communicator as you can. Make it easy for

the other side to contact you: Thus, ensure you have easy access to e-mail (perhaps through a Palm Pilot or other PDA) as well as a cell phone. (You can even buy a single device that combines both.) Also, always return messages promptly. Last, make sure you have periodic contact with the other side.

SPEAK CAREFULLY. Be careful of what you say, especially overly revealing "off the cuff" comments. Try to avoid negative words and phrases, like "I can't" or "I'm not sure." And be aware of your casual speech habits; many of us are sloppy speakers, interposing "like" in every sentence. Watch out for throwaway phrases, such as "To be honest with you. . . ." Are you saying you are not honest at other times?

Another aspect is enunciation. If you talk rapidly, this could hamper communications and also create the feeling that you're a sly, fast-talking type. Mumbling is another no-no.

DROP NAMES. Remember the names of the people you deal with and say them often when you discuss matters. People like to hear their names. It helps generate rapport.

LISTEN UP. Most people like to blab, and given enough time they *will* say too much—and give away their hand. As the old saying goes, "You can learn a lot just by listening." Slow down and ask the other side questions. Pay more attention to the *other* party. Negotiators often focus on their own interests. But, by seeing things through the viewpoint of the other side, you might be better able to fashion workable strategies.

NOTE NONVERBAL COMMUNICATION. Studies show that about 55% of communication is nonverbal—body language, facial expressions, and other nuances. Pay close attention to the other side's unconscious messages.

When they appear nervous, for example, it's probably a poor time to bring up the touchiest terms of the deal.

MASTER TELEPHONE AND E-MAIL. A large percentage of the overall communications a deal entails are conducted via e-mail and telephones. This is efficient, of course, but there are drawbacks. In particular, there's the loss of nonverbal cues. So, when communicating by way of technology, try to eliminate any possibility of your messages being misinterpreted.

Here are some telephone tips:

- **Phone tag.** Phone tag can be extremely frustrating in an M&A deal. A good way to reduce this problem is to use voice mail or e-mail to set up an appointment to speak in "real time."

- **Call screening.** If you have a secretary, let him or her know what types of calls have priority.

- **Holding.** If you must put a caller on hold for an extended interlude (more than a minute), you should periodically come back on the line and say, "I haven't forgotten about you. . . ." And don't keep someone on hold for five minutes and *then* say you'll have to call them back later. Establish time limits for interruptions.

- **Voice mail.** When leaving messages, be sure to specify the date, time of the call, your name, title, and phone number—repeated twice, slowly. If you are leaving an involved message—which I don't recommend—don't ramble. Write some notes before you make the call so you don't waste the message recipient's time.

- **Phone log.** This could be a notebook in which you plan your callbacks, indicating the objectives of the call, questions to ask, and follow-up information. Also, record the time and date of the call.

It is common to forget whether you actually called a person.

- **Attitude.** Even though callers cannot see each other, try to find ways to project a positive attitude. One technique is to smile when you talk. Another technique is to stand up and walk around. Also, get a headset. This will free you up to write or type notes as you talk.

- **Background noise.** Find ways to reduce audible distractions.

- **Silence.** Provide cues that you are listening, such as saying "OK," "Uh-huh," and so on.

- **Wrap-up.** At the end of the call, sum things up. You want to ensure that both of you are thinking the same things.

Here are some e-mail tips:

- **Signature line.** This should appear at the end of every e-mail you send. The signature line makes it convenient for people to respond to you by other communication media, such as cell phone or fax. Most e-mail programs provide for easily set up signature lines. If you choose to be creative with your signature lines, bear in mind that M&A deals and frivolous mottoes don't mix well. This is the standard format:
  Full name
  Professional title
  Company name
  E-mail address and Web site (if applicable)
  Phone, fax, cell, pager, and so on

- **All caps.** DON'T USE THIS FOR YOUR MES-SAGES. IT IS CONSIDERED SHOUTING (AND IS VERY ANNOYING). Allsew, use a spall chucker befare yuu sind yaw emale.

- **Attachments.** Before sending large attachments—say, anything over one megabyte—get the permission of the recipient. Some people still have slow modems and do not appreciate having their computer tied up by lengthy downloads.

- **Subject lines.** Try to be as descriptive as possible. This increases the chances the e-mail will be read promptly. Keep it to four or five words.

- **Emoticons.** You can express emotion in an e-mail using certain symbols. For example, the symbol ":-)" indicates that you are being lighthearted. But use these shorthand glyphs sparingly. The other side may not recognize the symbols. And some people cringe at the sight of them.

- **Links.** If you send a Web link to another party, include the *http://* before the rest of the URL. Some e-mail programs need this.

- **Security.** Most likely, your e-mail is unsecure, so try to send very little sensitive information this way. There are e-mail programs that can encrypt messages for security, but the recipient must be familiar with the process.

- **Responses.** When you reply to a message, include the text from the original message but erase the rest. This helps reduce the clutter the recipient has to wade through.

- **Think before you send.** Once you send your e-mail, it is a permanent record. Even if you delete an e-mail from your inbox, the message is probably saved on outside servers—and of course the recipient has it on his or her computer. So before you send any message, think through the consequences.

- **Flame.** *Do not* send angry messages. And if you receive a flame, don't respond via e-mail. Instead, call the other person or meet face to face to resolve the matter.

- **Autoresponder.** This feature automatically sends a reply that you have composed to anyone who e-mails you. It is a very useful way to indicate you are out of the office or will be out of town for a certain period.

- **Organize e-mail.** Top e-mail programs—such as Microsoft Outlook Express—allow you to categorize your messages. Making smart use of this technique can save you loads of time and hassle. You can set up folders, segregated by deal or any other applicable categories.

CHAPTER 5

DEAL STRUCTURES

There is no such thing as a "cookie-cutter" merger transaction. Virtually every M&A deal is unique in some way, and finding the right price is only one element among numerous variables that must be hashed out in negotiations. In fact, the way a deal is structured is just as important as the total dollar amount.

In the broadest sense, "structure" ultimately includes every element of the deal that will be reflected in the merger agreement, from intellectual property transfers down to office supplies. In chapter 7, we'll look at the panoply of elements in considerable detail. But in this chapter, I will discuss the basic structural issues that a seller and buyer should be considering from the start—that is, before even making contact with the other party. (In some sense, this chapter is a "down payment.")

Structural considerations include the form of payment (cash, stock, promissory notes, or a combination), tax implications (especially for the seller), liabilities (the buyer's interest in protecting himself from inherited liabilities), and follow-up participation (where payment is partially contingent on the seller's continuing role at the company). These are all complex issues and could take several months to resolve. And keep this in mind: Both sides will ultimately need to compromise on many of these issues. No party will get the perfect deal.

It's important that sellers know the rudiments of how M&A deals work so they're not unpleasantly shocked when negotiations begin. Often, I've seen the business owner enter deliberations with this mind-set: "My company is great; I want a lot of money, and it's gotta be cash." They expect a big check with a big number on it; I call it the "all-cash fantasy." And then they find out it's not that simple. Typically, their first rude awakening is when the buyer names a price. This may completely turn them off, effectively putting the kibosh on a deal. Or it might make them so distrustful that negotiations turn into a protracted and unfriendly process. (And sometimes, this will then turn the buyer off!)

So, some preliminary understanding can be crucial. One of the functions of a good broker is to try to bring a seller's expectations down to a realistic level. In fact, a really smart broker tries to underpromise and overdeliver.

THE BASICS

Before I discuss the individual types of deal structures and considerations, let me present the following overview of the key points.

- There are three ways to structure a deal:
    1. Purchase the company's assets
    2. Purchase its stock
    3. Engage in a statutory merger (called a "reorganization")

- Most deals are either stock transfers or mergers. Asset purchases are a distant third—generally, you see these only when distressed companies are being dismantled. A "statutory merger" is not essentially different from a stock purchase; it's just the technical name for a type of transaction with particular tax consequences.

- A significant percentage of deals involves payment in the form of stock; rarely do you see all-cash deals, although in some stock deals, there may be some cash. The cash component is known as the "boot." Personally, I don't recommend straight-cash deals. Getting some equity component is smart; after all, the buyer might be the next Microsoft! In fact, when you see a lot of cash deals happening, it's an indication that buyers think their stock is undervalued—which is probably the best time to get *paid* in stock.

- Most deals are tax exempt for the seller (and virtually all are for the buyer). The lawyers and accountants come up with a structure that's entirely tax free. Since cash is taxable in most situations, this explains why stock-only deals are so common.

- For buyers, much of the M&A process concerns allocating liability risks. A large component of the merger agreement—the "deal structure" portion—is devoted to protecting the buyer and providing recourse to go after the seller if major undisclosed problems arise after the deal is inked. (M&A people have described many an owner as an "overeager seller, undereager discloser.") But even when sellers proceed in the best faith, nearly always something unforeseen will come up. Sometimes buyers will structure the deal to include a set-aside fund to pay for such eventualities.

- One way buyers get around liability issues is by creating a shell entity to buy the other company. This is especially common in deals involving public companies. The upside is that it's an effective way to limit liability exposure; the downside is that it runs the risk of fraud—if there's a class-action suit or creditors go after it.

- In addition to the options I just mentioned, there are numerous other non-payment-related factors—contingency agreements, noncompete agreements, performance timetables, and so on (These will be discussed in chapter 7.) The point is that the seller—and, to a lesser extent, the buyer—should not become so focused on price that he neglects the many other deal structural elements that also determine how well the deal works out for the players.

- Another key issue for the buyer is ensuring that the seller helps make the transition run smoothly. With some businesses, if the owner/founder walks away, the company falls apart; employees and customers need the continuing participation of the previous owner to get over the hump phase. So, increasingly often, deal structures mandate a follow-up role for the seller. One common way to do this is with an earn-out clause, which stipulates that payment is contingent on the company's continuing performance level. Obviously, this is a component that demands intensive negotiation efforts to get it right; otherwise, the seller could be taking a terrible, sometimes tragic, risk.

- Deal structure should be considered early in the negotiations, preferably before an LOI is signed. If possible, in fact, the LOI should include a description of the deal structure. (See the "Basic Transaction" passage in the section "Letter of Intent" in chapter 4.) If the seller or buyer has a top-priority requirement concerning structure, it's best to know whether the parties can accommodate each other before they waste too much time and effort.

- As the deal proceeds through due diligence and more intensive negotiations, the deal structure very likely will undergo some change. The result will be reflected in the merger agreement. Just as price is fluid during the M&A process—influenced by market and industry developments and expanding knowledge about the target company—other deal structure elements are subject to modification.

DEAL STRUCTURE OPTIONS

Now we'll take a look at the three main types of deal structures. To explain them, I'll use the following hypothetical situation:

Sight Lines is a leading manufacturer of eyewear, with over $1 billion in annual sales. The company's stock is listed on the New York Stock Exchange. CUNow, on the other hand, is a small designer and manufacturer of high-end eyewear. The company, which is owned 100% by the founder, has sales of $10 million. But there is a problem: CUNow has been sued for infringing on a patent. The estimated cost to settle the suit is $500,000. Both companies have been involved in preliminary negotiations and want to sign an LOI. The big stumbling block is deciding on the deal structure.

Asset Purchases

In an asset purchase, the seller transfers all or most of the assets of its business or subsidiary for stock or cash (or a combination of the two). Using the example above, Sight Lines will determine the assets of CUNow, such as leases, real estate, patents, trademarks, equipment, and inventory. The LOI and merger agreement will itemize each of these assets. For these assets, Sight Lines is willing to pay the founder $20 million in cash.

In asset sales, the buyer benefits the most. Here are the key advantages:

LIABILITIES. The buyer assumes only those liabilities that he explicitly agrees to in the LOI and merger agreement. So, if these documents don't make mention of the patent infringement suit, the CUNow company, and perhaps even the founder, will still be on the hook for this.

There are some exceptions to this no-liability rule. The more consumer-friendly states, such as California, don't allow buyers to avoid liability in regard to a product liability case. Also, an asset purchase cannot bypass a collective bargaining agreement. (In chapter 9, we discuss in more detail the handling of unions in an M&A transaction.)

STEPPED-UP BASIS. Taxwise, the cost basis of an asset is the cost to the buyer. In an asset purchase deal, the cost basis is the purchase price of all the seller's assets. This can lead to significant tax advantages. For example, suppose Sight Lines buys CUNow's assets for $20 million. According to the IRS, that $20 million is the cost basis. Let's say after two years Sight Lines sells the CUNow division for $35 million. The gain on this transaction for Sight Lines is $15 million, which is the sales price of $35 million minus the cost basis of $20 million. The maximum capital gains tax rate is 20%, so Sight Lines would owe $3 million and net $12 million of profit from their two-year investment of $20 million. In the business world, this is a *very* favorable outcome.

Unfortunately, the seller will likely suffer a big tax disadvantage. In most cases, the founder of a company has little or no cost basis in a company. For example, suppose CUNow's founder launched his business with a mere $20,000. That would be considered his cost basis. So if he sells the business for $10 million in cash, his gain will be $9,980,000, and he'll owe $1,996,000 in tax when the deal is signed. This might not seem like a terrible result, but remember that the founder probably spent between 10 and 20 years building his business; forgoing 20% of the "prize" is not likely to go down easy. (On a happier note, however, the deal can be structured to be tax free, as discussed below.)

To do an asset sale, the shareholders of the seller must vote on the matter. In the case of CUNow, it's a moot point. But sometimes the voting requirement presents problems, such as when there are over a hundred shareholders. According to Delaware law (where most public companies are incorporated), the deal must be approved by a majority—regardless of whether the company is private or public. Of course, one way to get around this is to sell a smaller portion of the company's assets. A safe benchmark would be selling 50% or less.

Essentially, the buyer is purchasing each asset as if it's a separate transaction. For most assets, this legal transfer of title is no problem. But there could be complications for assets that are nonassignable. In these situations, the buyer must renegotiate the contract. If it is a supplier agreement, the supplier may use this opportunity to jack up the price. This often happens with leases. In the due diligence process, this type of issue should surface, and the buyer should get a sense of whether price increases are likely. If so, this could be leverage to lower the price of the acquisition.

Finally, you need to be aware of the Bulk Sales Act. Each state has its own version, although they are all very similar in scope. The Bulk Sales Act is meant to prevent fraud—such as an owner selling his company's assets for cash and then skipping out on all the creditors by leaving the country.

For example, California's Bulk Sales Act is triggered if a company sells more than half its current inventory. In such a situation, the company must give notice by filing a form with the recorder's office and publishing a statement in a newspaper in the municipality where the inventory is located. The notice must appear at least 12 days before the bulk sale. If a company fails to provide this notice, all the company's creditors can demand payment in full.

Stock Purchases and Statutory Mergers

As the name indicates, a stock purchase is when the buyer purchases all or a majority amount of shares from the seller and thus merges the operations of the two companies. Payment takes the form of cash, the buyer's stock, or a promissory note (backed by the seller).

Using our example, suppose Sight Lines decides to purchase CUNow for $15 million in cash and $5 million of Sight Lines stock. CUNow's founder will deliver all his shares to the buyer, and in turn he'll receive the cash and stock certificates from Sight Lines.

As this is obviously a merger of two companies, you may wonder how it differs from a statutory merger. The big difference is that a statutory merger (which is, somewhat confusingly, called a "reorg" for short) is when the buyer bases the merger on existing state merger laws where the buyer is incorporated. Here's how a reorg works: The boards of directors of both buyer and seller must first approve the merger. Then the shareholders of both companies are notified and vote on the matter. Typically, it takes a majority vote from both. If the shareholders approve the merger, the buyer files a certificate of merger with the secretary of state.

Let's take a look at the relative advantages and disadvantages of stock purchases and statutory mergers.

The Advantages to the Seller

LIABILITIES. In a stock purchase, the buyer assumes all the seller's liabilities. In our example, therefore, the buyer would be responsible for the patent infringement case. However, the merger agreement may have indemnification for unknown liabilities.

But a buyer can structure a statutory merger to limit exposure to the seller's liabilities by making the seller's operations a subsidiary. The liabilities of the seller remain the liabilities of the subsidiary, not the buyer company.

TAXES. If the transaction is taxable, then the seller will face the same consequences described with an asset purchase above. But for the most part, a stock purchase or statutory merger can be structured to be tax free. (See below.)

The Disadvantage for the Seller

RISK. See the section "Payment Types" in this chapter.

The Advantages to the Buyer

BULK SALES ACT. This does not apply to a stock purchase or statutory merger.

ASSIGNABILITY. The types of problems with transferring leases or other types of agreements encountered with asset sales generally don't apply with a stock purchase or statutory merger. But be careful: Sometimes a seller will have some contracts with "change of control" clauses that prevent assignability even for these deals.

HOSTILE TAKEOVERS. The way these are done is through stock purchases. A statutory approach is likely to fail since it will be difficult to get the seller's board of directors to agree. By doing a stock purchase, however, the buyer is making an offer directly to the seller's shareholders. To make this enticing, the buyer will offer to pay a premium over the current market price. (See chapter 11 for a full discussion of hostile takeovers.)

The Disadvantages to the Buyer

APPRAISAL RIGHTS. In a stock purchase, if you want to buy 100% of the company, you need to buy the shares from all the shareholders. However, there may be some shareholders who refuse to sell. A statutory merger, on the other hand, avoids this problem since it requires only a majority vote.

But there is something else to consider: appraisal rights. This allows a shareholder to dispute the merger in court and perhaps to even stop it. In most cases, however, the holding-out shareholder of the seller will work out a separate deal with the buyer—yes, for a higher price. (See chapter 12 for more detailed information about appraisal rights.)

CARRYOVER BASIS. Instead of the advantageous stepped-up basis that applies in asset sales, buyers in stock buys and reorgs are saddled with carryover basis. That is, the buyer gets the basis that the seller had in the assets of the company, which is usually less than the purchase price.

TAX-FREE TRANSACTIONS

Any stock purchase, statutory merger, or asset purchase that involves a buyer's stock as payment can be structured to be tax free to the buyer. The seller is not always so blessed, but the incentive is strong: The seller wants to defer tax payments, naturally, and the buyer wants the seller to be happy. A lot of deals would fail to materialize if most sellers had to face a big tax hit right afterward. In fact, though, most M&A transactions are structured as tax free for the seller.

Example: The founder of CUNow merges with Sight Lines for $20 million in stock. After three years, he decides to sell some of the stock. He will have to pay capital gains on the difference between his cost basis and the sale price. If he sells shares for $100,000 and has a cost basis of $10,000, then his gain is $90,000. His capital gain tax will then be $18,000 ($90,000 times 20%).

Keep in mind: Only the stock part of the purchase price qualifies as tax exempt. If a seller receives cash or any other type of property (such as real estate), then he is taxed on the value of these assets when the deal closes.

Unfortunately, the rules regarding tax-free transactions are exceedingly complex. Even the vocabulary sounds contradictory at times. It was the IRS, for instance, that termed an M&A transaction a "reorganization."

The section of the IRS codes that defines the parameters of tax-free M&A is 368. Its general requirements include the following:

PURPOSE. The transaction must be for a bona fide business purpose, not as a way to get favorable tax treatment.

CONTINUITY OF INTEREST. This means that the target company must have a continuing business interest in the surviving company. This is met if the target shareholders receive equity in the surviving company—which can be either voting or nonvoting common and preferred stock.

CONTINUITY OF BUSINESS ENTERPRISE. This means the buyer must pursue a significant amount of the target's historic business or must use a significant portion of its business assets.

Structure

The four main types of tax-free transactions mirror the three basic categories described above. So, when some-one is trying to decide on a tax-free transaction struc-ture, he would apply the same analyses.

The four main ways to structure tax-free transac-tions are the following:

"A" REORGANIZATION. This is a statutory merger and also the most common form of tax-free transaction. One restriction is that the merger must be done under fed-eral or state law; foreign mergers are not allowed.

In this transaction, the consideration (that is, pay-ment) for the seller can be cash and stock, provided that at least 50% of the consideration is stock in the surviving corporation. The stock need not have any voting rights

Example: Sight Lines decides to purchase CUNow for $20 million—paid as $5 million in cash and $15 mil-lion in Sight Lines stock. CUNow's owner will not pay any taxes on the transaction, except on the capital gains for the $5 million in cash.

"B" REORGANIZATION. This is basically a stock pur-chase. However, the buyer must use its own stock. No other asset can be used for the purchase price.

The transaction must result in the control of the target, which is at least 80% of the total number of all voting and nonvoting shares. An interesting twist, how-ever, is that the transaction need not be done all at once. Rather, the acquirer can devise a plan to buy the stock over time. This allows buyers to structure M&A deals in such a manner that the seller has a stake in helping the buyer after the deal.

Example: Sight Lines agrees to purchase CUNow for $20 million, in two stages. In the first stage, Sight Lines will buy 90% of the founder's voting and nonvoting shares for $18 million of Sight Lines stock. If the founder agrees to stay for one year, he will receive an additional $2 million in stock. The founder will owe no taxes on any of the $20 million.

"C" REORGANIZATION. This is an asset purchase. But the only asset the buyer can use as payment is its own stock.

The guideline is that the buyer must buy either 90% of the fair market value of the seller's net assets or 70% of the fair market value of the seller's gross assets.

"D" REORGANIZATION. This is a statutory merger. But instead of merging with the parent (that is, buyer), the target merges into a subsidiary of the parent. The shareholders of the seller can receive stock and cash as payment, but at least 50% must be in stock. The stock does not need to be voting shares.

PAYMENT TYPES

There are a myriad of types of methods to pay for an acquisition, including uncommon forms, such as real estate. In determining payment type, buyer and seller must integrate many factors—including the price of the deal, tax implications, management retention, and so on.

Following is a look at the most common types of payments.

Cash

As the old saying goes, "Cash is king." The procedure in small deals (say, $1 million or less) is that at the time of the signing of the merger agreement, the seller will get a certified check. It certainly is a great feeling, almost like winning the Lotto!

For bigger deals, the more common approach is for the purchaser to wire the cash into the seller's bank account. The seller should be sure that the buyer transfers the funds into an interest-bearing account and make sure the funds will earn interest immediately. For example, suppose the funds are wired on a Friday but the bank is closed until Monday. The seller will forgo three days' interest. This can be a significant concern if the deal was for $100 million.

Doing an all-cash deal certainly makes it easier for both sides to negotiate a merger agreement. There is no need to discuss registration rights of securities. There will be fewer representations and warranties from the buyer. (See chapter 7 for more on this subject.) There will also be no need to discuss the terms of dealing with common stock or with promissory notes (as discussed below).

But keep in mind that all-cash deals are rare. Rather, it is much more common for a deal to have a part of the purchase price in cash (say, 10% or 20%) and the rest as stock or a promissory note.

The Buyer's Advantages

ATTRACTIVENESS. It is easier to convince the seller to sell. For example, if Corp. One bids $100 million in stock and Corp. Two bids $100 million in cash, the cash deal has a much better chance of prevailing. Once again: Cash is king.

DILUTION. It is not dilutive to existing shareholders. For example, Sight Lines decides to buy CUNow for $10 million. Sight Lines' shareholders own 10,000,000 shares. Suppose it will take 1,000,000 shares to buy CUNow. These will have to be new shares issued by Sight Lines. So now there are 11,000,000 shares outstanding. An existing shareholder who owns 2 million shares would see his equity percentage fall from 20% to 18.18% (2 million divided by 11,000,000).

The Buyer's Disadvantages

PRESERVING CASH. It is often hard to pay cash because a company needs to preserve cash to continue to grow its operations.

UNMOTIVATED EMPLOYEES. Cash deals can immediately make the seller very rich and thus not particularly motivated to work hard for the new merged company. It is typical for a seller's employees—at least those who made a lot of money from the deal—to eventually leave and perhaps even retire.

The Seller's Advantages

CERTAINTY AND STABILITY. That is, the value of the deal will not plunge as it might with a stock purchase.

The Seller's Disadvantages

TAXES. The seller will have to pay taxes on the net gain of the transaction. If the seller invested $1,000,000 to form the business and sells it for $2,000,000, there is a $1,000,000 gain. This is taxed as a capital gain, which has a maximum rate of 20%.

Common Stock

If a company does not have much cash flow or borrowing capacity, then an acquisition based on common stock is a good alternative.

Typically, when the merger agreement is signed, the seller's shareholders deliver all their stock certificates—endorsed in the name of the buyer—to the buyer. The buyer delivers its own stock certificates to the seller; sending some by mail is permissible.

The Seller's Advantages

UPSIDE. If the stock soars, the seller's shareholders benefit. After all, consider how well owners of companies that sold out to Microsoft 10 years ago made out: If they held on to their stock, they would have made over 10,000 times the initial purchase price.

TAXES. Look at "Taxes" under the section "Stock Purchases and Statutory Mergers" above.

The Seller's Disadvantages

VOLATILITY. The market for common stock is volatile. What can soar can also plunge. The seller is taking a risk on the future prospects of the buyer's stock performance.

LIQUIDITY. Usually, there are restrictions on when the seller's shareholders can sell the buyer's stock. (This is discussed in more detail in chapter 7.)

The Buyer's Advantages

INCENTIVES. If the managers of the seller get substantial amounts of stock as a result of the merger, they are "incentivized" to operate the new company as well as possible.

CHEAP CURRENCY. When the equity markets are soaring, common stock can be a cheap way to buy companies. This was especially so during the late 1990s.

The Buyer's Disadvantages

DILUTION. Dilution is especially significant if the buyer's stock is already at a low valuation. (See above for basic explanation.)

Example: Suppose Sight Lines has a total market valuation of $250 million. They want to buy CUNow for $10 million—which represents 4% of the value of Sight Lines. However, if the company's value had slid to $100 million (in a hyperactive bear market, for example), the acquisition would be much more dilutive, accounting for 10% of Sight Line's valuation.

DUMPING. If the company issues a large amount of stock in a variety of mergers, that stock may be dumped on the market over time, depressing the price of the buyer's stock.

CONTROL. A buyer must be careful about this issue. For example, suppose Sight Lines decides to buy CUNow, which is owned 50% each by two founders. In the deal, the founders wind up owning 30% each of Sight Lines. Assuming the two vote in sync, they would essentially be in control of Sight Lines.

One way to deal with this problem is to issue preferred stock. A hybrid of debt and equity, preferred stock has a dividend that must be paid before common shareholders get paid their dividends. Also, in the event of a liquidation, the preferred-stock shareholders get any assets before the common shareholders do. By issuing preferred stock, the buyer can reduce the voting power of the shares. This can be perpetual or for a fixed period of time (say, two years) to keep control of the company under current management.

Example: In March 2001, LaBranche & Co. purchased Peck McCooey Financial Services. In the deal, shareholders of Peck received approximately $285 million in common stock and $100 million in preferred shares.

Debt

With this form of payment, the buyer takes a promissory note from the seller. The buyer is responsible for both interest payments and repayment of principal. Whereas there's no preset way to structure the terms of promissory notes, the buyer would generally be inclined to lengthen the term of the payment of principal in order to help preserve cash flow. And conversely, the seller would prefer the money sooner. As a rule of thumb, the promissory note term will range from five to 10 years. Or a deal can be structured in which the buyer pays off the promissory note in stages—perhaps the first 20% will have to be paid after two years, another 20% after four years, and so on.

Important Issues Associated with Promissory Notes

INTEREST PAYMENTS. Basically, the higher the risk of default of the buyer, the higher the interest rate will be set. If the buyer is a public company with a formal credit rating—such as from Moody's or S&P's—then the seller will generally tag the interest rate to the buyer's current debt outstanding.

If the company is private or doesn't have a credit rating, then this is a fertile area for negotiation. One approach is to look at the corporate bonds of a similar company in your industry. You can find such yields at *bonds.yahoo.com*. The seller would then add three or four percentage points on top of this rate.

One interesting twist: Sometimes the buyer doesn't want to pay off the interest in cash because that would deplete precious cash flow. An alternative is to pay with more shares. But since stock is riskier than cash, the interest rate would be set higher—perhaps even another 2% to 4%—than it would be for cash payments.

EXISTING DEBT. The seller must be concerned about the buyer's ability to pay off the new debt. The main question is how much debt the buyer already has and whether the buyer's cash flows are sufficient to take on the additional liability.

Another factor is the debt's priority. The seller would want the contract that sets forth the terms of the promissory notes to stipulate that its notes have senior priority rather than second or third. That is, it must be paid off before any other debt.

COLLATERAL. A promissory note may or may not be secured by the company's assets. Of course, the seller will try to secure his promissory note against as many assets as possible—and preferably hard assets, such as real estate, equipment, and inventory.

A seller may also put his shares in an escrow account as security for the promissory. Here's how it works: James sells his 100%-owned company, JJ Inc., to Ralph Corp. In the transaction, all of Jim's JJ Inc. shares are put in an escrow account. If Ralph Corp. defaults on the promissory note, then Jim can essentially get his company back. However, there may not be much left of it if the buyer mismanaged the JJ Inc. assets.

NEGOTIABILITY. Suppose Jack has a promissory note and sells it to you. However, you realize that Jack actually did not own the note, and the company that is paying interest on the note refuses to pay you. You have no recourse unless the promissory note is considered "negotiable." Basically, negotiability must be expressed as a term in the promissory note contract.

The seller of a company tries to make promissory notes negotiable. Why? Because it is easier to sell to third parties (after all, they know they will get payment on the note). Negotiability is only an issue for notes from private companies. A public company buyer's promissory notes are automatically negotiable.

Keep in mind that the seller may also have out-standing loans. You need to read these agreements carefully and see if you can find a change-of-control clause. This stipulates what happens if the seller is purchased. In some cases, the creditor requires repayment of the loan (there may even be a premium above this amount required). This could be devastating to a buyer if it does not have cash readily available for handling this payment. If you see a prepayment clause, it is a good idea to contact the creditor and see if something can be worked out. If not, you can use this prepayment as a negotiation tactic with the seller to get a lower price on the M&A transaction.

Assume the above problem does not exist and you assume the loan. The loan has an interest rate of 12%. However, because of the size of your own company, you know you can get a loan for 10%. Thus, it is worthwhile considering refinancing this 12% loan at a lower interest rate.

Example: In September 1999, a buyout fund managed by Donaldson, Lufkin & Jenrette purchased Charles River Laboratories for $443 million. About $400 million was in cash, and the rest was a promissory note for 13½% interest.

Earn-Outs

An earn-out is when all or part of the payment is deferred into the future, contingent on the acquired company achieving certain milestones, such as sales or profit levels. Among other things, earn-outs can be a great way to bridge the price gap between a buyer and a seller.

Example: Suppose you own 100% of ZZ Inc., and its profits are $1 million for the current year. The buyer, AA Inc, and ZZ agree that the purchase price should be valued at five times earnings, which is the industry standard for this type and size of merger. This would mean a purchase price of $5 million. But the founder believes that earnings will increase 50%, to $1.5 million, over the next year, which would raise a deal's value to $7.5 million. But AA Inc. is skeptical and does not want to pay the price. An alternative would be to structure an earn-out so that if earnings do in fact increase by 50% in the next year, AA will pay ZZ's founder an additional $2.5 million.

Ultimately, the earn-out is to the benefit of the buyer. If the company does not perform as expected, the buyer will not have wasted extra money or stock in a purchase price. Then again, if the seller's operations grow tremendously, both sides will benefit. The seller gets more compensation, and the buyer receives additional profits from the growth.

Interestingly enough, a smart buyer can often get an earn-out by playing on the emotions of the seller. After all, many sellers will be extremely optimistic about the future prospects of their business. It often verges on hype. Well, the buyer can then say, "I really hope this company grows as much as you say it will. But how do I know? What if the growth doesn't happen? In that case, I will have overpaid for the company. Why don't we use an earn-out that gives you higher compensation if the growth pans out?" With this, it is hard for the seller to back off. After all, didn't he say the company was going to do very well? If this is so, why should he be afraid of an earn-out?

The Important Issues Associated with Earn-Outs

"GRAVY." If the seller meets his goals, the upside can be tremendous. Actually, a seller may know that the goals that are established for the earn-out are relatively easy to achieve and that the earn-out can be easy money.

TAXES. Taxes on the earn-out are deferred—none are owed on the compensation until the year it is earned.

CHANGE OF CONTROL. Suppose you sell your company and get an earn-out that pays you compensation over three years. But after a year from the acquisition, the buyer is purchased. What happens to your earn-out? This needs to be specified in the merger agreement. One approach is to actually make the earn-out payable in full. After all, your original deal was with the first buyer, not the company that just bought it. How do you know that the new buyer will support your division? There is no way to know this when you negotiated the original earn-out.

FAILURE TO MEET GOAL. Taking the example above, suppose that the founder increases the earnings by 49%. According to the formula, he would not get the additional $2.5 million. A solution is to have a sliding scale. For example, if earnings increase 20%, then the amount is $500,000; if the increase is 50%, then the amount is $1.25 million; and so on.

RESOURCES. Will the acquirer provide the target with enough resources to achieve the earn-out goals? To help avoid this problem, it is critical that the seller develop a business plan, one that will forecast sales on the basis of a budget of expenses. This plan should be used as the basis of the earn-out; that is, the buyer will be responsible for funding this budget. When constructing the budget, the seller needs to be conservative. It is never easy to meet forecasted expenses.

EMPLOYMENT AGREEMENT. The purpose of such an agreement—which is commonly requested by sellers—is to ensure that the seller's management can't be fired willy-nilly and denied its earn-out. (The term of the employment agreement should be at least as long as the term of the earn-out). The buyer benefits as well because it can retain current management—which is likely to be the most qualified to run the operations. (There is a detailed discussion of employment agreements in chapter 7.)

CALCULATIONS. A huge consideration for both the buyer and the seller is the calculation of the earn-out. Ideally, from the seller's perspective, the earn-out would be based on an increase in sales. That would be a fairly straightforward, relatively low-risk target.

But a buyer usually won't agree to such an arrangement. After all, the founder may be tempted to boost sales temporarily and jeopardize the long-term prospects of the company. For example, the founder may sell a product that provides for free maintenance service for five years. This may stimulate sales but would mean a loss of revenues over the years from zero maintenance revenues.

Rather, an earn-out will usually be based on net profits. One approach is to base this on Generally Accepted Accounting Principles (GAAP), which is the recognized standard for accounting in the United States. On the surface, this makes sense for both parties. Then again, the seller may have some disadvantages. An acquisition may involve "goodwill" (the cost of an acquired business in excess of the fair value of its identifiable net assets), which must be taken as an expense. Goodwill, though, is a noncash expense. If this is applied to the sales of the seller's division, it could greatly depress the net profits. In many cases, a seller will not include goodwill in the net profit calculation.

In some cases, the buyer will even apply the acquisition expenses to the earn-out calculation. Such expenses, which can run well over $100,000, would appreciably depress net earnings. A seller will try to exclude these from the net profits calculation.

Another consideration for the seller is the allocation of overhead expenses. These are the general administrative expenses, such as HR, accounting, legal, and so on.

The buyer may be tempted to allocate a large proportion of these expenses to the seller's operation in order to depress the net earnings. A solution is for the seller to factor in reasonable expense amounts for overhead in the business plan.

Another difficulty is determining the source of revenues or profits. For instance, suppose XYZ has a technology that produces revenues of $1 million per year. ABC buys this company in a deal that involves an earn-out based on the net revenues of XYZ. Now, suppose that in the following year, direct revenues from XYZ increase by $500,000. Also, ABC is using the XYZ technology in another division, resulting in $1 million in additional sales. Is this $1 million part of the earn-out? It depends on how the contract is drafted. It would certainly be to the advantage of the seller to be able to book these additional revenues.

Example: Stephen and Susan Schutz started a greeting card company in 1971. Slowly, the company built a loyal following (the cards were sold door to door). Then in 1996, the couple's son, Jared, convinced them to go on the Internet. So they launched Bluemountain.com, which became a leader in online greeting cards. In December 1999, Excite@Home purchased Blue Mountain for $350 million in cash and $430 million in stock. By that time, Bluemountain.com was the 14th-most-trafficked Web site. Remarkably enough, the company spent no money on marketing or distribution. An earn-out was applied to the transaction. The couple and son would receive an additional $270 million in stock contingent on the company achieving certain traffic milestones (that is, the sending of e-greeting cards).

CHAPTER 6

DUE DILIGENCE

Due diligence is the process of investigating a firm before it is purchased. It is complex and time consuming—but vitally important. This is the buyer's opportunity to delve into all aspects of the seller's business and thereby determine whether the purchase is a smart move. In fact, good due diligence should accomplish a number of crucial goals:

- Ensure there is no reason the deal should be aborted—for example, if the companies are fundamentally incompatible
- Detect any irregularities in the seller's operations—financial, legal, or other
- Determine how much the target company is really worth—that is, find out whether there are reasons to adjust the official valuation
- Provide insight on how the postmerger integration should be handled—such as what and where resources will need to be allocated

- Find out how easy (or difficult) it is to interact with the target company's management

- Discover possible alternatives to acquisition

For the most part, it is the buyer that conducts the due diligence. After all, the buyer wants to make sure that the company to be acquired is legitimate and sound. It's not at all uncommon for a seller to downplay its weaknesses or even to hide significant problems. This is especially pertinent when the target company is privately held, as there are no public filings or oversight from the SEC. But there are also dangers involved in buying a public company; if the seller is committing fraud, even its accountants don't necessarily know.

For a buyer, part of the art of doing due diligence is to not make it seem like a criminal investigation even as you rigorously examine every aspect of the target's business. On one hand, it's crucial to take nothing for granted or on face value; there's a saying that goes, roughly, "The only way to find the unexpected is by expecting it." If you approach due diligence as a formality and just go through the motions, it is likely you will miss indications of a seller's weak points or even improprieties.

At the same time, if you didn't assume that things are on the up and up, you wouldn't be interested in the company in the first place. The price of due diligence should not be destruction of the trust that allows deals to run smoothly. It is a delicate balance. But in general, a seller with nothing to hide will be forthcoming in response to a buyer's requests for information and assistance.

Another important point is that if you uncover problems that the seller failed to disclose (as is very likely), that doesn't mean the deal should fall through. The seller was not necessarily acting in bad faith; it just might not have known about the condition. Actually, such problems are effective negotiation tools. If it's a problem you would need to pay to have remedied, you might request a lower price. For example, suppose you hired a consultant who found hazardous waste on the seller's property. The costs for remediation would be about $500,000. You could then easily negotiate that this amount comes directly from the original offer price for the seller.

THE DUE DILIGENCE PROCESS

Typically, due diligence doesn't begin until a letter of intent and a confidentiality agreement have been signed. (See chapter 4 for information on drafting the letter of intent; see last section of this chapter about the elements of a confidentiality agreement.) It should be obvious that confidentiality is of utmost concern in all discussions and exchanges of documents between buyer and seller. Any inadvertent disclosure of sensitive information to competitors could be greatly damaging.

It is important that both parties accommodate the other by providing information in an open and honest manner. If a seller tries to hide anything, it will only lose credibility if the buyer finds out (and in many cases, it will). Besides, neither party wants to prolong the due diligence process unnecessarily. The substantial allocation of resources required—of both buyer and seller—could eventually downgrade company operations. Or, if the process gets bogged down, the buyer may get concerned and ultimately back out.

It's helpful to understand due diligence as a two-stage process: pre-M&A due diligence (research that can be done without talking to or visiting the seller) and in-person due diligence (which requires input from the seller).

Pre-M&A due diligence starts before a seller is contacted. As discussed in chapter 2, a buyer should develop screening criteria for selecting buyout candidates. This means doing extensive research of the industry. It is smart to track all the key companies in the industry and collect as much information about each: management, products/services, sales/profits, market share, product features, and so on.

Conducting in-person due diligence will comprise a combination of activities:

- Meetings
- Phone calls and e-mails
- Document exchanges
- On-site visits to the seller's (or buyer's) business location(s)

The buyer needs to form a due diligence team, which should include an investment banker or broker, an attorney, and a CPA. If the buyer is a company, then the resources of its senior management team should be deployed. If the deal entails special concerns—such as potential environmental liabilities, antitrust matters, or highly complex information systems integration—it is a good idea to bring in consultants that specialize in these respective areas.

It is highly advisable to have a single "point person" for all the due diligence information. This manager will be responsible for collecting and codifying all the various reports and documents pertaining to the process.

The length of the due diligence process can vary. With small companies (say, below $100 million in sales), it can take a few weeks. For larger companies, it can take several months, especially if there are complex issues, such as environmental liabilities or antitrust matters.

CHECKLISTS

To help manage the complexity of due diligence, a buyer should use a checklist. You can buy your own checklist or use one from a deal professional, such as a broker, an in-

vestment banker, or an attorney. Most checklists deal
with a company's finances, marketing, and legal aspects.
But a good checklist should also encompass a range of
strategic factors that will help you determine whether
the other company is a good fit and whether it has a
long-term future.

The following sections offer in-depth analyses of
each section of a due diligence checklist. To compile this
chapter, I've distilled the most relevant questions from a
number of checklists, both general purpose and industry
specific. Having this chapter as a resource doesn't mean
you shouldn't bother purchasing a full, detailed checklist, but it will provide an excellent start.

Of course, the entire list won't apply to all companies. With the help of your team, you can tailor a checklist to the characteristics of the seller. In fact, at the
beginning of due diligence, the buyer should discuss the
checklists with the seller, both to hone the lists and to
prepare the seller to help. To help build momentum, it is
a good idea to start with easier sections, such as the delivery of corporate documents.

Now we'll discuss each checklist category in detail.
As you'll see, quite a few of the areas require no pre-
M&A diligence, just in-person.

Financials

The buyer should certainly focus a lot of effort on investigating the seller's financials. Unfortunately, some companies are tempted to play fast and loose with their
financial data, so much care and some healthy skepticism is advised in this pursuit.

In fact, it is a good idea for the buyer to have the
CPA perform an audit on the seller (assuming the financials are unaudited). While an audit can be expensive—
usually more than $20,000—it can uncover hidden
problems in a company's finances that would more than

"SELLER BEWARE"—
DUE DILIGENCE WORKS BOTH WAYS

Though this chapter focuses on the traditional situation, in which the buyer performs the due diligence, smart sellers know that it's a two-way street. After all, for both parties it's important to truly understand each other, to make sure that the other is strong and a "good fit," and to uncover possible alternatives to acquisitions. And most important, the seller doesn't want to get burned. Nothing could be worse: You give a huge chunk of your life's energies into building a company, and then you sell it to a con artist who "pays" you with a small lump of cash and a big pile of worthless stock certificates.

A seller has a lot at stake when you sell your company. True, if you sell for 100% cash, the risks are minimal. But this is rare. You are likely to have your compensation be based on the stock of the buyer. In a way, selling a company is similar to buying stock for a portfolio: The seller wants a stock that will grow.

But instead of having to start to investigate a prospective buyer from scratch, the seller should be informed ahead of time. That is, the seller should have its own set of screening criteria (assuming they consider M&A as a potential strategy, as everyone should) and keep abreast of the marketplace. So, when the seller is approached by a buyer, it won't have to scramble.

In performing due diligence, the seller should employ the same checklists as the buyer and ask equivalent questions. Areas of emphasis include the following:

Financials. Has the buyer's growth been better than its peers? Also, check for danger signs, such as increasing receivables. How much cash does the company have? Does it have enough cash to pursue its goals? Also, perform a ratio analysis on the company.

Strategy. Do you believe in the buyer's goals and strategies? Do you think the company is headed in the right direction? Does the buyer have a history of M&A strategy, and if so, how have the acquired companies or "brands" fared?

Products/services. Does the company have a competitive product line? Will your product line enhance the company's growth?

Management. Finally, do you think the buyer has a strong management team? Do they have prior experience with growing strong companies?

justify the outlay. Perhaps, for example, much of the inventory must be written off or sales are being recorded too aggressively.

If the company is public, you have access to the required SEC filings. But these are often incomplete. Thus, it is simply too risky to rely solely on these financials for a buyout. You should get the internal documents, which involve cash flow projections, sales forecasts, and budgets.

Analyzing the financial statements involves hundreds of questions. Because of its scope, this section is organized differently from the ones that follow. The first checklist below covers the general issues, but then we delve into each key financial statement separately and in depth.

FORENSIC ACCOUNTING

The goal of a traditional audit is to determine whether a company is complying with GAAP. Unfortunately, such audits are ineffective at detecting if a company is engaged in fraud—even massive fraud, such as was the case with HFS before it merged with CUC. No buyer would want to acquire a business guilty of such abuses, but what can be done?

There is an emerging trend to have much more in-depth audits—known as forensic audits. A forensic specialist looks beneath and behind the numbers, trying to uncover possible manipulation or fraud. Here are some telltale factors indicating the need for a forensic audit:

Background investigations. Has current management engaged in any past fraud?

Internal controls. These are policies intended to prevent corporate fraud. If such controls are lax or lacking, a company could be in jeopardy.

Regulators. Has the company had past run-ins with regulators?

Turnover. Has the company had much turnover with its auditors, attorneys, or CFO?

Sales. Is documentation of sales inadequate?

Buyer Team Involved
- Founder/buyer, CEO, CFO, CPA, investment banker or attorney

In-Person Due Diligence
(for General Financial Considerations)
- Request monthly and annual financial statements for at least the past three years, compara-

tive financial statements for each division, a list of banks and other financial institutions the company deals with, auditor's reports, and debt agreements.

- Are there any personal guarantees by the owners of the business for certain debts?

- How are the financial statements prepared? Do they use GAAP (Generally Accepted Accounting Principles)?

- How reliable are the financials? What is the process for the accounting? Are there checks and balances to guard against bad reporting? If there are problems, how fast can they be changed? What will the costs be?

- Is the accounting system integrated with other parts of the company, such as the sales department?

Balance Sheet

The balance sheet shows the assets, liabilities, and equity of the company.

CASH. What is the cash position? Is it enough to last for the next few years? Has it been declining substantially? It can take about a year to integrate an acquisition, so it is a good idea to have enough cash to fund the operations for this period of time. Also, it is common for the growth rate to decline for a year after the merger because of integration issues. So, when forecasting the cash flows of the company, you should reduce the growth rate at least 15%. Under this assumption, will this company have enough money to continue at this rate for the next 12 months? In chapter 3, we took a detailed look at how to construct a cash flow forecast. Is the excess cash being invested in money market accounts? What are the company's cash management policies? Is the company earning a competitive interest rate from its cash balances? (Strangely enough, some companies will put large sums in non-interest-bearing accounts.) How much cash is in foreign accounts? How easy is it to get to this money? Are there currency controls?

CREDIT. What are the credit policies? Look at the aged trial balances for accounts receivables. Is it taking longer for the company to collect money from customers? Has the company been using rebates or discounts to encourage sales? Are any customers in default? How long does a customer have to pay bills? If you notice that, say, over the past six months, it is taking 20% or longer to collect bills, then there is likely a problem with the company's customers' ability to pay. Moreover, if sales are growing slower than receivables, this is another indication that there are problems with customers.

CUSTOMERS. How many customers are there? Does one or a small number of customers account for much of the sales? If one customer accounts for more than 10% of total sales, then this is a danger sign. The loss of the customer can have a big impact on the company's sales and the performance of the M&A transaction. What is the customer turnover? It is a good idea to call some customers.

INVENTORIES. Are inventories building up? Could the products be obsolete? What type of inventory accounting system is used? If, for example, you employ GAAP for your financial statements but the seller uses a different method, you will need to convert the seller's financials to a GAAP system—which can cost $20,000 or more from a qualified CPA. Do a physical count of the inventory. Has the company written off inventory? Should it? A qualified CPA should answer this question. But if the inventory is not likely to be sold, then it should be written off. And of course this inventory should have no bearing in terms of the valuation of the seller's company.

REAL ASSETS. Request the type and location of property, plant, and equipment. How have these assets depreciated? Has there been an appraisal of their value? At what capacity are the factories running? Are there zoning restrictions? What improvements have been made to the real property? For leases, when do they expire? Can they be terminated or renegotiated? What are the annual costs? What other types of assets does the company have? Has the company invested in start-ups? If so, what are the values of these companies?

PAYABLES. Analyze the accounts payables. To whom does the company owe money? List the vendors. Who are the biggest vendors? If a vendor is lost, can another one be found quickly enough and at a reasonable cost?

DEBT. List all the company's liabilities: notes, mortgages payable, credit lines, and bond issues. What are the payment schedules? Is there a big debt payment due soon? Are any assets of the company used as collateral for the loans? Did officers borrow from the company? How much? Is the company in compliance with loan covenants?

Income Statement

The income statement shows the revenues, expenses, and profit of a company.

REVENUES. How are revenues recorded? Is it a good technique? Is the company too aggressive? Has revenue been volatile? Are sales increasing because of price increases or volume increases?

EXPENSES. Review the expenses. Can the merger help reduce the expenses? This is a very important area. Saving expenses is a main reason for an acquisition. Typically, this is accomplished by consolidating duplicated expenditures, especially labor. Thus, when looking at the potential savings, list the different departments and combine the employees from the buyer and seller. For example:

Sales force	10 employees
HR	5 employees
Administration	9 employees
Marketing	3 employees
Product development	12 employees
Senior management	7 employees

Estimate how many employees you need in each department. (If possible, identify specifically which employees stay or get laid off.) Suppose that you can cut two employees from HR, one from marketing, two from senior management, and two from administration. Add up the annual salaries for each and then subtract the expenses from the layoffs (such as severance payments and outplacement services). The result should give you a rough idea of the savings. Assuming the average salary is $50,000, the potential savings would be $350,000 for one year.

Hint: With a private business, sometimes the founder will use the company for personal expenses. These expenses can add up. When looking at the financials, see what expenses are personal: cars, vacations, and so on. By eliminating these expenses, the company will automatically save money.

Financial Projections

These are the internal revenue and expense projections of a company. Of course, it is common for these to be quite optimistic.

- Request forecasts and projections, such as for cash flows, earnings, units sold, and so on. These are usually in the form of spreadsheets.

- What is the worst-case scenario for the next year? The best case? With the forecasting spreadsheets, run these scenarios. If there is a substantial drop in sales, will there be enough cash?

Modeling Techniques

It's unwise to take a seller's forecasts at face value because there's nearly always an inclination for the company to take an unrealistically optimistic view of things. Rather, with the financial information you gain from the due diligence, you should do your own financial modeling.

SENSITIVITY ANALYSIS. This shows how a change in sales affects other parts of the financials, such as gross margins and profits. Sensitivity analysis can be effective for looking at best-case and worst-case scenarios. If a company is in fact highly sensitive—say, because of high fixed costs—a slight reduction in sales could mean big losses. But the reverse is true as well.

BREAK-EVEN ANALYSIS. As the name implies, this shows how many units the company must sell to break even. This helps management establish milestones.

Example: If a company with annual expenses of $1 million manufactures a product that sells, on average, for $10 apiece, the company will need to sell 100,000 units to break even.

CASH FLOW PROJECTIONS. When making cash flow projections, look at items that could have a major effect, such as new plant investment or equipment or debt retirement.

RATIO ANALYSIS. With the company's financial statements, you can compute a variety of useful financial ratios, as described in the following section.

But keep two things in mind: First, you should look at the ratios in comparison to the overall industry. For example, a current ratio in the grocery industry may be far different from the auto industry. You can find industry ratios online, at sites such as MSN Investor *(money-central.msn.com / investor)* or *www.hoovers.com.* Second, it is a good idea to track the ratios over a period of time— say, three to five years. Are the ratios improving? Getting worse?

Useful Financial Ratios

The best way to present a series of ratios is to posit a hypothetical company equipped with a full set of financial numbers. Our theoretical company is XYZ Corp., a developer of high-end waxes for cars. The company distributes its products through retail outlets. Through due diligence, you were able to obtain the company's financial statements. See table 6.1.

Let's compute some useful ratios for XYZ Corp.

Liquidity Ratios

These measure the likelihood that a company will be able to pay its bills. A banker will look at the *current ratio* very carefully before extending a loan to a company. The formula is

$$\text{Current Ratio} = \text{Current Assets/Current Liabilities}$$
$$3.0 = \$1,500/\$500$$

If the ratio were less than 1.0, then the company probably does not have enough assets to pay off its short-term liabilities. In other words, if a company liquidates the current assets, there is still more debt that has to be paid off in the next 12 months.

Interestingly enough, the current ratio may overstate the liquidity of the company. This is true when inventory is difficult to sell. This is why it's useful to apply the *quick ratio,* which is essentially the current ratio excluding inventory :

TABLE 6.1.
BALANCE SHEET FOR XYZ CORP.

Assets (values are in thousands)

Cash	$500
Accounts receivables	$500
Inventory	$500
Current assets	$1,500
Buildings	$4,000
Equipment	$1,500
Total assets	$7,000

Liabilities and Capital (values are in thousands)

Accounts payable	$400
Accrued expenses	$100
Total current liabilities	$500
Long-term note	$1,000
Total liabilities	$1,500
Retained earnings	$1,500
Common stock	$4,000
Total liabilities and capital	$7,000

Income Statement (values are in thousands)

Revenues	$5,000
Cost of goods sold	($2,000)
Gross profit	$3,000
Selling expenses	($1,000)
Administrative expenses	($1,000)
Net income before interest and taxes (EBIT)	$1,000
Interest	($100)
Taxes	($300)
Net income	$600

Quick Ratio = (Current Assets–Inventory)/Current Liabilities
$$2.0 = \$1{,}000/\$500$$

Leverage Ratios

These measure how effectively a company is paying back
its debt. High ratios may limit a company's ability to
raise money. On the other hand, a low debt structure
may indicate a company is not aggressive enough. This
can be a big opportunity for a buyer.

The formula for the total debt to total assets—*debt
ratio* for short—is

Debt Ratio = Total Debt/Total Assets
$$21\% = \$1{,}500/\$7{,}000$$

You can also look at the overall debt in relation to
the company's equity—*debt-to-equity ratio* for short:

Debt to Equity = Total Debt/Total Equity
$$33.33\% = \$1{,}500/\$4{,}000$$

Now, even if these ratios are high, this does not
mean that the company cannot raise any more money.
Bankers will also look at the company's cash flows. For
doing so, a key ratio is the *times interest earned.*

Times Interest Earned = EBIT/Interest Charges
$$10 = \$1{,}000/\$100$$

In this case, XYZ has quite a bit of cash to pay for
its current debt load. Thus, it's likely to be able to raise
more debt.

Profitability Ratios

These measure the profitability of the whole firm. The
profit margin gives an indication of the profitability of
the operations—excluding administrative and selling expenses. If the company has negative gross margins, then
there could be serious problems. Either the company is
deliberately setting the prices low—to gain market
share—or the company is uncompetitive.

$$\text{Profit Margin} = \text{Gross Profit/Total Sales}$$
$$60\% = \$3,000/\$5,000$$

Another key profit ratio is the *return on total assets.* As the name implies, this shows how much profit a company derives from its complete asset base. If the figure is low, it may indicate that the company is not being efficient with its assets.

$$\text{Return on Total Assets} = \text{EBIT/Total Assets}$$
$$14\% = \$1,000/\$7,000$$

Next, there is *return on equity:*

$$\text{Return on Equity} = \text{Net Income/Shareholder's Equity}$$
$$15\% = \$600/\$4,000$$

Of course, showing strong growth from this ratio indicates that the company is in a healthy position. But be wary: The return on equity figure may be high because the company is carrying a large debt load.

Activity Ratios

These ratios show how efficiently a company is using its assets. For example, one of the hallmarks of Dell Computer is its strong activity ratios. The company has implemented sophisticated technology to create a highly efficient manufacturing powerhouse.

Here is the formula for the *fixed asset turnover* ratio:

$$\text{Fixed Asset Turnover} = \text{Sales/Net Fixed Assets}$$
$$0.90 = \$5,000/\$5,500$$

This provides an indication of how well a company uses fixed assets, such as land, buildings, and equipment. Some industries are capital intensive and as a result have low ratios (such as the auto industry). Also bear in mind that assets may be understated. Why? Because according to GAAP accounting, there is no adjustment for inflation. In other words, a piece of land may be valued as $1 million on a company's balance sheet yet may be worth $15 million in the open market.

For the *inventory turnover* ratio, a high number is generally better. This means less capital is tied up in inventory storage:

$$Inventory\ Turnover = Sales/Inventories$$
$$10 = \$5,000/\$500$$

The formula for *days sales outstanding* shows how long, on average, it takes a company's customers to pay bills. Of course, the shorter the period, the better:

$$Days\ Sales\ Outstanding = Receivables/(Sales/360)$$
$$38 = 500/13$$

Taxes

One potentially big problem is underpayment of taxes. If the IRS does an audit, there could be substantial back taxes, interest charges, and penalties. Therefore, a buyer must review a target company's tax situation carefully. Many companies keep two sets of numbers: one for the IRS, to limit tax liability by showing relatively low earnings, and another for investors, geared to demonstrate the company's strength. In such situations, the fundamental goal of the due diligence team is to find out "What's real here—taxes, or financials, or somewhere in between?"

Buyer Team Involved

- Buyer/founder, CEO, CFO, CPA, investment banker or broker

In-Person Due Diligence

- Request federal and state tax returns for the last three years. Reconcile these returns to the company's financial statements. Also, look at filings for sales taxes, unemployment, and social security payments.

- Is the company subject to special types of taxes?
- Have there been any notice of assessments from state or federal authorities?
- Does the company have any tax losses that can be carried forward? Any tax credits? How will an acquisition affect these?
- Was there ever an audit? If so, what were the results?
- What are the payroll practices? Is money being deposited in a timely manner?

Strategic Factors

In considering an acquisition, the strategic importance of the target company should be the first consideration. Often, a buyer will look at a company because it is cheap or profitable or has a strong, talented workforce. But too often, the buyer neglects to assess the company's overall competitive strength or weakness in relation to the industry. This is where fundamental problems may be lurking, so it's better to find that out before it's too late.

We break up the strategic checklist into two: (1) the industry and (2) the company itself. You need to have a good grasp of the general dynamics of the industry in order to assess where the target company lies. In looking at the company, one of the crucial strategic factors is how the public sees it. As the saying goes, "Perception is reality." This is absolutely true for companies. You want to buy a company with a favorable reputation rather than a firm that's despised.

Buyer Team Involved

- Buyer/founder, senior management, investment banker or broker

The Industry

Pre-M&A Due Diligence

- What are the main factors that are driving the growth of this industry?
- How fast is the market growing? What is the international growth forecast?
- What are the governmental regulations?
- Are there specific tax laws affecting this industry?
- Is the industry being commoditized (that is, are prices for the product falling because it is easy for others to manufacture)?
- Are there barriers to entry?
- What are the cyclical trends?
- What is the reputation of the industry?
- How competitive is the industry?

Competition requires close attention. Without doubt, every industry has competition. (If you don't think so, then look again!) In fact, it's essential that the buyer conduct an extensive competitive analysis. One reason for this is that in due diligence, target companies are often not forthcoming about the competitive environment. Instead, they tend to discount the competition.

Here are some things to include in your competitive analysis:

- List of the primary competitors; make sure you look at foreign competitors
- Look at their strengths and weaknesses for quality, products, technology, and market share
- Industry pricing

In-Person Due Diligence

- Who are the main suppliers? Have they been increasing prices?

The Word on Competition

To learn more about competition, it is worth reading *Michael E. Porter on Competition,* by Michael Porter (Harvard Business School Press, 1998). A Harvard professor, respected and innovative economist, and author of 14 other books, Porter is considered *the* competition guru, and this book is his masterwork on the subject. It is a collection of 13 key articles about competition, the premise being that all companies—local or domestic or international—must face competition head-on and master it. (Porter claims this applies to countries and individuals as well.)

- Do they have a business plan? When was the last time it was updated?

The Company

Pre-M&A Due Diligence

- What is the history of this company?
- Look at the press clippings for the past few years—is the company presented favorably?
- Are there any customer satisfaction surveys?

In-Person Due Diligence

- What is its mission statement?
- What sets this company apart from the competition?
- Is this company willing to make changes in its corporate values?
- What are its long-term goals?

Products/Services and Manufacturing

Many buyers are drawn to acquire a company by its product or product line. Perhaps the product can complement the buyer's current line. Or the buyer wants to enter a new business altogether. This area is also divided into two: (1) products themselves and (2) product manufacture. It is smart to visit the key manufacturing facilities and see the manufacturing process in real time.

Buyer Team Involved

- Buyer/founder, CEO, vice president of the product division involved, investment banker or broker, attorney (who can review sales and marketing agreements)

Products / Services

Pre-M&A Due Diligence

- Request product brochures, lists, and descriptions.
- Inspect the products. Use them. Test them. How do they compare to your products? To those of competitors?

In-Person Due Diligence

- What products are growing fast? Which ones are slowing? Is there a backlog?
- What are the current versions of these products?

Manufacturing Systems

Pre-M&A Due Diligence

- Does the industry have excess capacity?
- Are there raw material shortages?
- How does it compare with the industry?

In-Person Due Diligence

- How long does it take to build a manufacturing facility? What is the cost?
- What have they done to reduce costs?
- How do they increase productivity?
- Do they use just-in-time inventory or another type of system?
- Do they have a quality control system, and if so, what kind? Do they have a quality assurance team? What are the standards?
- At what capacity are the factories running? Are they currently constructing any new manufacturing facilities?
- How are labor relations? Any disputes?
- What is the wage structure?
- How is purchasing handled? Is it centralized? Do they use competitive bidding? How many supply sources are used?
- Are there intercompany purchases? If so, how are these priced?

Sales and Marketing

It is not uncommon to find an acquisition candidate with a strong technology base and product line—but inadequate marketing and sales. When conducting due diligence in this area, look for ways to make improvements. Remember, the costs for making such changes add to the bottom line of the acquisition.

Buyer Team Involved

- Buyer/CEO, sales/marketing vice presidents, investment banker or broker, attorney (who can review the contracts)

Pre-M&A Due Diligence

- Who is the price leader in the industry? Have prices been increasing or falling?
- Is there seasonality to the industry? How does the industry perform in recessions? Is the industry cyclical? Is the industry currently in an up cycle or a down cycle? How long does the average cycle last?

In-Person Due Diligence

- How do the company's metrics compare to the industry as a whole?
- Look at prior sales forecasts. Has the company been meeting or exceeding the forecasts?
- What are the current marketing and sales strategies? Have they changed in the past year or so?
- On what basis does the company compete? By price or quality?
- What sales have fallen through? Why?
- What are the pricing policies and strategies?
- What types of channels does the industry use? What channels does the company use? What are the most important ones? Which channels are the company seeking?
- Request contracts for the channel deals. How strong are these contracts? Can they be changed? Are there conflicts with the channels?
- Look at the direct sales force. How is it organized? How well qualified are the staff members? How long on average have the salespeople been with the company? What is the compensation?
- What is the discount policy? Are many discounts given out?

- What type of advertising does the company engage in? What are the expenses? Does the company expect to ramp-up expenditures? How does the company measure the effectiveness of advertising expenditures? Does the company use an outside advertising firm?
- How is the company's PR? Is it mentioned often in the trades? What are the PR strategies? Is there a PR firm?

Management Information Systems

The importance and challenges of technological compatibility should never be underestimated. In 1995, two healthcare plans merged and formed Harvard Pilgrim. Wall Street liked the play, and the stock price surged. But by 1998, the stock plunged, as the company had a loss of $94 million. One of the biggest problems was the integration of the two companies' information technology (IT) systems. The claims-processing system—which supported about 500,000 subscribers—was now supposed to handle 1.2 million. Harvard Pilgrim failed miserably, as the company took a $94 million operating loss in fiscal 1998. What's more, the CEO and CFO resigned.

Such stories are all too common. Integrating IT systems can be daunting, and it usually takes longer than expected. A critical factor is to first integrate the communications systems between the two companies. You need to make sure that phones, e-mail, and intranet are in sync.

On the surface, it would seem that integration is easier for two companies that are in the same business. But this is not necessarily so. For example, both companies may have different types of customer bases that require different IT setups.

Some M&A firms have so-called SWAT teams for IT integration. After all, a rapid conversion means more upside from a merger. One company with a SWAT team is FleetBoston Financial Group. Interestingly, the company only does big mergers since the costs of IT integration are large regardless of the size of the merger. Since 1995, FleetBoston has integrated the disparate IT systems of such major banks as Shawmut National, NatWest, and BankBoston.

In fact, major companies may hire consulting firms—such as IBM, Accenture, EDS, and so on—to help with the merger integration. It may be costly—running over $100,000—but it can make for a much smoother M&A transaction, especially if both companies have varying IT infrastructures.

Buyer Team Involved

- Buyer/founder, CEO, chief technology officer, chief information officer, investment banker or broker

In-Person Due Diligence

- Does the target use enterprise resource planning (ERP), such as SAP or Oracle? How much customization has been done to these systems? (Even if both companies have the same ERP system, this does not mean integration will be easy.)
- Do they outsource IT? If so, how much?
- Are different IT systems employed overseas? Within the United States? (It is common for companies to have a complex hodgepodge of different IT systems, making the integration task that much more cumbersome and problem prone.)
- Is your (the seller's) current technology infrastructure sufficient to support an acquisition target's customer base? What changes will need to be made?

- Will you keep the acquisition target's IT system? Will you only use parts of it?
- Are there key employees critical to the IT infrastructure of the target?
- What are the expenses of the IT system during the past few years?
- What are the success and failures of the IT system?

Human Resources

As explained in chapter 8, postdeal integration is extremely important for an acquisition, and HR is often a major stumbling block. The employees of both companies need to feel like they are part of a strong organization. Doing thorough HR due diligence, you can better plan the integration of two corporate cultures.

Buyer Team Involved
- Buyer/founder, CEO, vice president of HR, chief counsel, attorney, CPA, investment banker or broker

In-Person Due Diligence
- What is the work environment like? Company culture?
- Request organization charts, compensation records, personnel files, management contracts, and HR manual.
- What type of HR information technologies do they use?
- What types of benefits—health insurance, retirement, stock options, sick leave, disability, vacation, severance, deferred compensation, bonuses—do they offer? How do the benefits compare to the rest of the industry?

MERGER OF EQUALS

Sometimes, "M&A" focuses on the "M" rather than the more typical "A." In such instances, neither of the two companies is the buyer or the seller. Rather, the transaction is a "merger of equals." In this case, both parties will perform mutual due diligence. This was the case with the megamerger between the pharmaceutical giants Glaxo Wellcome plc and SmithKline Beecham plc—the combined value of which was a whopping $176 billion. In such a deal, both companies get roughly the same amount of stock in the new combined entity, and neither gets a premium price. In fact, both stocks fell when the merger was announced. Under the merger agreement, Glaxo shareholders got 58.75% of the new entity and SmithKline 41.25%. Glaxo's CEO became the CEO of the new entity, but both companies were represented equally on the board of directors.

In mergers of equals, the problems often emerge after the deal, during the integration phase. Leadership complications are common, with the big question being, "Who's going to be in charge here?" Sometimes it will take a year or two to determine which of the two companies is pulling its weight more and is, hence, the de facto "buyer."

As for due diligence, in the Glaxo/SmithKline merger, both companies knew each other well, with many of the employees having worked at both organizations. Each corporation had been gathering competitive intelligence about the other for many years. The companies were quite certain that the other was financially sound and generally free of legal wrongdoing. As a result, the due diligence teams were able to focus more on strategic issues rather than "the fundamentals" (that is, financials). Strategic matters include areas not evident in public documents: technology systems, management techniques, and so on—what I call "non-spreadsheet-type analysis." The attitude behind this due diligence could be summed up as "We want to learn more about your business, and have you learn more about ours, so everyone benefits."

- What is the turnover rate? Is there any pending employee litigation? How many—if any—key employees have been lost to competitors?
- Is there a labor union? Are employees requesting that a union be established?
- Are there any problems with federal or state labor regulations?
- Are there corporate training programs? Pay for employee education?
- Is there compliance with affirmative action laws? How diverse is the workforce?
- Employee communication? Newsletter? Intranet? Retreats? Orientation? Are there employee attitude surveys? Is there a "hot line" telephone number for employees?
- Does the company have any community involvement?
- What are the executive perks: company car, credit union, physical fitness programs, food service?
- What is the dress code?
- How many employees are contractors?
- Do they have an accident log?

- Is the organization flat or hierarchical?
- Is there a succession plan?
- What are the recruitment practices? What do they look for in an employee?
- Are there any unfilled positions?
- Are there any employee complaints?
- What are typical working hours?

Corporate and Financial Structure

The buyer needs a full understanding of the legal structure of the company, starting with whether the company is a corporation, partnership, limited liability company, or joint venture. It's crucial that all the associated legal work be airtight. More generally, you need to ascertain that the company has a sound system for storing essential documents. Also, the buyer must know where the company operates and how that affects its status. Plus, you need to know the company's overall financial footing—how much equity is owned by outsiders and so on. To grow, the target company probably had several rounds of external financing. You must know the legal nature of the debt the company carries.

Buyer Team Involved
- Buyer/founder, CEO, attorney, chief counsel, CPA, investment banker or broker

In-Person Due Diligence
- Request articles of incorporation; bylaws; minutes of all board, committee, and shareholder meetings; shareholder list; annual reports; and stock transfer books. Also, request any amendments to these documents. With this information, you can see if a company has been incorporated

properly (were the fees paid? were there director meetings?) Also, you can see if there are any anti-takeover provisions (such as in the bylaws). These are explained in more detail in chapter 11. However, the seller may waive this provision.

- Are there any subsidiaries, affiliates, strategic alliances, or joint ventures? If so, request the material legal documents.

- In what states and countries do they transact business?

- What are their business locations?

- List the advisers/consultants of the company: attorneys, bankers, investment bankers, auditors, transfer agents, insurance and real estate brokers.

- What are the procedures for record keeping? Is there a retention policy? Are key documents kept in areas outside the company's headquarters? Is there a privacy policy for customer records and for the Web site? Have there been any breaches of the company's internal databases? For private companies, record keeping can be sporadic. Months may go by without any records, for instance. If this is the case, that certainly should raise concerns. Why weren't records maintained? Were there any problems during this time period?

- Request a list of stock certificates, warrants, options, and debt instruments issued. Information should include shares issued, payments, and issuance dates. Also request buy-sell agreements, shareholder agreements, proxies, warrant agreements, right-of-first-refusal agreements, option agreements, and preemptive rights agreements. (From these documents, you can see how many shares are outstanding and need to be purchased to buy the company.)

Insurance

Insurance has an interesting twist: You hope you never have to use it. But a business without proper insurance coverage is in a precarious situation. If policies overlap, as they sometimes do in M&As, you could probably reduce overall coverage costs. (See later in this chapter for information about M&A insurance.)

Buyer Team Involved
- Buyer/founder, CEO, CFO, investment banker or broker

In-Person Due Diligence
- Request policies for property, liability, workers' compensation, key person, and director indemnification.
- What exactly is covered? What are the costs? Are the premiums expected to increase? What are the deductibles? Are there better alternatives?
- What are the insurance claims for the past five years?

Regulation and Litigation

Of course, if a target has not been abiding by certain laws and regulations, the acquirer could be subject to liability. One way to deal with this liability is to shift it to the seller through contract provisions in the merger agreement (known as "representations and warranties"). In chapter 9, we will look at this—and regulations in general—in great detail.

Of course, the United States is a litigious society. And since companies usually have large amounts of assets and cash, they are often targets of lawsuits. Thus, you need to make an assessment of the prior litigation and potential litigation exposure.

Buyer Team Involved

- Buyer/founder, CEO, chief counsel, attorney, investment banker or broker

Regulation

In-Person Due Diligence

- Does the company have a legal department? If so, what has been done to deal with the company's regulations?
- Or does the company consult with outside consultants and attorneys to help deal with regulatory concerns?
- Has the company complied with securities regulations?
- What are the pertinent environmental regulations?
- Are there special labor regulations specific to the company?
- Is the company under the jurisdiction of a federal agency, such as the FDA?
- Are there antitrust concerns?
- Are there foreign regulations involved?

Litigation

In-Person Due Diligence

- Request copies of pleadings for prior or pending lawsuits, settlements, decrees, orders, and judgments.
- For pending litigation, what are the potential damages? How are the cases progressing? Are

any of the lawsuits covered by insurance? If so, how much? Are there deductibles?

Past Acquisitions

You may be buying a company that has itself engaged in M&A activity. Review the documents for these transactions. And try to assess how these acquisitions have progressed. Also, the target may be involved in one or more joint ventures (JV). By buying the target, will this violate the JV or will the JV be terminated because the partners consider that you are too competitive with them?

Buyer Team Involved

- Founder/buyer, CEO, general counsel, CFO, investment banker or broker, CPA, attorney

In-Person Due Diligence

- Are there still integration questions?
- If an acquisition was a failure, will it need to be written off?
- Are there any potential legal problems, such as shareholder lawsuits?
- Has the target been the subject of buyout offers? What were the amounts? Why did the deals fall through? Has the target been actively trying to sell the business? If so, for how long?

Special Category 1: High-Tech Acquisitions

There is a high rate of failure for high-tech acquisitions, and one big reason for this, in fact, is insufficient due diligence.

A classic example is Novell's purchase of WordPerfect in 1994. At the time, Novell was the leading developer of networking operating systems. Even the mighty Microsoft recognized it would be extremely difficult to unseat Novell. But Novell's founder and CEO, Ray Noorda, wanted to diversify. So he purchased WordPerfect—at the time, a leading developer of word processing software—for $1.4 billion. He also bought QuattroPro, a frontline spreadsheet company, for $145 million. But WordPerfect was riddled with problems: For example, its transition from DOS to Windows was slow. The main problem was that Microsoft was coming out with more competitive products, investing a lot of resources into overtaking WordPerfect. Within 18 months, Novell recognized its diversification strategy was a huge mistake, and the company sold its WordPerfect and QuattroPro assets for about $180 million.

Of course, if done properly, high-tech acquisitions can be a great benefit. But there must be a strong emphasis on due diligence.

In the following sections, we will take a look at strategies. These are all basically in-person due diligence matters, and the buying team should include the founder/CEO, the CEO, the chief technology officer, the sales vice president, product vice presidents, general counsel, an investment banker or broker, and an attorney.

Developers

A critical part of the value of an acquisition is the technical staff. In fact, some companies will look at the price of an acquisition in terms of cost per engineer. As the old saying goes, "Your assets walk out the door every night."

- What are the qualifications of the staff? How many have master's degrees? Doctoral degrees? Who are the key employees?

- What are the procedures for documenting the development process? Do programmers document the code itself?
- What types of development tools does the staff use? Will it integrate with your tools?
- Is there a LAN-based system to keep track of changes to software or hardware products?
- Is the development team understaffed?
- Are there frequent backups of source code?
- What kind of virus policy is in place?

Products

In high-tech, a product line is subject to rapid obsolescence—to be replaced by a newer iteration or an entirely different product line. More than anything, you need to have a good feel for where the industry is going.

- How many versions are there for each product? When are the next updates?
- Do they meet their announced product release dates?
- Is there a list of bugs per product? Have they had to make any fixes?
- What criteria do they use for bringing out new features in a product? What is the priority?
- How do they factor customer feedback? Do they have usability studies? Focus groups?
- What percentage of the product sales is returned?
- Call several of the customers.
- Review complaint letters.
- How do they test software? Do they use in-house or outside applications for testing? Do they have a quality assurance team? At what point does the

quality assurance team come into the development process?

Technical Support

Some products can be a nightmare, especially if many customers call for technical support help. This area is a key factor affecting a company's reputation.

- How do they handle customer support? Is much of it outsourced?

- How many people are on staff for technical support? What is the response time? How successful is the staff with answering questions? How many calls, on average, does it take to answer a question?

- How do they log calls for technical support? Is the information put into a database? Is there a bug tracking system?

- What are the technical support procedures? Is there a manual?

- Are there technical support Web resources, such as Frequently Asked Questions (FAQs) and discussion groups?

- How do technical support communicate with each other?

- What are the hours for technical support?

Intellectual Property

Sometimes a company's ownership claim over its technology is questionable. Each type of intellectual property protection requires evaluation, as described in the sections below. But first, here are some general legal questions you should answer:

- What do the license agreements look like? Are the rights protected?
- Did some of the technology originate outside the company? Does the company own its technology?
- Are there copyright notices/patent notices on the software or hardware?
- Are all the software tools paid for? Does the company meet all licensing agreements with outside tool providers?

Patents

A patent is a right granted by the federal government to exclude others from making, using, or selling your inventions. The protection can last between 14 and 19 years, depending on the type of patent. If someone violates your patent, you can file an infringement suit. If you win, you can prevent others from using your invention or charge a licensing fee for its use. There are three types of patents:

Utility patent. This is the most common patent. As the name implies, a utility patent is an invention that produces something that is useful. This could be a process (a way of using DNA to create a new drug), an article of manufacture (a tire or computer chip), a composition of matter (a drug or new chemical), or a machine (a copy machine or fax).

Design patent. This is some type of design or shape. It can be intangible, such as a computer graphic.

Plant patents. These are asexually reproducible plants.

In order to qualify for any patents, however, the invention must be both "novel" (the first of its kind) and "unobvious" (to someone skilled in the technology).

With the rise of the Internet, patent law has changed radically. For example, Amazon.com patented its "one-click" system and then sued Barnesandnoble.com for using it. This new style of patent is known as a "business method patent." Another example is Priceline.com's unique reverse online auction. Although such patents have been widely criticized, that hasn't prevented companies from applying for such patent protection.

Here is the due diligence checklist relating to patents:

- List all the seller's U.S. and foreign patents—issued and pending.

- Has the company paid the required maintenance fees for the patents (without which the patent could be invalidated)?

- Has there been any litigation on these patents? If so, list the lawsuits.

- Is the company prepared to file more patents? What products could be patentable?

- Does it have an intellectual property policy?

- Is there anyone currently infringing on its patents?

- Are its products potentially infringing on any patents? Are there any lawsuits against its products? Are there threats of lawsuits?

- Did it compile—and save—lab notebooks that track the dates of the inventions?

- What are the terms remaining on its current patents?

- Are some or all of the employees that generated this intellectual property (the current patent portfolio) still with the company?

- List the contracts for all licensing deals for patented products. When do the deals expire? Can the rights be transferred?

- What has the company done for searches regarding its patents?

Trademarks

A trademark is a distinctive phrase, logo, graphic, slogan, or even Internet domain name that identifies a company or its products. Brands can have incredible power, such as can be seen with Starbucks or Coca-Cola. Unlike a patent, trademark rights can endure indefinitely. If another company infringes on the trademark, a company can sue for damages. You do not necessarily have to register a trademark with the federal government. It is advisable, however, to obtain a greater degree of protection.

- List all trademarks and service marks for both the United States and foreign markets. List any pending federal registrations.
- List when the trademarks were first used in commerce. Then, you might want to do a check on the Internet for the trademarks. Were any used by other companies before those dates?
- Has the company paid the renewal fees for the trademarks?
- Are there any planned or pending lawsuits? Have there been suits in the past?
- Is there a company policy for trademarks?
- Are there products that are *not* trademarked?
- Are there any restrictions on the use of the trademarks?
- List any licensing agreements for trademarks.
- Has the company sued—or been sued—over its trademarks? Is anyone currently infringing on them?

Copyright

This is a right granted from the federal government that allows an author of an original work to exclude others from using it for copying or commercial purposes. To qualify for a copyright, a work must be original. The copyright is in force as soon as the author finishes the work. The copyright lasts for the life of the author plus 70 years. Like a trademark, you can register your copyright with the federal government to better ensure protection.

In the high-tech field, the most commonly copyrighted product is computer software. After all, software is intangible—it is composed of lines of codes. (Although if the software helps operate hardware, it might be patentable.)

- List all copyrights for the United States and foreign markets.
- Have there been current payments for renewal fees?
- Is there a copyright policy?
- When dealing with subcontractors who create copyright material, does the company have contracts that grant the company full rights to the work?
- List any licensing of copyrighted work.
- Are there any restrictions on the use of the copyrights?
- Have there been any lawsuits on the copyrights? Has the company been sued for violating copyrights?
- What is the official copyright notice?

Trade Secrets

This is information—such as a design, strategy, device, or process—that provides a business with a competitive advantage. For example, the formula for Coca-Cola is a trade secret. Other examples are customer lists, supplier names, and manufacturing techniques. Businesses take great pains to protect such trade secrets. In fact, if a company fails to take reasonable steps to protect the information, a court is likely to invalidate trade secrets. Thus, companies will have a trade secret policy—such as marking files "confidential."

- List all trade secrets.
- Is there a company policy for the trade secrets?
- How does the company protect its trade secrets? Does it mark documents "confidential"? Does it make outsiders sign nondisclosure agreements? Does it use encrypted e-mail and secure document delivery?
- To whom has it disclosed trade secrets?
- Have there been any lawsuits or pending ones for trade secrets? Has the company been sued for trade secret infringement?
- How does it protect trade secrets with employment agreements? Does it conduct exit interviews? Are there noncompete provisions?

SPECIAL CATEGORY 2: INTERNATIONAL PURCHASES

As you can see, due diligence is exhaustive. For international deals, unfortunately, it is usually even more complex. Each country has its own legal and business-practice peculiarities. Hiring professionals with international experience is crucial. Here are helpful guides for handling due diligence for overseas firms:

ACCOUNTING. Some countries standardize their financials on the basis of American GAAP. If not, you need a specialist who understands the country's accounting system.

INSURANCE. Because of the high risks, an insurance company may not underwrite for certain risks—such as for environmental problems, directors and officers insurance, and so on.

ECONOMIC CLIMATE. How is the country's economy faring? Is the government strongly pro-business? Has the country been historically unstable? Is there a likelihood of war? Is inflation high? Is unemployment high?

CULTURAL SENSITIVITIES. Every country has a distinct business culture. Some are not especially amenable to foreigners, and thus companies are reluctant to disclose material information. In some countries, it may even be considered insulting to conduct due diligence investigations. In quite a few countries, bribery and influence peddling is a standard practice for businesses. It may be impossible for a business to thrive without this. But does your company want to be associated with these unsavory practices? It is a good idea to have someone who can translate not only the language but also the cultural values.

GOVERNMENTAL ROLE. Learn the governmental requirements for buying a foreign company. For example, you may not even be able to buy a majority stake. Have you looked at regulations and fees (inspections, registrations, licenses, value-added tax, and so on)? Can you repatriate profits? Are there currency restrictions? What is the tax structure? Are foreign acquisitions subject to a special tax? Also, do you think the government may start its own operations to compete with this business?

M&A INSURANCE

No matter how thorough the due diligence, some potential problems always fall through the net. This is partly the result of the growing complexity of M&A transactions, as today's participants must deal with such unknowns as environmental liabilities, tax rulings, and deals that fall through. What's more, the pace of deal making is increasing.

In light of such concerns, more companies involved in M&A deals are purchasing insurance products—known as M&A insurance or deal insurance. This is still quite a recent phenomenon; Lloyd's of London launched the first product in 1996.

Not everyone is a fan of M&A insurance. First of all, insurance can be costly. One reason is that an insurance company is relying primarily on due diligence information and public records. Actually, private companies have higher rates because they have no disclosure requirements.

Also, insurance should never be used as a substitute for good due diligence. On the surface, it does lower confidence in the transaction if insurance is purchased. Another problem is the perception of the insurance industry as being stodgy. Are such companies nimble enough to deal with the fast-paced nature of the M&A game? Finally, since these policies are new, there is little history of claims paying to enable companies to gauge the policies. So companies must wonder whether an insurance company would be resistant to pay a claim (such as by going to court).

Critical for effective insurance is to involve the insurer early in the process. If a policy is written up at the last minute, there could be problems—and the price of the policy may be higher. In fact, having the insurer involved may help refine the due diligence process.

The following companies provide M&A insurance:

- March & McLennan Companies *(www.marshweb.com)*
- Willis Group *(www.willis.com)*
- American International Group Inc. (AIG) *(www.aig.com)*

- ACE Insurance *(www.aceinsurance.com)*
- Chubb *(www.chubb.com)*
- Kemper Insurance *(www.kemperinsurance.com)*
- Travelers Property Casualty
  (www.travelers.com / smallbusiness)

M&A insurance comes in a wide variety of flavors:

TAX OPINION GUARANTEE INSURANCE. As seen in chapter 5, the tax treatment of an M&A deal can be critical. An adverse IRS ruling could be devastating—even making the deal unprofitable. An opinion letter from a tax adviser helps, but it isn't foolproof. Tax opinion guarantee insurance, however, will pay the taxes, penalties, and interest if there is an adverse ruling. Keep in mind that the IRS has the right to review a company's tax returns for a period of three years.

ABORTED BID COST INSURANCE (ABC). It is quite common for mergers to fall through. Unfortunately, the failed bidder likely had to pay substantial fees. With aborted bid cost insurance, a company can recoup this money. True, many M&A deals include breakup fees. But these are primarily for situations in which there is a higher bidder. Rather, ABC insurance allows for the collapse of financing or when regulators do not approve the transaction.

LOSS PORTFOLIO INSURANCE. In most cases, it is the buyer that deals with liabilities. But a seller can face them as well. With a loss portfolio insurance policy, the seller can combine the whole portfolio of insurance policies—such as for general liability, workers' compensation, and auto. The seller pays a one-time premium—which covers all liabilities up until the acquisition. The seller can take a tax deduction for the premium.

REPRESENTATIONS AND WARRANTIES. In most cases, a seller is required to set up an escrow account to cover losses for false representations. A buyer can use this type of insurance as an effective negotiating tool. That is, by reducing the amount the seller has to put into escrow, the buyer can lower the purchase price of the acquisition.

SUCCESSOR LIABILITY INSURANCE. Suppose you sell your company and several years later there is a product liability lawsuit for $10 million. Unfortunately, the insurance policy of the company you sold was not transferable, so you could potentially be liable for any judgments. One way to deal with this is to purchase successor liability insurance.

ENVIRONMENTAL INSURANCE. This type of protection (which may be included in the representation and warranties coverage) may cover not only the discovery of new contaminants but also existing environmental liabilities. It is invaluable to handle cost overruns for remediation of contaminated property, for example.

LOSS-MITIGATION INSURANCE. When buying a company, you may be assuming liabilities that are difficult to quantify, such as contingent liabilities. For example, the company may be involved in a patent lawsuit. If there is an adverse judgment, what will the exposure be? This type of policy protects the purchasing company.

HOSTILE TAKEOVER INSURANCE. Also known as strategic defense insurance, this type of policy covers the costs of fighting a hostile takeover.

THE CONFIDENTIALITY AGREEMENT

Earlier in the chapter, we discussed the use of confidentiality agreements in the due diligence process. But sometimes the other party is reluctant to sign such an

HOSTILE TAKEOVERS

Due diligence is particularly difficult in hostile takeovers because the target company will be very resistant to provide any useful information to make the bid successful. As a result, the acquirer will need to rely mostly on public information.

Some targets of hostile takeovers will use the buyer's lack of information as a tool to demand a higher price. Occasionally, what starts as a hostile takeover can ultimately result in a friendly deal—that is, as long as the price is right!

Here's an example: Sherritt Coal Partnership made a hostile offer in February 2001 to purchase Luscar, Canada's biggest coal producer. The original bid was $581.3 million. But Luscar thought this was a lowball bid. The dispute lasted two months, with both sides engaging in a tough advertising campaign. Sherritt accused Luscar of duping shareholders, and Luscar accused Sherritt of trying to raise coal prices. During this time, Luscar withheld its books from Sherritt unless a standstill agreement was signed. A standstill agreement means that the acquirer can purchase the company only on friendly terms. That is, management of Luscar must agree to the deal. Sherritt signed the agreement. After inspecting the books, Sherritt extended an offer to Luscar for $64.6 million more than its original bid. The deal went through.

agreement. In that case, explain how it protects both sides. Moreover, confidentiality agreements are a standard practice in the M&A game. If the other side still resists, it is probably wise to forgo the transaction.

Interestingly enough, some believe that confidentiality agreements are not enforceable. This can be a big mistake. For example, Salomon Brothers advised Dime Bancorp in its acquisition of North American Mortgage in May 1997. In the deal, Salomon received $1.5 million in fees. Salomon also signed a confidentiality agreement in which the firm would not represent any company or person that would make a hostile bid against Dime. Several years later, Salomon represented North Fork Bancorp in a hostile bid against Dime. When Dime sued to enforce the contract, a New York court ruled in its favor. A temporary restraining order was imposed, requiring Salomon to abstain from any advisory role until the confidentiality agreement expired.

The key elements of a confidentiality agreement are the following:

SCOPE. The seller will want to make the scope as broad as possible. It will typically say "all" information that is provided to the buyer. But the buyer will ask for (and usually get) exceptions for information that

- becomes available to the general public,
- was previously known on a nonconfidential basis by the seller, and
- must be disclosed for legal proceedings.

The seller should take steps to protect the confidentiality of the documents. For example, documents should be stamped with "CONFIDENTIAL." Furthermore, the seller should number all documents and keep a log of when and to whom documents were sent.

TERM. If a term is not put in the contract, there could be litigation as to when the receiving party can disclose confidential information. It is common to put a five-year limit on the information. But, of course, everything is negotiable.

NONSOLICITATION. A buyer might interview a variety of employees when conducting the due diligence. What if the deal falls through but the buyer then hires one of the employees? A seller can protect against this by prohibiting the solicitation of existing employees. There should be a time limit to this, such as for one year after the merger is terminated.

NONCOMPETITION. A seller may try to get a buyer to agree to not compete in its business. After all, the buyer will be privy to sensitive information, which can then be used to start its own division. From the buyer's standpoint, this provision is not only very limiting but really should be a deal killer. A buyer should not be prevented from entering new business segments.

USE OF CONFIDENTIAL INFORMATION. The seller will want to specify that the confidential information be used solely for the purposes of the acquisition and should not be "harmful" or "detrimental" to the process. So, what if in due diligence the buyer discovers bad information that results in a lower price or the deal being canned? Well, is this harmful? Not exactly. Perhaps a buyer should stipulate that "harmful" or "detrimental" does not include discovering information that would result in a lower price or the deal being terminated.

The seller may want disclosure of information limited to a fixed number of people—say, the buyer's investment banker, CPA, attorney, CEO, and CFO. While this can help guard against information leaks, it can also hinder the due diligence process. For example, the buyer may want to use a consultant to research environmental matters. Thus, the seller may indicate that it will need to provide written approval to allow the buyer to share confidential information with anyone outside the stipulated parties.

TERMINATION. If the merger is terminated, then the confidential information is either returned to the seller or destroyed.

PREEXISTING AGREEMENTS. There may already be a confidentiality agreement in place between the parties. Perhaps the companies have a prior agreement—such as for a strategic alliance or a joint venture. So, when crafting a confidentiality agreement for the M&A transaction, you might want to integrate this prior agreement and perhaps even replace it.

CHAPTER 7

THE MERGER
AGREEMENT

After the letter of intent (LOI) is signed, it is time for both sides to begin drafting the merger agreement (MA)—the binding contract that seals the deal. Essentially, everything in the M&A process culminates in the MA, which you could visualize as a funnel capturing all that hard work—valuation, due diligence, negotiations, industry analysis, and so on. Unless it is a distressed company being sold or a hostile takeover, the MA also represents a meeting of the minds, a codified set of careful compromises between good faith and opposition.

As you'll see, the MA is a comprehensive document. In fact, it's quite common for an MA to surpass 100 pages. But don't let this intimidate or deter you. Remember, the MA must protect both the buyer and the seller. Not only is an M&A transaction complex, but a definitive MA needs to anticipate the unknown. That's a lot of ground for one document to cover. Interestingly, price actually occupies a small part of the document; the more complex, meaty portions are about allocating liabilities and risks.

During the drafting of the MA, the buyer will continue to perform its due diligence. In fact, as things are uncovered—such as hidden liabilities—the MA will usually incorporate these discoveries. Negotiations for the MA are something like a tug-of-war, where the seller wants to lessen its liabilities as much as possible and the buyer wants to avoid or be compensated for any known or unknown liabilities. The process can be long and contentious and will most likely be frustrating for both parties. But if it is rushed, either party can be denied key benefits of the acquisition.

Just as with the LOI, MAs traditionally are drafted by the buyer. But if the buyer would prefer not to handle this task, then the seller can seize the opportunity to be the drafter. As I pointed out in discussing the LOI, the party who does the drafting definitely has some leverage advantages. Of course, financial constraints can be a decisive factor because drafting an MA will require a lot of billable attorney hours.

Most important, both sides need qualified professionals involved, as the legal and financial issues are certainly daunting. And the stakes are high: An MA is the definitive contract between the buyer and seller. It is imperative that both sides approve of every dotted "i" and crossed "t." Once this contract is signed, all that remains is the closing (though of course the M&A process continues, through integration, seller earn-out efforts, and so forth.) If either side is dissatisfied with any part of the signed contract, that's hard luck. So even if the deal is for a small, straightforward business and the contract is only 10 pages long, it would be highly foolish for either party to not have an expert attorney involved—at the very minimum, to go over the document carefully and identify any potential weak spots, ambiguities, or disadvantageous terms.

Those involved in the drafting of the MA include the following (for both the buyer and the seller): CEOs, sen-

---

NEGOTIATING TIP

If you are dealing with a buyer that is public, there is a clever negotiating tactic the seller can take: Look up the buyer's EDGAR filings and look for the S-4 forms, which often disclose the MA. Compare these documents against the one the buyer presents you for the buyout offer. If there are discrepancies, this may indicate the buyer is willing to negotiate on these points.

---

ior managers, attorneys, investment bankers or brokers, and CPAs. Expect that the drafting process can easily take several months or so.

In this chapter, we will go over each element of the contract's structure, in sequence. They are as follows:

- **The Parties.** Lists the buyer(s) and seller(s).

- **Definitions.** Defines key terms of the MAs.

- **The Offer.** This is what the buyer is willing to pay the seller.

- **Representations and warranties.** These are facts that a buyer or seller indicate are true.

- **Covenants.** These are promises of a buyer or seller regarding actions that will be taken (such as delivery of certificates or payment for the acquisition).

- **Conditions.** These are promises by a buyer or seller that are to be performed before the closing. If the conditions are not met, the deal is off.

- **Indemnification.** If the representations and warranties are breached, indemnification will set forth the remedies.

- **Registration rights.** The seller will want to be able to sell the stock he receives as consideration.

Finally, we will look at employment agreements. Though these are essentially separate contracts, they are adjuncts to the MA. Plus, they're critical for many acquisitions in which the buyer wants to retain key employees.

To illustrate the key parts of an MA in this chapter, I provide sample text taken from an actual MA. The passages are from a September 2000 MA wherein Quest Software bought Fastlane Technologies for about $100 million in stock and cash. Quest is a leading enterprise software developer, building applications primarily for the Oracle database system. And Fastlane develops enterprise software for Microsoft platforms.

THE PARTIES

All the owners of company shares in the M&A transaction should be listed, as shown below. What's more, the corporation of Fastlane is named as a party. This means that if the acquisition falls through, Quest can sue the company (as well as the individuals). If the merger goes through, however, Fastlane will become a part of Quest and thus cannot be sued.

> THIS ACQUISITION AGREEMENT dated as of June 28, 2000, BETWEEN:

> ERIC KITCHEN, an individual residing in the City of Halifax in the Province of Nova Scotia; DAVID SEGUIN, an individual residing in the City of Kanata in the Province of Ontario; ALCATEL NETWORKS CORPORATION, a company constituted under the Canada Business Corporations Act; 10729 NEWFOUNDLAND LIMITED, a company incorporated pursuant to the laws of the Province of Newfoundland; and ONTARIO TEACHERS PENSION PLAN BOARD, a non-share capital corporation governed by the laws of the Province of Ontario (each,

individually a "KEY SHAREHOLDER" and collectively, the "KEY SHAREHOLDERS")

—and—

RONALD P. DIZY, as the Shareholders' Agent

—and—

FASTLANE TECHNOLOGIES INC., a company continued under the Canada Business Corporations Act (the "COMPANY")

—and—

881229 ALBERTA LTD., a company incorporated pursuant to the laws of Alberta (the "PURCHASER")

—and—

QUEST SOFTWARE, INC., a company incorporated pursuant to the laws of the State of California ("QUEST")

It is also a good idea to mention the names of the spouses of the sellers in the transaction. That way, the spouses will not have a claim against the buyer in the event of a divorce.

DEFINITIONS

This sets forth definitions of key words in the MA. Examples from the Quest agreement include the following:

"HARDWARE" means all computer hardware, peripherals, machine tools, administrative equipment, testing equipment, and all other equipment owned, leased, or used by the Company or its Subsidiaries other than Software.

"SOFTWARE" means all of the computer software programs (or portions thereof) and all components thereof, including Proprietary Software and Licensed Software and all related source and object codes, related documentation, and all derivatives and versions thereof, including all those in development, used, developed, marketed, distributed, or licensed by the Company or its Subsidiaries.

Beware the tendency to define virtually *everything* when drafting an agreement. An excess of definitions is likely to cause confusion. A good guide is to try to keep the definitions to no more than 100 terms. In the Quest agreement, there were fewer than 90 terms defined.

The following are a few important definitions to keep in mind when drafting an MA:

"ENVIRONMENTAL LAW" means any federal, provincial, local, or other statute, regulation, or rule, any judicial or administrative order or judgment or written administrative request of any Governmental Authority, or any provision or condition of any permit, license, or other operating authorization of any Governmental Authority, applicable to the Company or any of its Subsidiaries, the Company Business or the Assets, and relating to protection of the environment, persons, or the public welfare from actual or potential exposure (or the effects of exposure) to any actual or potential release, discharge, spill, or emission (whether past or present) of, or regarding the manufacture, processing, production, gathering, transportation, use, treatment, storage, or disposal of, any chemical raw material, pollutant, contaminant, or toxic, corrosive, hazardous, or nonhazardous substance or waste.

This is an intentionally broad definition ("any federal, provincial . . ."). As a public company, Quest is required to make extensive disclosures regarding environmental matters. Also, Quest made this definition so inclusive because it wants the leverage to shift undisclosed environmental liabilities onto the sellers.

On the seller's side, it can try to limit this paragraph by instead specifying certain laws that will be applicable to the company.

The following definition is broad as well ("any applicable . . ."):

"HAZARDOUS MATERIALS" refers to any hazardous or toxic substances, wastes, or materials, defined as such or governed by any applicable Environmental Law.

Does this paragraph mean that the seller is responsible for substances that may be deemed "hazardous" in the future? This is unclear. Therefore, a seller might want to include something like "excluding any substance that may be considered, in the future, to be classified as hazardous."

"INTELLECTUAL PROPERTY" denotes all: (i) inventions, discoveries, designs, and improvements thereto (whether patentable or not), and all patents, patent applications, and patent disclosures and utility models, together with all re-issuances, continuations, continuations-in-part, revisions, extensions, and re-examinations thereof; (ii) trademarks, service marks, famous names, trade names (in each case whether registered or not), Internet domain names, and corporate names and applications, registrations, and renewals related thereto (or portions thereof); (iii) copyrights, including moral rights, and applications, registrations, and renewals related thereto; (iv) trade secrets, confidential business information, know-how, and any designs, methods, processes, techniques, and systems relating to know-how; (v) databases; (vi) industrial designs; (vii) integrated circuit topographies or mask works; and (viii) other intellectual property rights of any kind whatsoever.

Again, the above clause is certainly expansive, and for good cause. A key reason for high-tech acquisitions is intellectual property. It is vital that this definition be very broad to ensure there is no question that the buyer owns all available intellectual property assets. Quest has a big interest in protecting as much of the intellectual property as possible.

THE OFFER

All valid contracts must have an offer and acceptance. In this MA, Quest is making the following offer to shareholders of Fastlane:

> Within 10 days of the signing of the agreement, Quest will mail all shareholders an offer to purchase all outstanding shares of Fastlane.
> The offer expires in 21 days after the date of the mailing of the offer.

Quest offered to pay $100 million for Fastlane, of which 65% was in stock of Quest and the remainder in cash. Quest has the right to change the terms of the agreement but cannot reduce the price of the deal unless key shareholders agree.

A key clause is as follows:

> In the event that less than all of the Company Shares and Options have been tendered to the Offer, the Company agrees to use all reasonable commercial efforts to enable the Purchaser to acquire the balance of the Company Shares and Options as soon as practicable after completion of the Offer.

For example, Fastlane could require a disruptive shareholder to sell shares back to the company.

In the MA, Quest agrees to make payment via wire transfer. If the purchaser incurs transaction expenses (such as payment for advisers to go over terms of the deal) that exceed $150,000, then the seller is responsible for the difference, which will come out of the purchase price. If the transaction costs exceed 1% of the purchase price, then the buyer has the right to terminate the agreement.

The MA specifies a closing date. This is the day when both parties meet for the seller to exchange shares and the buyer to make its payment. At this time, ownership is shifted from the seller to the buyer. Determining the closing date requires the parties to strike a balance. On the one hand, the process should not be rushed. M&A transactions can be complex, and issues must be dealt with in a rational manner. On the other hand, delay can be very harmful: While the buyer's (and seller's) energies are diverted, operations could suffer and competitors gain momentum.

The seller will want payment made via wire transfer, which gets the money into its bank account as fast as possible. But he should make sure the money will be placed in an interest-bearing account immediately. If, for instance, the money is deposited on a Friday night after the bank is closed, the seller will miss out on interest payments for two days (or three if Monday's a holiday). This can be very significant. Suppose you just sold your company and pocketed $100 million in cash—yes, every day makes a difference!

REPRESENTATIONS AND WARRANTIES

Representations and warranties are clauses in an MA in which both parties disclose material information about finances, litigation, and the ability to do the acquisition. If the buyer or seller violates any of these representations or warranties, then the deal can be canceled. The indemnification section (explained below) covers potential damages if any representations or warranties are violated.

Protection afforded by representations and warranties may extend beyond the buyer and seller. For example, if there is a third party involved—such as a lender or an investor—then the representations and warranties protect them as well.

When negotiating the MA, discussions over the representations and warranties are usually the most time consuming. This is especially true with private companies. Because they're not required to disclose information to the public, there could be many hidden problems that will later surface.

As for the buyer, he wants many representations and warranties. After all, he is taking on tremendous risk. First, the buyer is paying cash or stock for the company. Second, he could be exposed to hidden liabilities from the seller's company. The more representations and warranties, the more options the buyer has to back out of a deal.

On the seller's part, as well, there's a desire for representations and warranties—but its focus is different. If the deal is all cash, for example, the seller will want representations and warranties focused on making sure the buyer has the authority (and the cash) to do the deal. If the deal is for stock, then the seller will want representations about the financial and legal condition of the buyer.

There are negotiating techniques for the seller to reduce the impact of a buyer's demands for representations and warranties. One approach is a materiality clause. That is, a limit is placed on the representation and warranty. For example, suppose there is a representation and warranty that there are no threatened lawsuits. Then, a few weeks later, a lawsuit is filed for $20,000. Most likely, this will have little effect on the seller, yet the buyer could potentially use this as a way to back out of the deal. A materiality clause could stipulate that the seller represents that there are no threatened lawsuits over $100,000. Or, instead of specifying a number, the clause could state "material lawsuits." In this situation, "material" is left undefined, so it would be up to a court or arbitration panel to decide. This poses the risk that the seller will be responsible for something it thinks is not material. As you can see, it is these complex issues that make it an absolute necessity to have competent legal counsel.

Another key phrase is "ordinary course of business." For example, suppose the buyer does not want the seller to take on huge amounts of debt. It could use a materiality clause and indicate an amount. Or the clause could state that the company can incur debts as long as they are "in the ordinary course of business." This is a good solution because it allows the seller flexibility to run its business in a way that does not detract from its overall performance.

A seller would prefer to specify that its representations and warranties are based on the "best of his knowledge." True, if the seller does learn about an uncovered liability or other problem, it must disclose this to the buyer. Then again, if the seller does not know about any potential liability—say, environmental exposure—then he is not responsible. It is not easy to convince a buyer to allow the knowledge qualification. But if possible, the seller should use it to limit the reach of the representations and warranties.

Here's an example of a representation and warranty:

> Except as set forth in Section 7.23 of the Disclosure Schedule, each of the Company and its Subsidiaries has in a timely manner filed all Tax returns required to be filed by it, and has paid all Taxes required to be paid by it when due, and adequate provision has been made in the Financial Statements for all Taxes of any nature whatsoever for which the Company or any of its Subsidiaries may at any time in the future have any liability or obligation in respect of operations, activities, or transactions occurring prior to the Closing Date.

The representations and warranties can be extensive—potentially hundreds of pages long! To limit the size, it is common to use the above format to set up a disclosure schedule. This is a list, appended to the end of an MA, of references to documents that disclose pertinent information. For example, section 7.23 might have a list of some tax returns that were not filed on time.

Let's look at the typical clauses for the representations and warranties of the seller, which make up the vast majority of this portion of the MA:

CORPORATE STATUS. This represents that the seller is in fact a legitimate company that has been incorporated properly and has all the powers necessary to conduct business (such as selling itself to another company). Moreover, this affirms the company does not plan to file for bankruptcy or to liquidate.

CAPITALIZATION. This discloses the total amount of outstanding stock. This is important, as the buyer wants to make sure it is buying the whole company. An agreement may state that the number is as of a certain date since the seller may have issued more shares (or reduced shares) in the meantime.

Moreover, the seller represents the following:

- All shares have been validly issued in accordance with all applicable securities laws.

- There are no obligations to repurchase or redeem stock by Fastlane.

NO CONFLICT. This clause represents that the seller has entered no agreements that would somehow impair Fastlane's capacity to enter the merger, such as with a violation of the company's by-laws or articles of incorporation; a contract with a third party (such as, for example, the company having signed a deal that has a "right of first refusal"); a legal obligation that would terminate or impair Fastlane's intellectual property; or liens or restrictions on the assets or shares of Fastlane. These are all elements that are triggered if there is an acquisition.

A seller may want to limit the scope of the representation by indicating that it does not include actions triggered by the buyer or actions that are committed after the merger is closed. Also, it is critical that the seller disclose any potential risks of a triggering event that would stop the merger. This can be done in a disclosure letter to the buyer.

FINANCIAL STATEMENTS. The financial statements that the seller has provided to the buyer are of course critical for the buyer's decision. The buyer should require a representation from the seller that the statements are indeed accurate. Here's an example of a representation:

> The internal financial books and records of the Company and its Subsidiaries from which the Financial Statements were prepared contain all financial information of any material nature in respect of the Company and its Subsidiaries, the Company Business and the Assets and do not contain any information that is false or misleading.

PROPERTIES. Fastlane does not own any real property, but it did represent it was in complete compliance with its leases. But if a seller does own real property, it is important for the buyer to get a representation to that effect. There should also be a list of any restrictions, such as mortgages, liens, and even environmental liabilities.

Fastlane did have equipment, so it made a representation that the equipment was in good operating condition and did not need any repairs but for those in the ordinary course of business. It is a good idea for a seller to go beyond the representation and do an inspection of the equipment to see if it is really in good operating condition. Presumably, this would have occurred during "corporate cleanup" (see chapter 1).

ACCOUNTS RECEIVABLE. Fastlane had agreed to disclose all accounts and notes receivable and the aging of the accounts (that is, how long the debts have been outstanding). Fastlane represented that the list was "correct and complete" and the accounts receivables were the result of "bona fide, arm's-length transactions in the ordinary course of business consistent with past practice." Quest also requested that the receivables list be updated when the deal closed. The reason is that there can be substantial change in accounts receivables (as new sales are made and Fastlane collects the money from past sales).

Fastlane also represented that its disclosure for "doubtful accounts" (those that are unlikely to be collected) is "reasonable and adequate." Sometimes the buyer will negotiate a clause that will reduce the purchase price of the acquisition if the doubtful accounts are higher than expected (say, 10% or more than what was represented by the seller).

INDEBTEDNESS. This lists all of Fastlane's outstanding debt agreements and represents that the list is "true, correct, and complete." The company also represents that it is not in default on any of these agreements.

LITIGATION. This clause represents that there is "no litigation, arbitration, or other judicial or regulatory proceeding [that is] pending or, to the knowledge of the Company, and its Subsidiaries, threatened by or against the Company or any of its Subsidiaries. . . ."

This is broad. Does it potentially include future litigation? Also, it is common for companies to be "threatened" with litigation. Listing all examples could prove difficult and even impossible. A way to limit the scope of this clause is to eliminate "threatened" actions. Another idea is to limit disclosure to only those lawsuits in which the seller is named as a defendant. If not, according to the current litigation clause, the seller would be responsible for lawsuits even if it is not named in the suit!

EMPLOYEES AND EMPLOYEE BENEFIT PLANS. This clause represents that the seller has provided complete material employee information to the buyer, such as position, salary, age, sex, length of service, benefits entitlement, and accrued holiday pay or paid vacation entitlement. The seller also represents that all the following have been disclosed: employment agreements, consulting agreements, director agreements, pension plan arrangements, benefit arrangements, union contract, employee stock option plans/agreements, and personal service contracts.

Fastlane represents that it has no unions. (For more information about the implications of unions, see chapter 9.)

Fastlane represents that all contractors and employees have been classified according to "all applicable laws." If not, there could be tax consequences for the buyer. That is, if the contractor is actually an employee, then there are likely to be penalties paid and back withholding. Also, by using "all applicable laws," this is broad enough to encompass the labor laws not only in the United States but also in Canada (which is where Fastlane is based).

Fastlane represents the following:

> The consummation of the transactions contemplated by this Agreement will not entitle any current or former employee or consultant of the Company or any of its Subsidiaries to severance benefits or any other payment, or accelerate the time of payment or vesting, or increase the amount of, compensation due any such employee or consultant.

In a sense, when the merger closes, the employment agreement with Fastlane will terminate. This person will then become an employee of Quest. So, strictly speaking, this "termination" may entitle the employee to severance. However, the above clause prevents that possibility.

INSURANCE. Fastlane represents that it has disclosed all its insurance policies, including the amount of coverage, issuing company, expiration date, and amount of premiums due over the life of the contracts. Fastlane also represents the following:

- The policies have been in "full force and effect . . . without gaps."
- There are no claims pending in which the coverage would be "questioned, denied, or disputed by the underwriters."
- The company is not in default of any of the policies.
- All policies "can be maintained in full force and effect without substantial increase in premium or reducing the coverage thereof following the Closing."

It is very important to investigate who owns the policy. So, make sure that all the underwriters are contacted and that the necessary forms are filled out to transfer the ownership of the policies (the underwriters will have the forms).

CONTRACTS AND PERMITS. Fastlane represents that it has disclosed all "Material Authorizations" and "Material Contracts." These terms are covered in the definition section, taking up over a page. Generally, material authorizations include licenses, permits, and franchises. The phrase "material contracts" is quite extensive, including leases, marketing agreements, reseller agreements, distribution agreements, licensing agreements, warranties, and escrow agreements. These contracts are either oral or written. And they are subject to limits. For example, only leases of $25,000 or more for a 12-month period are disclosed. Placing dollar amounts on contracts is a good idea for the seller, since it limits the scope of the representation.

Fastlane represents that there have been no defaults with its material contracts or authorization "with or without notice or lapse of time." This is very broad. Essentially, it means that the seller must notify Quest of any potential default of contracts.

CORPORATE RECORDS. Fastlane represents that it has provided Quest with articles of incorporation, by-laws, minute books, shareholder agreements, and share registries.

In some cases, however, a private company seller may not want to represent the accuracy of the minutes because of the informal manner in which meetings were conducted. But from the buyer's standpoint, it is very important to have the seller back these statements. If the corporate records have not been kept properly, this likely means that the financial statements are in doubt.

POWERS OF ATTORNEY AND BANK ACCOUNTS. Fastlane represents that it has provided a list of all persons who have power of attorney as well as all bank accounts.

ENVIRONMENTAL MATTERS. Environmental law violations can be devastating to a buyer. In chapter 9, we take an in-depth look at the maze of federal environmental laws. Because of their serious nature, environmental issues often have a separate section in the representations and warranties.

> Neither the Company nor any of its Subsidiaries (i) has received any notices, directives, violation reports, actions, or claims from or by any Governmental Authority concerning the Company or any of its Subsidiaries and any Environmental Laws or any person alleging that conditions at any real properties leased by the Company or any of its Subsidiaries have resulted in or caused or threatened to result in or cause injury or death to any person or damage to any property, including damage to natural resources, and, to the knowledge of the Company and its Subsidiaries, no such notices, directives, violation reports, actions, claims, assessments, or allegations exist.

The clause uses broad phrasing: "any notices, violation reports, actions, or claims." A seller might want to try to place limits on this by introducing a "materiality" clause. Thus, it could say "material notices. . . ." Both sides can then define "material." Perhaps it will be any-thing above $100,000 in damage.

Next, a key phrase is "the knowledge of the Com-pany." This provides some degree of protection to Fast-lane. That is, it limits the representation to only those violations that it is aware of. After all, with environmen-tal matters, there could be problems that the seller has inherited. For example, the company may have bought real property that the prior owner contaminated.

> There has been no spill, discharge, release, contamina-tion, or cleanup of or by any Hazardous Materials used, generated, treated, stored, disposed of, or handled by the Company or any of its Subsidiaries at such real proper-ties and, to the knowledge of the Company and its Sub-sidiaries, no spill, discharge, release, contamination, clean-up of or by Hazardous Materials has occurred on or to such real properties by any third party.

In this clause, the seller represents that there has been no contamination by "any third party." This is tem-pered by the phrase "to the knowledge of the Company." But it is worth trying to limit this clause by limiting ex-posure for any third parties.

INTELLECTUAL PROPERTY. Fastlane represents that it owns all rights—free and clear of all liens—to all its in-tellectual property. The company also represents that it has not received any notice of infringement on the intel-lectual property of another company.

Fastlane provided Quest with a complete list of its software technologies as well as licenses to use others' technologies. Keep in mind that licensing is a common part of high-tech companies. Technology builds on other technology. It is rare that a company builds technology that they own 100%.

Once you get the licenses, read them all carefully. Will they expire soon, and can they be renewed—and on better or worse terms? Are the licenses flexible enough to take the technology into new directions? Has the seller been upholding these licenses? If not, there could be a potential infringement lawsuit.

Quest wanted to ensure that Fastlane's intellectual property matched the claims made in its marketing materials and any other representations to customers. Fastlane indicated it knew of no defects that would result in the failure of its products to perform "substantially in accordance with the functional and performance characteristics" of its product line. The use of the word "substantially" is very important. After all, technology is never perfect.

An interesting twist is that Quest also extracted a representation from Fastlane that the intellectual property did not contain any "viruses, worms, Trojan horses, or other material known contaminants."

Other representations include the following:

- Employees of Fastlane have no claims to intellectual property.

- The intellectual property has not been abandoned (that is, that the company has properly registered its trademarks, patents, and copyrights).

- Fastlane has the necessary paperwork and approvals to export its intellectual property outside the United States and Canada.

- Fastlane has taken all actions that are contractually required or reasonable to protect intellectual property, such as nondisclosure agreements and proprietary rights agreements (which indicate that employees, partners, and consultants have no ownership rights to the company's software).

- Fastlane represents that there has been no known infringement of its intellectual property.

AFFILIATE RELATIONSHIPS. Fastlane represents that no officer, director, or shareholder has directly or indirectly any interest in any entity that purchases from or sells to Fastlane.

Since the clause also includes "indirect" relationships, it is broad. This could result in Fastlane's shareholders, officers, and directors making lots of disclosures about possible conflicts to Quest. So it's a good idea to place some limitations on the clause. For example, in the case of Fastlane, the clause does not apply if a person owns no more than 1% of the outstanding stock of a publicly traded company that is involved directly or indirectly in a transaction with Fastlane.

Some sellers have a conflict policy that requires a person to sign a document that discloses the conflict. If this is the case, the buyer should request this information.

BROKERS OR FINDERS. Fastlane represents that there will be no costs incurred for brokers or finders. However, if there was a finder or broker, the compensation should be disclosed as well as which party will pay the fee.

COMPLIANCE WITH LAW AND REQUISITE APPROVALS. The company represents that it has been abiding by all laws, rules, regulations, and licensing requirements.

Of course, the buyer wants this representation to be as broad as possible, including compliance in the past, present, and future. A seller should try to limit this, perhaps by placing time limits. For example, compliance may be from January 1, 1995, to January 1, 2002, and so on.

TAXES. Fastlane represents that it has been in compliance with the relevant tax laws by

- filing returns on time,
- paying taxes on time,
- withholding sufficient taxes, and
- not incurring any actions by any taxing authority.

NO UNDISCLOSED LIABILITIES. Fastlane represents it has disclosed all liabilities to the buyer. A seller should certainly attempt to limit this far-reaching clause. For example, the seller may say it will represent that it has no "known" liabilities. But the buyer may be unwilling to take this risk, affirming that it is really the seller who has the best ability to understand the liabilities of the company and that therefore the liability should be with the seller.

KEY SHAREHOLDERS. Each key shareholder represents that he legally owns the shares disclosed and can sell them. All shares are free and clear of all liens, encumbrances, litigation, bankruptcy, and other restrictions.

Now, let's take a look at the representations and warranties of the buyer:

CORPORATE STATUS AND ENFORCEABILITY. Quest represents that it is a valid corporation and has the authority to make the acquisition.

CAPITALIZATION. Quest represents that it has enough shares authorized to close the acquisition and that it owns these shares free and clear.

LITIGATION. Quest represents that there is no pending or threatened litigation, arbitration, or regulatory approval that would have a material adverse effect on the acquisition. This is an important clause for the seller because litigation can prove harmful to the prospects of the combined entity and thus reduce the value of the shares.

GOVERNMENTAL APPROVALS. Quest represents that no governmental approvals are required for it to execute the MA and transfer the shares.

BROKERS OR FINDERS. This is the same as in the seller's section above.

There was no representation regarding the financial condition of Quest. But Quest is a public company, and so it is required to release this information to the public anyway. But if Quest is not public, the seller should get a representation on the finances of the buyer. The representation would be the same type that Fastlane made above.

DEFERRED CLOSINGS

When the buyer and seller sign the MA, both sides are affirming the representations and warranties are valid as of that date. But quite often the signing of the agreement and the closing don't happen simultaneously. It is, in fact, common for several months to elapse. (Possible reasons include the need for shareholder approval, an IRS opinion, and so on.)

So what happens if a big lawsuit hits during this time? Or if the seller's company deteriorates?

Two sections—covenants and conditions—are designed to handle deferred closings. That is, they ensure that the representations and warranties, as well as any other necessary promises, are in effect at least until the closing.

Conditions and covenants are commonly confused. For example, a seller can covenant that there will be no loans made to its officers until the closing. Or this can also be stated as a condition. In both cases, if there is a breach, then the buyer can cancel the deal without any liability. The difference is that if the restriction was specified as a covenant, the buyer could also sue for breach of covenant and get damages.

So as you can see, the distinction between a condition and a covenant is no casual negotiation point. Whether you're the buyer or the seller, when there's a matter over which you have little control—say, getting antitrust approval for a deal—then you should try to make it a condition.

Suppose that the buyer and seller agree to make antitrust approval a condition. And then, after much time spent on a deal, the federal government expresses many questions about the antitrust implications. During this time, the seller's business has been showing signs of weakness, and so the buyer wants out of the deal anyway. The buyer makes no effort to get antitrust approval, and the federal government rules against the transaction. In this situation, the buyer would face no liability.

The seller will likely feel wronged, though. And there is a solution. The MA could have provided a "best efforts" clause that requires the buyer to make concerted efforts to obtain antitrust approval. By failing to do so, the buyer would have breached the covenant and be liable for damages.

In fact, just such a clause was included in the MA between GE and Honeywell. This is why the CEO of GE made tremendous efforts to get European antitrust approval.

Let's take a closer look at covenants and conditions.

Covenants

A covenant is a promise from a buyer or seller to do or not do something. There are two types of covenants:

NEGATIVE. The party agrees to *not do* something, such as hike salaries. However, such covenants can actually prove harmful to the companies that make them. Let's say a key executive gets an outside offer during the lag between the MA signing and the closing. In this case, it might be in the best interest of the seller—and, ultimately, the buyer as well—to increase the executive's salary. To counter such an eventuality, negative covenants commonly have permission clauses that allow the seller to disobey a covenant if the buyer grants permission.

AFFIRMATIVE. The buyer or seller agrees to do something, such as provide the latest financial statements or deliver stock certificates. There is usually little argument over these matters. After all, a deal cannot happen unless basic functions are performed by both parties.

Let's take a look at key covenants:

ACCESS TO ASSETS AND INFORMATION. Fastlane promises to provide full and complete access to its books, records, accounts, files, software, and documentation. The company also grants the cooperation of its employees, consultants, officers, agents, and advisers to help conduct the necessary due diligence. Fastlane also agrees to assist in meetings with customers, suppliers, creditors, or even competitors.

To facilitate an acquisition, it is important for the seller to be committed to make full disclosure. In many cases, a savvy buyer will uncover things that have not been disclosed. This means a loss in credibility of the seller. And in return for full disclosure, a buyer might be amenable to being less stringent in its representations and warranties.

But there are instances when full disclosure is not the best policy. For example, if the seller is currently involved in a lawsuit, the disclosures of the lawsuit must be very circumspect. If not, the seller may lose its attorney-client privilege in the lawsuit, which could be devastating for a case.

GENERAL MAINTENANCE AND RESTRICTED ACTIVITIES. Fastlane is required to carry out its business in the "usual, regular, and ordinary course of business consistent with past practice." In other words, Quest does not want Fastlane to engage in activities that would adversely affect the health of the organization.

Fastlane promises to do the following:

- Maintain good standing under the laws.
- Maintain good relations with employees, suppliers, customers, licensors, licensees, and business associates.
- Maintain accurate books and records.
- Pay all amounts due for expenses.
- Maintain full insurance coverage in accordance with good industry and business practices.

Quest also required a number of negative covenants. Fastlane is prohibited from the following unless there is written consent:

- Accelerate, amend, or change the exercise rights of options and warrants.
- Sell, trade, abandon, or mortgage any principal assets, such as software and hardware, that are material to the company's business.
- Purchase assets of any kind in the ordinary course of business other than capital property less than $25,000 and office supplies less than $50,000 in the aggregate.
- Incur liabilities other than trade payables and other liabilities incurred in the ordinary course of business.
- License the source code.
- Commence any litigation other than for the routine collection of bills.
- Implement a new accounting method.
- Terminate or amend any plan for the benefit of employees.
- Transfer to any person or company Fastlane's principal assets.
- Acquire or merge with another company.
- Declare or pay dividends.

- Issue new shares (unless those specified under current stock option or warrant agreements).

- Forgive or waive claims to anything in excess of $25,000.

It is crucial that the seller make sure that the necessary people in the organization are aware of the covenants. For example, the purchasing department should be made aware of any limits and that they should notify senior management if the limits are exceeded.

The phrase "ordinary course of business" is not clear-cut. Should it be the ordinary course for the past six months? The past year? The past two years? Again, this is really a matter for the courts or an arbitration panel to decide. However, as seen above, the phrase can be limited, such as including price limits in the covenant.

REQUISITE APPROVALS AND REASONABLE EFFORTS. This applies to both the buyer and the seller. They agree to the following:

- Make the necessary filings to facilitate the transaction.

- Make all reasonable efforts to facilitate the transaction (for example, pay fees, make calls, deliver documents, and so on).

BREACH OF REPRESENTATIONS AND WARRANTIES. This covenant also applies to both sides. It requires either party to promptly notify the other if it becomes aware of an event—or threat of an event—that would result in the breach of representations and warranties.

EXCLUSIVITY. This is the so-called no-shop clause. That is, the buyer shall not take any action to solicit any new buyers unless the transaction is terminated. Also, the seller is obligated to disclose any unsolicited offers to Quest.

Conditions

A condition is a promise by a buyer or seller to perform an action before the closing. If the condition is not met, the deal can be canceled. But the buyer or seller has the right to waive any of these conditions. For example, suppose a condition indicates that the seller must have no pending litigation at the closing. However, a lawsuit is filed in small claims court against the seller for $1,000. In this case, the buyer may deem this immaterial and continue with the transaction.

Typically, a deal's conditions require the delivery of key documents, such as the following:

- Stock certificates (or cash or other form of consideration)
- Books, records, accounts, files, and software
- Approvals
- Executed noncompetition, proprietary rights, escrow, and employment agreements
- Any written resignations of officers or directors

Usually, the conditions will echo the types of clauses described in the representations and warranties section above. Casting such requirements as conditions is known as the "bring-down condition." In other words, if there have been any breaches of representations and warranties, then the injured party can kill the deal. In many cases, however, breaches don't drive the injured party to walk away from the deal. Rather, they create an opportunity to negotiate better terms, such as a lower price.

Because of the length and complexity of MAs, there is opportunity for inconsistency between conditions and representations and warranties. For example, suppose the representation and warranties for litigation are "as of September 10, 2001." There is also a bring-down clause regarding this representation and warranty. But then the deal is delayed, and by November 5, 2001, there is a material lawsuit filed against the seller. Which clause is in effect? The representation and warranty or the bringdown clause? It is not clear in this instance. Rather, the attorneys drafting the contracts should have made attempts to make all the clauses consistent with each other.

There was no need to secure financing in the Quest transaction because Quest used its stock to buy Fastlane. But assuming there was financing, Quest would probably include a "financing out" condition. Basically, if the buyer cannot raise enough money to make the purchase, the buyer can walk away from the deal without any liability. From a seller's standpoint, of course, this is a very poor arrangement. Sellers should resist the inclusion of such a condition. After all, the seller has spent a great deal of time and resources trying to close the deal. One compromise solution is to require the buyer to pay a termination fee to the seller if the financing is not obtained.

INDEMNIFICATION

Indemnification sets forth the damages owed in the event of a breach of representations and warranties.

Keep in mind that there is usually no indemnification section if the seller is a public company. This is because a public company has numerous shareholders, some of whom may own only 100 shares or fewer. Imagine trying to go after all these shareholders if there is a breach of representations and warranties. It would be highly impractical. But if the seller has only several major shareholders, then these people may enter separate indemnification agreements.

Here's part of the indemnity clause from the Quest deal, in which the seller agrees to the following:

> . . . indemnify and hold harmless the Purchaser and the Company and its Subsidiaries from and against any and

all liability, loss, costs, expenses, claims, or damages of any nature, including legal costs on a full indemnity basis, accountants' fees, and all other reasonable costs and expenses of litigation, investigation, defense, or settlement of claims (including costs of all appeals related thereto) or threats thereof and amounts paid in settlement to the extent of the amount of such liability, loss, cost, expense, claim, or other damage suffered or incurred by the Purchaser or the Company or any of its Subsidiaries (whether directly or by virtue of any third party claim) by reason of the breach by the Company or any of the Key Shareholders of any representation, warranty, covenant, agreement, or other obligation of the Company or the Key Shareholders or any of them hereunder.

How does the above clause apply? Let's take an example. Suppose the seller fails to disclose a $50,000 loan, and the buyer discovers this after the deal closes. The buyer can sue for damages for at least $50,000 from the sellers. What's more, the buyer can also get damages for any "reasonable costs" for pursuing this claim (such as legal fees).

Liability for representations and warranties should not go on indefinitely. Thus, Quest specified time limits that extended from one to four years, depending on the clause in question. For example, the four-year limit applies to taxes. Why four years? Well, probably because it corresponds with the IRS's statute of limitations for prosecuting tax cases. For such things as the corporate structure and intellectual property, Quest specified a two-year limit.

Escrow Funds

Suppose that Lou, who owns 100% of a business, decides to sell out to HiLo Co. for $5 million in cash. Within a year, he loses most of the money in bad investments and heavy gambling. Then HiLo discovers that Lou had mis-represented the scope of a lawsuit, which will cost HiLo $500,000 to settle. Assuming there is an indemnification clause, HiLo can sue Lou. The problem is, Lou is now ba-sically broke.

To handle this scenario, an escrow fund can be set up. Quest did this by putting 10% of the purchase price in shares in a separate escrow account. The shares stay in this account for at least one year after the closing as long as there is no judgment that will need to be satisfied (the escrow stays in effect until there is resolution). How-ever, no shares can be taken out of the escrow account unless there are aggregate claims of at least $100,000. This amount is called a "basket." That is, there is really no indemnification until claims exceed $100,000.

Each party should negotiate for this provision. Es-sentially, it's tantamount to a materiality provision. After all, no deal is perfect, and there are likely to be some unknown claims after the deal is closed—yet these claims usually aren't material.

As a general rule, a basket ranges from 1% to 5% of the purchase price, and a bank usually handles the es-crow fund. The basket clause should be drafted very carefully (again, with the help of an experienced attor-ney). For example, suppose Roberta sells her company to Chief Corp. for $10 million and there is a $100,000 (1%) basket. After nine months, there is a claim for $150,000. Does Jane owe $150,000, or is the $100,000 waived and she really owes $50,000? This is not necessarily clear. Rather, it should be spelled out in the MA.

On the seller's side, he should negotiate for a "found assets" clause. For example, suppose after the merger there is a claim for $100,000. However, the seller actu-ally uncovers an asset—which was not disclosed in the MA—that amounts to $20,000. The seller can reduce the claim to $80,000.

An escrow fund does not cap the liability of the seller. For example, let's say the value of the escrow fund is $1 million yet the breach amounts to $2 million. This means the sellers will be personally responsible for the $1 million difference.

REGISTRATION RIGHTS

As we learned in chapter 5, after a merger is completed, the shareholders of the seller will get stock certificates from the buyer (assuming the deal is for the buyer's stock). However, the seller usually cannot sell any of the shares yet. If the shares are from a public company, the seller can deposit these in a brokerage account but cannot sell them. The shares are probably restricted in some form, either mandated by federal securities laws or because a company doesn't want the seller's shareholders to dump shares and thus depress the stock price.

Here's a look at the different types of restrictions:

CONTRACTUAL RESTRICTION. This is also known as a "lockup agreement." Here, the seller agrees to hold some or all of his shares for a certain period of time. The exact terms depend on the negotiating power of both sides, but the time period is usually more than one year. The reason is that the buyer can instead issue restricted securities (which are explained below). If the lockup is more than two years, a seller should be very skeptical. This is a long time to wait before selling stock. Of course, compromises are possible. For example, 50% of the shares can be sold after one year and the remaining 50% after the second year.

REGISTRATION RIGHTS. A smart seller will try to negotiate for "registration rights" in the MA. This means that the shares will be registered with the SEC and thus allowed to be sold without restriction. The registration statement is a Form S-3, which is what Quest filed within a month of the merger with Fastlane.

Two types of registration rights can be negotiated in an MA:

- **Demand rights.** These are the most advantageous to the seller. Basically, demand rights means that the seller can determine when the shares must be registered.
- **Piggyback rights.** In this case, the seller's shareholders will have their shares registered whenever the buyer decides to file a registration statement. So, if the buying company decides not to register the stock, the seller's shareholders are out of luck.

The registration statement lists the seller's shareholders and how many shares they can sell without restriction. However, the buyer may agree to register a certain portion of each seller's holdings (say, 20% or so). The rest of the securities would be considered restricted.

From the buyer's standpoint, registration rights have some drawbacks. First of all, filing a registration statement is expensive—ranging from $50,000 to $100,000. Here's what it cost Quest:

Registration fee	$66,381
Accounting fees and expenses	$10,000
Legal fees and expenses	$10,000
Printing expenses	$10,000
Miscellaneous	$3,619
Total	$100,000

Also, it takes time and energy to draft the registration statement. This time could have instead been used to operate the business or pursue other acquisitions. Thus, a seller needs leverage to obtain registration rights. In other words, the buyer has to consider the seller an important acquisition. If it is relatively immaterial, the seller should not expect registration rights.

RESTRICTED SHARES. These are shares issued to the seller that must comply with Rule 144 from the federal securities laws. Basically, restricted shares have not been registered with the SEC and thus cannot be sold until certain conditions are met. All restricted shares will have a statement on the backside of the certificates—called a legend—that indicates that the shares are restricted.

Now, as for Rule 144, first you must determine if the seller shareholder is an affiliate or a nonaffiliate. Basically, an affiliate is a person who has some degree of control over the seller. For the most part, affiliates include officers, directors, and major shareholders of the seller (that is, those who own at least 10% of the outstanding stock).

If a nonaffiliate holds on to the stock of the buyer for two years, then the restrictions are essentially gone. However, a nonaffiliate must have had this status for at least three months before selling the securities.

For shares to be sold within the two years, the following terms must be satisfied:

1. Both an affiliate and a nonaffiliate must hold on to the stock at least one year in order to sell it.

2. The company of the buyer must be subject to the reporting requirements of the SEC for at least 90 days before a sale of the restricted securities. And the company must have filed all the necessary documents with the SEC for the last 12 months.

3. Both affiliate and nonaffiliate shareholders are subject to volume restrictions. The restrictions are for any three-month period (the volume restrictions go away when a nonaffiliate has held on to the stock for at least two years). The volume restrictions also include securities of the same type that were not restricted (that is, you sold bought and sold shares on the open market).

The sales may not exceed the greater of either 1% of the shares outstanding or the average weekly reported volume of trading for the past four weeks.

4. An affiliate or a nonaffiliate must file a Form 144 with the SEC and the respective stock exchange if the amount of securities for any three-month period is more than 500 shares or has a purchase price more than $10,000.

5. A sale must be a so-called brokers transaction, which means your broker will require that you fill out a form before you sell your shares.

If the above requirements are satisfied, the affiliate or nonaffiliate will be able to sell their shares. In other words, if you can negotiate registration rights in your acquisition if you are a seller, do so.

EMPLOYEE AGREEMENT

In many M&A events, the seller's executives will become executives of the buyer. In a sense, a buyer is buying not only assets but also key people. Not only should these people help ensure the continued growth of the acquired company, but they may offer managerial expertise to the whole company.

To retain these executives, a buyer will have them enter into employment agreements that set forth the duties, compensation, and term of the service. These contracts will usually have noncompete provisions, preventing the employees from becoming potential competitors.

Managers tend to favor such contracts for a variety of reasons:

- They have probably spent a lot of their time and energy building the company and want to make it grow even more.

- Usually, they will have substantial amounts of the buyer's stock and want to make sure it appreciates. This means running a sound business.

- They will have a sense of security, knowing that they cannot be fired without consequences. (Employment agreements typically have severance provisions and termination clauses, discussed in more detail below.)

CONFLICTS OF INTEREST. When should the employment contracts be negotiated? Be careful about this. Here's the problem: Suppose Sand Corp. is in negotiations to purchase Gravel Co. Before the price of the deal is agreed on, Sand Corp. has offered Gravel Co. executives lucrative employment agreements. So these executives now would be very inclined to do the deal—even if it is not a good price for shareholders. Thus, it is a good idea for the seller to refrain discussing employment agreements until an LOI has been signed.

However, the situation is quite different if Gravel Co.'s management also constitutes the company's majority shareholders. In this case, the conflict is less apparent since management definitely has an incentive to sell the company at a good price. Besides, they also have control of the company.

For each executive of the seller company that is negotiating an employment agreement, it is a good idea to get a personal attorney. Using the seller's corporate attorney poses a conflict of interest since this attorney is representing the company, not the individuals.

CHAFING FOUNDERS. Keep in mind that for most private companies, the founder did not have an employment agreement. He ran the show any way he wanted. If he wanted a company car, he got one. If he wanted a golf membership, he got one.

But after he sells the company, he is an employee. Psychologically, this is a big shift. In fact, when the founder reads the employment agreement, he might get downright mad. He will have to perform duties for the company. There will be termination clauses. In other words, he has constraints—and many founders do not like the feeling, not one bit.

The buyer should be sensitive to these issues and try to be patient. In fact, it is a good idea to have the founder's attorney write the first draft of the employment agreement to try to minimize the tension.

To illustrate how an employment agreement works, we'll be using a new example. In April 2001, Autobytel purchased Autoweb for about $15.6 million in stock (both companies sell cars over the Internet). In the deal, the CEO of Autoweb, Jeffrey Schwartz, became a senior executive with Autobytel (the official title was vice chairman).

Here's a look at his employment contract:

TERM. Most employment agreements will have a term. After the term has expired, there may be an evergreen provision that allows the contract to be renewed automatically for another year unless both sides agree not to do so. In the Autobytel agreement, the term is three years. Contracts typically range from three to five years.

DUTIES. These are usually broad in nature. The Autobytel agreement includes duties such as the following:

- ". . . devote his full business time, attention and energies to the business of the Company."
- ". . . shall use his best efforts to promote the interests of the Company."
- " . . . shall report directly to the Chief Executive Officer of the Company."

If the agreement calls for part-time work, it is a good idea to indicate the minimum number of hours the employee is supposed to work per week. There could also be a clause providing for telecommuting, indicating that for a certain number days of the week, the employee can work from his home office.

COMPENSATION. This includes base salary and bonus. Schwartz will receive a base salary of $275,000 per year. The board of directors can review the salary but cannot reduce it. As for the bonus, the board also determines this. For Schwartz, it is based on hitting certain objectives (the bonus structure was not disclosed).

BENEFITS. Schwartz is entitled to "all ordinary and customary perquisites afforded to executive employees," such as (perhaps) a company car and other perks. Also, Schwartz will be eligible for retirement plans, profit sharing, savings plan, insurance, disability, medical, and dental. Vacation time, sick leave, and personal days will be negotiated as well.

INCENTIVE COMPENSATION. These are employee stock options. In Schwartz's prior employment agreement with Autoweb, he had an acceleration clause. That is, all his stock options vested when Autoweb was bought. This is a very smart clause to have. Thus, Schwartz preserved 375,000 options that were converted into Autobytel options. Schwartz also negotiated 300,000 more options for Autobytel stock that vests over three years. There was also a performance option of 250,000 shares. He gets these shares if he stays with Autobytel for seven years or certain goals are hit. These two option grants had accelerated clauses.

EXPENSES. Autobytel will reimburse all of Schwartz's "reasonable and authorized" business expenses. However, this does not include expenses for private clubs or civic organizations unless approved by the CEO of Auto-bytel. Business travel costs are reimbursed, but there are limitations. If a flight is for four hours or less, Schwartz will be reimbursed for coach class. Flights that are longer will qualify for business class.

TERMINATION. No doubt, this is very important to any employee. In fact, there are several pages of termination clauses in Schwartz's contract.

The employer has the right to terminate an em-ployee for "cause." The employer will try to make this as broad as possible. But an employee will fight hard to narrow the definition. Here is how "cause" is defined in the Schwartz agreement:

- "Any conviction of, or pleading of nolo contendere by the Executive for any misdemeanor involving moral turpitude which if committed at the work place or in connection with employment would have consti-tuted violation of Company policy or felony."

- "Any willful misconduct of the Executive which has a materially injurious effect on the business or reputation of the Company."

- "The gross dishonesty of the Executive which has a materially injurious effect on the business or reputation of the Company."

- "Failure to consistently discharge his duties under this Agreement which failure continues for thirty (30) days following written notice from the Com-pany detailing the area or areas of such failure."

However, Schwartz has the opportunity to cure any problems within 15 days of his receipt of the notice from the company.

An employment agreement may talk about the em-ployee's right to terminate the contract with "good reason." However, this type of clause is only for those executives who are in very high demand, such as Schwartz. In his contract, "good reason" is when the employer does the following:

- "Materially modifies, reduces, changes, or restricts his salary, bonus opportunities, options, or other compensation benefits or perquisites, or the Executive's authority, functions, or duties as Vice Chairman of the Company."

- "Deprives the Executive of his title and position of Vice Chairman."

- "Relocates the Executive without his consent from the Company's offices at 18872 MacArthur Boulevard, Irvine, California, 92612-1400 to any other location in excess of fifty (50) miles beyond the geographic limits of Irvine, California."

- "Involves or results in any failure by the Company to comply with any provision of this Agreement, other than an isolated, insubstantial and inadvertent failure not occurring in bad faith and which is remedied by the Company promptly after receipt of notice thereof given by Schwartz."

So, if Schwartz is terminated without "cause" or if he terminates his contract on the basis of "good cause," he is entitled to a lump-sum payment equal to the highest annual base salary. He also gets continuance of his benefits for 12 months.

What if another company takes over Autobytel and fires Schwartz? Well, he has protections for "change of control." If he is not fired, his employment agreement is extended automatically for another three years. If he is terminated, Schwartz is entitled to a lump-sum payment equal to twice the highest annual base salary. His benefits will also continue for 12 months.

Since this payment is contingent on a change of control, the IRS considers it a parachute payment. If the payment is 2.99 times the average taxable income over the past five years, then the employer will not be able to deduct the payment, and the employee will be subject to a 20% excise tax. However, Schwartz negotiated a gross-up clause. In other words, if he is subject to the tax, Autobytel will pay it.

INDEMNIFICATION/INSURANCE. Executives of public companies are potentially liable in shareholder lawsuits. Although these lawsuits may be frivolous, they still must be dealt with and can be very expensive. An employee should require his employer to provide indemnification against such suits and to provide officers and directors liability insurance. This is what Schwartz did.

NO MITIGATION OR OFFSET. Ordinarily, if an employee is terminated, he must use his best efforts to lessen the damages. That is, he should seek alternative work. The severance payments would then be reduced by the amount of compensation from the new employment. But with Schwartz, he was able to negotiate a "no mitigation or offset" clause that does not require him to find work and, if he does find work, ensures his severance won't be reduced.

NONDISCLOSURE. Any employer wants certain information to remain confidential. A nondisclosure clause will require that the employee not disclose such information. The clause, though, should define confidential. This is how it was defined in the Schwartz agreement:

- "The business, operations, or internal structure of the Company or any division or part thereof."
- "The customers of the Company or any division or part thereof."
- "The financial condition of the Company or any division or part thereof: trade secrets, technical data, marketing analyses and studies, operating, procedures, inventory lists."

NONCOMPETE CLAUSE. Unless you are an extremely sought-after executive, expect to have this clause in your agreement. Basically, the employer does not want you to highjack what it has developed and bring it to a competitor.

Courts generally do not look favorably on noncompete agreements. The prevailing legal belief is that employees should have the right to work where they want. What's more, courts consider an employer to have more leverage when negotiating a noncompete. So, in general, courts will limit the impact of a noncompete—such as the duration of the restriction, the geographic area, and the types of activities it forbids.

The Schwartz agreement contains a noncompete that has a term of one year from the date of termination. During this time, Schwartz cannot do the following:

- "Own or have any interest in or act as an officer, director, partner, principal, employee, agent, representative, consultant, or independent contractor of, or in any way assist in, any business which is engaged, directly or indirectly, in any business competitive with the Company in those automotive markets and/or automotive products lines in which the Company competes within the United States at any time during the Term, or become associated with or render services to any person, firm, corporation, or other entity so engaged ("Competitive Businesses"); provided, however, that the Executive may own without the express written consent of the Company not more than two (2) percent of the issued and outstanding securities of any company or enterprise whose securities are listed on a national securities exchange or actively traded in the over the counter market."

- "Solicit clients, customers or accounts of the Company for, on behalf of, or otherwise related to any such Competitive Businesses or any products related thereto; or solicit any person who is or shall be in the employ or service of the Company to leave such employ or service for employment with the Executive or an affiliate of the Executive."

CHAPTER 8

POSTMERGER
INTEGRATION

The importance of postacquisition integration cannot be overstated. The main reason so many mergers either fail or fall short of expectations is a lack of adequate efforts to integrate the purchased company into the buyer's existing operations. You could say that once the deal is inked, the *real* work has only just begun. In a sense, the merger was the courtship; now both sides must find ways to make the marriage work.

Basically, it is now up to the buyer, and the challenge he faces is formidable. Too often, the buying company underestimates how long it'll take to get the two companies to act as one. When you take ownership of a second company, you've essentially created a new organization. So you have to manage two: your old one and this new entity.

With many—I'd say most—mergers, the biggest problem areas to integrate are human resources and technology. That's where nearly everyone will run into some degree of trouble and often catastrophe. But integrating a

newly bought company encompasses everything, so unforeseen snags can occur anywhere; like sailing a boat in
interesting waters, you need to be alert all the time and
alert to everything that's happening.

It's nearly impossible to conduct an effective integration without thorough planning. With a well-formulated
plan, you will have some benchmarks against which to
gauge your progress. With a lot of acquisitions that
looked good on paper, their ultimate demise was the lack
of an integration plan. Sometimes the effort to formulate
an integration plan leads the buyer to scrap the deal—
which is a very difficult decision to make because of the
momentum that's accrued after a letter of intent (LOI) is
signed and due diligence is in gear. Much more commonly, sufficient planning allows the buyer to contend
with problems in an intelligent and systematic fashion.

When devising the plan, there must be constant attention to a concept developed at GE (which, of course, is
renowned for effective merger integration). The concept is
known as "metricizing." The point is that everything needs
to be measured; if you cannot measure it, you cannot manage it. So, with your integration plan, make sure everything
can be tracked. This shows whether you are succeeding.

The time to compile the plan is during due diligence.
Two goals of due diligence are to decide whether it's
really a good idea to purchase a company and to figure
out the right price, but a third, equally essential aim is to
understand the target company, with an eye to your post-
purchase efforts. A smart buyer notes both similarities
and differences and visits the trenches, asking employees
and managers loads of questions—and listening carefully
to the answers. From these investigations, a picture and
plan should take shape. Remember: In the integration
process, assumption is the mother of all disaster.

Unfortunately, many companies neglect to pay sufficient attention to postmerger issues. And many pay the
price. According to a study from KPMG Transactions Services, the majority of companies fail to adequately pre-

pare for integration. Further, KPMG found, even among those companies that *did* plan, that the process was still "haphazard." It should be no surprise that in the survey sample, only 30% of the deals created shareholder value.

Of course, even having a sound plan is no guarantee that you will avoid serious problems. The bottom line is that integration is tricky and tough. Some of the process requires a "knack"—that is, a combination of insight into how companies work and how people function in organizations along with the ability to manage change effectively. It's not a skill that can be readily taught. But experience is an excellent coach; a buyer's first acquisition tends to be the hardest one, with ensuing purchases going much more smoothly. (But once again, there's no guarantee; many a top-rank CEO has crashed and burned thanks to a mishandled acquisition.)

Though the thrust of this chapter is directed at buyers, it's important for sellers to be aware of this information as well. That's obvious when the seller is to remain active in the company or if he's been paid with the buyer's stock, where he would have a personal stake in the buyer's health. Or it might be a matter of pride, where the seller wants his former company to stay healthy and profitable. And he wouldn't want his ex-employees who stay on to have too rough a ride. Finally, when buyers find the integration phase difficult, some are likely to blame the seller, as irrational as that may be, and try to make trouble. At the least, the new owner could damage the ex-owner's reputation. So, in many cases it's a good idea for a seller to keep apprised of the buyer's progress, especially in the first year after the sale.

POSTDEAL PRIMER

Before we delve into the integration plan, take a careful look at the following list of important points. Try not to

TROUBLE SIGNS

Usually, it's highly advisable that the seller be a big participant in the integration planning. If that is not possible, then the seller is wise to self-protect by distancing from the buyer.

During the due diligence and negotiating process, sellers should beware of the following danger signals:

- The buyer is being unrealistic about the time or effort required to merge his new acquisition. And as a result, he hasn't allocated sufficient resources to handle the inevitable snags. This is especially worrisome if you're getting paid in stock and/or there's an earn-out arrangement.

- The buyer is overoptimistic about the likelihood that everything will "click"—including often-gnarly areas such as IT.

- Buyer impatient to make radical changes right away, such as relocating your company.

- Buyer makes no effort to contact or communicate with the personnel at your company. (Sometimes this is a moot point, such as if it's understood that all the current staff members and managers will be terminated.)

- When you ask the buyer questions (as you should) about how he plans to manage the integration, he hasn't been thinking about such questions.

- Buyer "wouldn't even consider" bringing in outside consultants to help with the integration.

- If the buyer isn't listening to you or your recommendations, it probably means they're going to take total control—which they usually do. Arrogance breeds problems.

be discouraged by the barrage of pitfalls I present. Remember, most acquisitions do work out well; it just might take a little longer than the buyer expects. If you really digest the following cautions and suggestions, you will be far, far ahead of the pack.

KEEP THE SELLER AROUND. An often-critical aspect of integration is ensuring the seller stays involved. One common way to do so is with an earn-out stratagem (see chapter 5), but other methods exist, such as lockups on the stock. More and more buyers are going this route, reasoning that the ex-owner can remedy sensitive situations with employees, customers, suppliers, and so on. This makes sense; many times a phased transition is the best way to go, with the seller available to reassure, motivate, provide information, and generally maintain the business's continuity despite new ownership. However, this can also backfire. Ego problems—on both sides—rear up very frequently, and the resulting clashes make bad situations worse. Trying to have two chiefs is a formula for disaster. Even good advice goes unheeded when personal power stakes are on the line. Sometimes, keeping the seller around could actually delay or undermine a healthy integration. The buyer needs to make clear that he's the new boss, even if he makes some mistakes.

DON'T BE IMPATIENT; SPEED IS CRITICAL. Yes, these are seemingly contradictory ideas. By nature, integration is meant to be temporary. If not, there is certainly a big problem. Then again, speed is relative. It can take a good year, if not longer, to get the two companies to work together. Trying to hasten this flow raises the likelihood of making serious errors. In general, avoid sudden, radical changes. Big moves—such as relocating the company's entire manufacturing operations—should be carefully considered before implementation. Maybe it's more important to keep manufacturing close to the area of highest customer concentration, for example. From the customer's standpoint, they really expect no disruption. If they experience it, though, they may go to the competition.

CONSIDER LEAVING WELL ENOUGH ALONE. Take a very careful, all-angle look before making huge changes in your new property. Many buyers assert their ownership by moving quickly to convert the acquired company. They'll absorb a brand rather than keep it alive. Watch out—that could be a colossal mistake! Sometimes it's a good idea not to rock the boat but to watch the company, monitoring it closely for a year or two. This applies especially with a small company: You don't want to squash its spirit.

When you aim to consolidate, you run the risk of dilution. A classic example of this was Webvan. Warren Buffett's strategy is the exact opposite, one based on the "if it ain't broke . . ." doctrine. His reasoning is that at a profitable and sound company—as virtually all his purchases have been—"management is smarter than me" when it comes to running that business, so let them do their thing. This doesn't *always* work, but it has worked often and well enough to make him the country's second-richest person.

BEWARE OF COMPETITOR END RUNS. While you're focused on integrating your new acquisition, it's an ideal time for your competitors to make a run on the market. For example, when HP announced it was buying Compaq, Michael Dell said he was delighted to hear it because he would assault them on their core business while they were distracted by the deal making.

BE FLEXIBLE. What a buyer thought was synergistic in the new company might prove not to be. A buyer can plan all it wants, and it will still have to contend with some surprises. Perhaps you'll discover the "crown jewel" buried deep down in the company, where you didn't expect to find it. (This is quite rare, though.) Or

MINIMAL INTEGRATION

Actually, there may not be much need for integration. Perhaps the buyer wants to keep the target fairly independent—perhaps because the parent company does not have many core competencies in the target's industry or there are few opportunities for synergy. Also, for financial buyers, there is no need for integration, unless the seller is being integrated into another company controlled by the financial buyer.

Example: Warren Buffett is a big believer in this philosophy. He has made his fortune by M&A. And, even though his empire has more than 60,000 employees, Buffet's company has only 13 employees who manage the companies (all from Buffett's home office). Businesses that he has bought are in diverse industries: Executive Jet (time-shares for corporate jets), Nebraska Furniture Mart, FlightSafety International (training company), Ben Bridge Jeweler, the Buffalo News, Dexter, and See's Candies. According to Buffett, "We have embraced the 21st century by entering such cutting-edge industries as brick, carpet, insulation, and paint. Try to control your excitement." Buffett gives management wide autonomy. He says, "Our operating managers continue to run their businesses in splendid fashion, which allows me to spend my time allocating capital rather than supervising them (I wouldn't be good at that anyway)."

sometimes you find you've bought a headache. In all cases, your integration plan should change over time as you learn more.

RESPECT DIFFERENCES. Be *extremely* careful about transferring assumptions from your existing company to the new one. Unless the acquired business is in the exact same field as your existing one(s), then very different dynamics might apply. Even a different line of products in the same industry could be an entirely other ballgame—for example, if you're been a food distributor specializing in bulk staples and you acquire a gourmet line. Even the best M&A players can run into trouble when they go into a different situation. Of course, in some very simple industries—such as video rentals—once you get the knack and have a formula down, it works. Wayne Huizenga would say he does a deal at breakfast, another one at lunch, and yet another at dinner. But this is extremely rare.

CUT WITH CARE. One of the most common and damaging mistakes is to lay off crucial employees from the acquired company. The problem is, you don't always know who the important staff members are. Even as you think you're consolidating costs by eliminating duplication, you could in fact be shooting yourself in the foot. The problem is that it's not always easy to identify the crucial people. Even the seller might not have an accurate idea, and job titles can be misleading. This is a very complicated, delicate matter, and it makes for a good argument for leaving an acquired company alone until you have a strong grasp on its work force functions.

Example: In October 1995, the graphics software company Adobe Systems purchased Frame Technology. While Adobe's products are geared for consumers, this was not the case with Frame's software, which was quite complex and required much hand-holding. Not realizing this, Adobe terminated Frame's direct sales force. Since Adobe's direct sales force didn't have the expertise to deal with the new customer base, Frame's business started to suffer. Adobe had to take a $31.5 million restructuring charge, and the stock price fell more than 50%.

HUMAN ISSUES ARE PARAMOUNT. The buyer often has to tend to two populations in transition: current workers at his existing company and the corps from the new property. Not only are there numerous potential problems, but many personnel issues are very difficult to foresee, notice, diagnose, or counteract. First, there's the home front. In most situations, current employees should be informed once a deal is signed so that they feel they're "in the loop." (See the section "Communication.") All change creates anxiety, and the buyer's personnel sometimes feel threatened by an impending merger and the possible fallout. Also, sometimes the old and new employees are deeply resistant to working with each other. You see this happen when a business acquires its arch rival; workers at both companies have spent many long years perceiving each other as "the enemy," and that prejudice can't always be dispelled. The longer such animosity has been engrained, the harder it is to overcome.

Generally, the greater challenge is dealing with the workers at the acquired company. (Of course, if the buyer plans to lay everyone off, it's something of a moot point—although this must be handled carefully for legal reasons and to prevent workers from doing anything to sabotage the organization.) But when a staff is to be merged into an existing company, the "new" people need a lot of reassurance and motivation. It's likely to be hard no matter what, especially when some bloodletting is involved (which is usually the case). But above all, the buyer must be careful not to lose key people. The motivating force needs to come from the top—not from the HR department—so charismatic buyers are way ahead of the game. Communicate with the new staff directly, face to face, as early and genuinely as possible. And consider introducing the workforces to each other before any physical relocation begins. In fact, after M&A deals are finalized, quite commonly the buyer throws a "closing party" at which managers from both companies can meet. Both teams are brought in, congratulations are

WORDS FROM THE FRONTLINE

"Having been more than a casual observer of mergers and acquisitions over the past 18 years, I have seen the impact of poor integration planning numerous times. From the people side of the equation, it can start with the not-so-gradual deterioration of a once-productive workforce. When they get fed up with the disconnects, key players start to leave. No one really pays much attention—'There are more where they came from.' And then good customers leave—'They, too, can be replaced; it's no big deal.' The unraveling continues. And the promising investment spirals downward."

—Patti L. Hanson, SPHR,
human resources consultant

shared all around, there's mutual toasting, and the overall effect is to create a positive spirit: "Here's to the start of a beautiful relationship."

Bottom line is that there are no pat, one-size-fits-all answers to most of the human problems encountered during integration. I can tell you what to look out for, but each situation is unique. It helps to have a good handle on the nuts-and-bolts aspects of HR integration—which we go through in this chapter—but some human relations issues will always be downright thorny.

DON'T BE TOO PROUD TO BRING IN AN EXPERT. As M&A transactions are coming to a close, there's a lot of momentum, relief, and heightened hopes. Buyers' egos tend to be riding high at this point, and as the integration process gets into gear, they resist bringing in outside consultants to assist because they think they can handle it all. This can be a costly mistake. In fact, a good integration plan should factor in the possibility of consultant assistance. If, say, several productivity benchmarks take a nosedive, this could be a signal that an outside HR expert should be brought in. But most commonly the big headaches are IT related, and outside consultants aren't hired until the situation is already bad—the company's lost some customers, suppliers are annoyed, and so on. Buyers simply should assume these consultants will be necessary—and include this in the technology portion of the integration plan.

OVERALLOCATE RESOURCES. Another big reason buyers run into major integration problems is that they haven't factored in sufficient resources—in terms of money *and* personnel time. It's smart to reserve additional money above what you've estimated. As I said, technology incompatibility alone can be a killer and can lead to unforeseen expenses that drastically drive up the cost of integration. Another facet here is that *growth can kill;* if you suddenly have a surge in sales, for example, such "success" can be brutal. The company has to scramble to upgrade its accounting systems, increase manufacturing capacity, or make other rapid adjustments that are nearly impossible to do right without excellent planning. Always err on the side of caution.

THE INTEGRATION PLAN DOCUMENT

As I've emphasized, it's critical to the success of postmerger integration to craft an integration plan document. It should be a joint effort, with representatives from both the buyer and the seller (yes, integration is a team sport). Try to have the CEOs of both companies involved as well as some of the senior managers. Moreover, make sure the HR vice presidents participate actively. A great deal of the integration plan is about

WEBVANITY TRUMPS WEB SANITY

In its mid-2000 acquisition of Home Grocer.com, Webvan seemed to make every mistake in the e-book. Its overriding mistake was failing to realize that in a market segment with a relatively untested and unproven business model, it's wise to move carefully. In established, profitable businesses, it can make sense to pressure competitors, but not in an embryonic sector where players were still scrambling for market share. The underlying problem? Too much money to burn, which is always a dangerous temptation. Webvan chose to build up an expensive infrastructure and to rapidly expand nationally—two big bad moves.

Webvan immediately absorbed HomeGrocer under its own moniker, a catastrophic decision resulting in the company losing a large swath of HomeGrocer customers. These clients were happy with the service, and the brand had very favorable name recognition in its geographical areas. Since San Francisco–based Webvan and Seattle-centered HomeGrocer hadn't overlapped much at all, there was no good reason to eliminate the brand. If anything, there was ample room to *leverage* Home Grocer's regional name recognition. "Infinite expansion creates infinite dilution," as one industry newsletter put it.

Opting for expensive technology instead of labor, Webvan's system didn't work any better than HomeGrocer's more low-tech approach. What happened is that customer service plummeted for HomeGrocer customers. Because Webvan had devoted too many resources to its acquisition strategy, its own core competency foundered.

One foolish mistake was to eliminate Home-
Grocer's appealing peach logo. Webvan would have
been smart to adopt the symbol, not to discard it.

Webvan's fiery crash a year later came as no
surprise to many analysts, as the company had
seemed to be nearly *deliberately* making every
wrong move in the book.

dealing with HR matters, especially layoffs and compensation. Finally, at least one attorney who specializes in
HR should be present.

Start as early as possible, preferably when the LOI
is signed. Developing a solid integration plan can take a
month or so. And remember, the plan is not set in stone.
It is a guide. If you learn that additional steps need to be
taken, then do so.

The plan should cover the following issues:

Cultural fit. You need to understand the culture of
both parties.

Compensation/benefits. This is the integration of
the compensation and benefit structures of both
companies.

Organization integration. This is the process of
determining who the key employees are of the
seller.

Communications. How do you communicate the
integration to both parties?

Technology. IT systems are notoriously complex
and resistant to integration; this subject is a
realm unto itself and beyond the scope of this

book. It is very helpful if you have a very experienced IT vice president who has been through a variety of integrations. Having an outside consulting firm can be extremely helpful. They may spot issues that you miss. Generally, make sure there are sufficient backup systems in place so that if the integration fails, you can rely on this backup. It may take a few tries to get everything working. Also, there is some description of IT issues in chapter 6.

For every particular category and itemized activity, establish a start date, completion date, list of people involved, and desired outcome. There are many good project management software tools to help you keep track of the scheduling required to organize this complex process, including Microsoft Project. There should also be periodic updates on the progress of the integration plan (such as on a weekly basis). Finally, conduct a postmortem analysis when the integration has been completed. What were the problems? What were the lessons learned? What worked?

Now we take a comprehensive look at each of the elements.

Cultural Fit

Like all buzzwords, "corporate culture" has become quite fuzzy. That's partly because of the concept itself, however, because corporate culture is an all-encompassing blend of both tangible and intangible factors. It denotes the totality of how a given company operates, especially internally. Its meaning is obvious when one compares greatly divergent organizations—say, IBM and MTV. But differences can be a lot harder to make out.

No two corporate cultures are exactly alike, even when the companies are in the same industry. And culture

CULTURAL VARIABLES

A wide range of factors help define a company's culture. Depending on the organization and the industry, some elements count for more than others in determining a business's operating style. A prospective buyer should weigh the following factors in devising an integration strategy:

- Overall quality: for example "conservative, sober, buttoned down" versus "freewheeling, visionary"
- Style of meetings and decision taking—for example, formal or impromptu
- Ethical/moral code—"hyperscrupulous" or "a little loose"
- Physical environment—open air versus segmented, cubicles versus offices, industrial park versus downtown, and so on
- Hierarchical structure—tightly drawn versus flexible (and, by extension, degree of worker "empowerment" to make decisions independently)
- Work hours—average number of hours per week
- Workload
- Dress code
- Average age of employees
- Political leanings
- Communication style
- Degree of risk taking
- Employee sentiments about the business—loyalty, enthusiasm, and so on

clashes can be extremely destructive in an acquisition. If employees of the buyer and seller are fighting with each other or are confused about the strategic direction of the new company, that's a recipe for disaster. So the main goal for a buyer should be to understand the similarities and differences and work with them.

Here's an example of two companies that made major efforts to bridge the culture gap during their integration:

Example: In January 2000, AOL and Time Warner agreed to a megamerger. Both sides realized that one key to the merger's success would have to be effective integration of two divergent cultures: the relatively free spirit of AOL and the more conservative tone of Time Warner. For example, AOL's CEO Steven Case was known to wear denim (and even Hawaiian) shirts and khaki pants, while the (now ex) CEO of Time Warner, Gerald Levin, always stuck with wearing suits. When they actually announced the merger, it was seen as a good sign that Case was wearing a suit and Levin a sports coat with an open shirt. That sent a clear signal, with powerfully positive psychological effects. Even though the deal would have to undergo a lengthy regulatory process, AOL nonetheless began the integration process right away by naming AOL Vice Chairman Ken Novack as head of a four-person integration team. No stranger to M&A, Novack helped deal with the acquisitions of CompuServe, ICQ, and Netscape. In fact, Novack learned a lot from the past deals. Netscape had some particular tough lessons. There was a clash of cultures, and many top Netscape people left, even one of the cofounders, Marc Andreessen, who then went on to found another company called LoudCloud. Although it is still early, it appears that AOL and Time Warner have done well with their integration. In fact, one critical element was having Steve Case step down as CEO and having Gerry Levin take over the top spot for the new company. In other words, there would be a clear leader. It also indicated that Case had a strong desire to make the deal work. Then again, Levin has extensive experience with merger integration. He was brought on as chief operating officer at Time Warner to *integrate* the $14 billion deal between Time and Warner.

In some cases, cultural issues can be too divisive to overcome. One hopes the participants will realize and acknowledge this before it's too late. Keep in mind that it is extremely difficult to change the behavior of an organization.

Example: Founded in 1996, Redback Networks is a leading provider of advanced networking solutions. By 2000, the company had revenues of $334.8 million. Redback's culture is hard driving, with workers commonly arriving early in the morning and leaving late at night. When Redback was in the process of buying another company, its human resources VP, Carrie Perzow, participated in the due diligence process. When she did her onsite visits, she saw that employees would come to work at 9:00 A.M., always go to lunch at noon (when the bell rang), and leave at the same time. She saw this as an ominous sign that the target company's workforce wouldn't deal well with Redback's culture of intensity. So the deal was canceled.

Clearly, the time to recognize serious cultural discrepancies is before the deal is signed. Even if the buyer still wants to move forward, the realization could have a far-reaching impact. For instance, the buyer might decide that it's best to keep the purchased business separate, meaning that some expenses will not be consolidated as he expected. Therefore, the buyer might well choose to lower the bid.

Life Cycle Stages

Making such determinations is a tricky task. Fortunately, there are tools available (other than intuition) to help. One of the most powerful methods is simple: Look at the companies' places in the life cycle. As a business goes through its different stages, the culture will change. The way the stages typically unfold is as follows:

START-UP COMPANY. This is a young company that is less than five years old, with sales levels of no more than $10 million. A start-up will usually have a freewheeling decision-making process. In fact, not much time is expended on decision making. After all, start-ups need deals, and they're likely to sign just about any one that comes along. Anything to make money interests start-ups since they are usually capital constrained. The founder has a tremendous amount of control and tends to not delegate responsibilities. This means a company can move extremely quickly and also be innovative.

HYPERGROWTH COMPANY. This company is hitting critical mass. Its age ranges from five to 10 years, with revenues between $10 million and $100 million and a strong growth rate—usually over 100% per year. Cash is generally not a difficulty. But the management structure—or lack thereof—may be problematic. The founder probably still has much control but may not be establishing adequate processes and infrastructure to scale up the company's growth.

MIDSIZE COMPANY. The company has been in existence over 20 years, and the growth rate has moderated (although it can still be growing strongly, say 25% to 50% per year). There is likely to be professional management, and the founder is onto the next venture. Management responsibilities are delegated within the organization. The company has a strong infrastructure and management processes.

MATURE COMPANY. The company has a strong brand name, but its growth rate has slowed considerably, say 5% to 25%. Management is still strong, and the infrastructure and management processes are solid. But the company is at a critical point. Will the company be able to find new markets and rejuvenate the growth rate? Or will the company begin a decline?

DECLINING COMPANY. As the name connotes, the company is seeing reductions in its growth rate and will more often than not be losing money. The organization has become bureaucratic and political, making it difficult for others to deal with. The brand is losing its allure, and the company has difficulty finding good talent.

But both mature companies and declining companies often present excellent opportunities. A new, visionary leader can be very instrumental in turning things around. In other words, the old management should be swept away, replaced by new, rejuvenating blood. The best way for this to be effected, of course, is by acquisition.

Understanding how a company proceeds through its developmental phases enables you to make wise acquisitions and integrate organizations effectively—even when the combination of companies seems odd. Here are some tips for combining these different cultures in an acquisition (or even when engaging in an alliance).

First of all, the cultures of start-ups and hypergrowth companies tend to be similar. They move at a fast pace and are aggressively seeking to expand their existing markets.

However, expect tougher integration of start-ups or hypergrowth companies with midsize companies. They are moving at different paces, and it is important for the midsize companies to deal with established managerial processes and infrastructures.

If a start-up or hypergrowth company merges with a mature company, there can be many challenges. The cultures are probably very different. In fact, the mature company may keep the target fairly independent so as to not damper the innovation and growth.

A combination of a midsize and mature company will have an easier time with managerial and infrastructure integration. In fact, a merger can be an effective way for the mature company to increase its growth rate. As for the midsize company, it will have more access to marketing and distribution channels as well as capital.

Unfortunately, declining companies have a difficult time. Their culture is probably stifling and not attractive to any type of company. A declining company may have to pay a high price for an acquisition or even do a hostile takeover. Then again, if the declining company can demonstrate that it has a plan to turnaround the operations, then this may make it easier to convince a target to sell out.

Compensation and Benefits Integration

It is extremely rare for a buyer and seller to have the same compensation and benefit programs—in fact, it's virtually impossible. Thus, you will need to spend quite a bit of time dealing with the differences. Obviously, pay and benefits are matters of immense concern to employees, so this part of the integration needs to run smoothly. Even if the new employees don't like *every* modification from their old plan (and they won't), it's critical that you present the overall package clearly and conclusively. And of course, if you want to avoid a stampede out the door, it's critical that the new deal be fairly equivalent to their old one.

Assuming you've conducted the due diligence process thoroughly and systematically, you should have all the necessary documents to analyze the other side's compensation and benefit programs. The first step is to look at the features of both and make line-by-line comparisons (see the following table of such comparisons covering employee stock option plans). The main areas to compare include salaries, pensions, medical insurance, life insurance, dental insurance, disability insurance, time off, and stock options:

Terms	Buyer	Seller
Type of plan	Incentive stock option	Nonqualified
Vesting	25% for four years	20% for five years
Eligibility	Only full-time employees	Includes part-time employees

Compensation

Overall compensation comprises some combination of the following components:

Base salary.

Bonus. This is based on the performance of an employee and is usually paid on an annual basis.

Stock options. This gives an employee the right to buy a quantity of the employer's stock at a fixed price.

Severance agreements. This is compensation for an employee who leaves the company, is laid off, or gets fired. If the job loss is the result of a merger, then such severance is known as a "golden parachute."

Paid time off. This includes vacations, holidays, personal days, and sick days.

SALARY. Within most industries, pay scales are quite similar. So when there is a merger, the variance between compensation levels might well be relatively small. This is an ideal situation, as it minimizes the degree of adjustment for everyone concerned. But let's take a look at what happens when this isn't the case.

If the buyer's compensation is generally higher than the seller's compensation, offering an immediate salary boost can have a big impact in terms of building trust and helping retain employees. However, the buyer should not feel it is imperative to immediately raise the seller's

---

Key Integration Resource

Integrating separate workforces can be a very complex and subtle process, and the ultimate success of the merger could well ride on how well the buyer pulls it off. If I were to cover all the aspects in sufficient detail, this book would have to be twice as long. Fortunately, there is a great book about how to deal with the myriad issues of integration: Patti Hanson's *The M&A Transition Guide: A 10-Step Roadmap for Workforce Integration* (John Wiley & Sons, 2001). Hanson, a senior human resources consultant, has spent more than 18 years dealing with merger integration issues. At her Web site *(www .hr-integration-tools.com),* she offers free download of her integration Excel spreadsheets.

---

employees' salaries. Instead, some buyers choose to phase it in. For example, salary boosts could coincide with favorable performance reviews; perhaps the seller's employees will get proportionately larger raises for the same level of performance.

If the buyer's compensation is generally lower than the seller's compensation, one approach is to reduce the compensation of the seller's employees. Of course, you should expect lots of dissatisfaction and anger if you do this. On the other hand, if the seller's employees continue making more, then the buyer's employees will feel dissatisfied. One idea is to keep the seller's company as a separate division.

In general, realize that any change with an employee's paycheck can be stressful. One potential hot spot is timing. People plan their lives around paychecks, so if you change a paycheck from weekly to biweekly, expect lots of complaints.

With regard to executives, the compensation should be handled on an individual basis. For example, suppose that the seller company provided its executives with a country club membership but that the buyer does not provide this benefit. If you want to retain the executive, you might have to throw in this perk.

STOCK OPTIONS. There are two types of options—nonqualified and incentive. In some cases, a company will have both. But if the acquiring company has only nonqualified stock options, what happens to the target's incentive stock options? Actually, they could be canceled and replaced with nonqualified stock options.

The integration must also deal with potentially different vesting periods and special clauses (such as for change of control).

Example: In April 2000, Autobytel purchased Autoweb for about $15.6 million in an all-stock deal. Both companies retail cars over the Internet. The new company would have sales of about $100 million. Autobytel agreed to assume the outstanding options of Autoweb—whether vested or unvested. These include the 1997 Stock Option Plan, the 1999 Equity Incentive Plan, the 1999 Employee Stock Purchase Plan, and the 1999 Directors Stock Option Plan. Instead of allowing employees to buy shares in Autoweb, the options permit employees to buy shares in Autobytel "on substantially the same terms and conditions as were applicable prior to the effective time of the merger."

If the buyer decides to terminate the seller's option plan on the M&A transaction, this is probably not a big problem if the options are underwater (that is, if they have no value). But if the options do have value, expect much dissatisfaction and perhaps even litigation. (See chapter 9 for an example of litigation over canceled stock options.)

SEVERANCE. Executives are likely to have severance agreements. If an executive is laid off as the result of a merger, these agreements must be upheld. If not, expect litigation. For those executives who stay on board, you may consider structuring a new severance agreement to improve the chances of retention. This is known as a "golden handshake."

It's rare for nonexecutives to have severance agreements. However, it could be good policy to provide some type of severance for laid-off employees. After all, these workers are likely to remain in contact with employees that stayed on at the merged company. Word will definitely spread if they were treated harshly.

PAID TIME OFF. Elimination of vacation days is typically the big concern of the seller's employees. After all, employees make plans on the basis of their allotted vacation times.

Pension Plans

The main piece of federal legislation that governs pensions is the Employee Retirement Income Security Act of 1974 (ERISA). Like many federal laws, it has been modified a lot since its inception. It is also exceedingly complex.

First, let's take a look at the different types of pension plans a company may have:

DEFINED BENEFIT PLANS. For each employee, an employer sets aside money to be invested for the employee's retirement. When the employee retires, he or she will get a fixed amount every month.

DEFINED CONTRIBUTION PLANS. With these, which usually take the form of a 401(k) plan, an employee sets aside a certain amount of money from his or her paycheck to different investments, such as the company stock or mutual funds. In some cases, the employer may match these contributions.

In order to keep these two types of pension plans exempt from federal taxation (that is, for them to be *qualified* plans), an employer must abide by a variety of regulations. It's beyond the scope of the book to describe all these rules, but some are that (1) the plan must be for the exclusive benefit of employees or their beneficiaries, (2) the plan's eligibility requirements must be nondiscriminatory, (3) they must have maximum contribution limits, and (4) they must have minimum vesting. And there are quite a lot of other requirements.

Why is it important that a plan be exempt? Well, suppose you purchase ABC company, which has a defined benefit plan. And let's say it did not abide by the rules. If you are responsible for this plan, you will have to pay the back taxes and interest. This could be a huge liability. Thus, before buying a company, it is imperative to determine if the pension plans are in compliance with current federal regulations.

In a stock sale or merger, the presumption is that the buyer assumes the seller's pension plan unless specified otherwise. This means the buyer is responsible for all the liabilities of the pension plan. Because of this, a buyer will try to get representations and warranties for such things in the merger agreement. As for an asset sale, the presumption is that there is no assumption unless specified otherwise in the merger agreement.

Regardless of what the buyer does with the plan, any benefits that the seller's employees have earned cannot be reduced.

Most companies have their plans managed by a major financial institution. Many of these firms have consultants that will help with the integration issues of merging different benefit plans. So make sure you have the contact information for the seller's financial service providers and use these resources. It is extremely helpful.

Defined Contribution Plan Scenarios

BUYER KEEPS SELLER'S PLAN SEPARATE. This especially makes sense if the seller's business is to remain independent. Or perhaps the buyer considers the seller's benefits too generous but does not want to reduce these benefits for fear of losing employees. Since there is really no plan integration, there is little initial work. However, there will be more ongoing administrative costs.

BUYER MERGES SELLER'S PLAN WITH ITS OWN. Again, before doing this, make sure that the seller's plan is in compliance with federal regulations. If not, the merger can create problems for the whole plan. Also, defined contribution plans have antidiscrimination rules. That is, if the executives are getting most of the benefits, the plan is considered disqualified. Before merging two plans, make sure it does not result in discrimination problems.

Another danger point: When merging plans, do not eliminate so-called protected benefits, such as vesting schedules and withdrawal options (for example, being able to take money out using joint survivor annuities and so on). Benefits not protected include loans and company matches.

The bigger the plan, the more leverage you have with service providers; it's easier to get better terms and service since your account is big. Moreover, having one unified plan makes administration and employee communications easier.

Interestingly enough, some companies offer comprehensive plans in order to make it easier to consolidate plans for M&A transactions. This is, in fact, what Cisco has done.

BUYER TERMINATES THE SELLER'S PLAN. Be careful! Any time you terminate either pension or medical benefits, you run the grave risk of litigation—even if you have the right to terminate these benefits.

For defined benefit plans, an employee cannot take money out of his account until he reaches at least 59½ years of age, subject to a 10% penalty as well as the taxes on the amount. But what if the defined benefit plan is terminated? Typically, an employee will be able to make a withdrawal without paying a penalty, but the taxes are still owed. To avoid paying the taxes, an employee can roll over the account into an IRA. However, the seller's employees will not be able to contribute to the buyer's defined contribution until one year after the transaction is closed.

Finally, there is the so-called same-desk rule. That is, if the employee continues in a job that is substantially similar to the one at the seller's, then there is no penalty-free withdrawal. The exceptions to this rule include asset sales or the sale of a single division.

Defined Benefit Plan Scenarios

BUYER MERGES SELLER'S PLAN OR KEEPS IT SEPARATE. You will face the same issues as with the defined contribution plan discussed above. That is, if both plans are merged, there must be planning in terms of what features and benefits to keep and which to eliminate. While doing this, any protected benefits should not be terminated. If after the merger both seller and buyer are kept as separate, then the buyer may want to keep the two plans separate as well.

BUYER TERMINATES SELLER'S PLAN. All benefits that have accrued in the seller's plan will vest. In other words, an employee of the seller can distribute these benefits to himself. For example, suppose you work for ABC for 15 years and XYZ buys the company. Over this time, you accrued a pension benefit of $1,500 per month when you retire at age 55. XYZ terminates the pension plan. However, you still have the right to the $1,500 when you retire at age 65. The buyer may not reduce these benefits.

To provide these pension benefits, the seller establishes a fund. The employer contributes to this fund in
order to generate enough assets to pay the pension distri-
butions to its employees. If the fund's investments perform well, it may be overfunded. That is, there are more
funds than are needed to meet the forecasted pension liabilities. So let's assume that ABC has a pension and that
it has a surplus of $100 million (this is the amount by
which it is overfunded). If XYZ terminates the plan, can
it pay off all current liabilities and take the $100 million
for itself? Well, this is very difficult to do. First of all, the
pension contract must provide this right. And this right
must have been in existence for at least five years.

Even if those conditions apply, there is a big problem of taxes. A 50% excise tax is levied on the amount
withdrawn from the plan. What's more, the amount distributed is also subject to income taxes. Thus, it is very
rare for a company to get the surplus.

Of course, there are many pension plans that are
underfunded. There are two versions:

Underfunded on a termination basis. If the
seller's pension plan is terminated, there are not
enough assets to pay off accrued benefits. In this
case, the buyer is responsible for the shortfall,
unless it can show it is in financial distress. Keep
in mind that the government is very reluctant to
make such a determination.

Underfunded on an ongoing basis. If the pension
plan is terminated, the current accrued benefits
can be paid off. However, if the pension is not terminated, there will eventually be a shortfall.

Medical Plans

There are two main types of health insurance plans:

INDEMNITY PLANS (ALSO KNOWN AS "FEE FOR SERV-
ICE"). With such a plan, an employee has the option to

choose any doctor, hospital, or lab. Such a plan, though, will have a deductible (say, about $200). After this, there are co-payments for any claim (for example, an employee may pay 20% for any procedure done). However, because of the flexibility, indemnity plans cost more than managed care plans.

MANAGED CARE. An employee may select only those doctors, hospitals, or labs that have contracts with the HMO (health maintenance organization) or PPO (preferred provider organization) the company belongs to. The plan also has a list of the types of medical procedures that are covered. There are no deductibles. As for copayments, they are fixed, usually very modest charges (say $10 to $20 per procedure).

The three main scenarios are the following:

1. Buyer has insurance; seller does not. By providing medical coverage—regardless of the type—the employees of the seller will be very happy. It will be a strong factor in getting the support of the seller's employees.

2. Buyer has no insurance; seller has insurance. If the buyer does not provide any type of medical insurance to the seller's employees, this will likely increase employee dissatisfaction and probably lead to turnover. Then again, this may not be a concern for the buyer. Perhaps the buyer wants to lay off many people anyway. Cutting medical benefits does lower costs.

3. Buyer has insurance; seller has insurance. In this case, having the comparisons between the two plans is important. Inevitably, there will be differences—some major.

Suppose the buyer converts the seller's employees to the buyer's plan. However, there is a 60-day waiting period to become eligible. What if an employee gets sick during this time? Is there coverage? This will be a big concern for the seller's employees.

There is a federal law called COBRA (Consolidate Omnibus Reconciliation Act). The medical policies of the seller will continue until the seller's employees are transitioned to the new medical policy. However, either the seller's employees or the buyer must make the payments for the COBRA coverage. (Usually the buyer does.)

Just as with a pension plan, a company can also get deductions for medical plans, regardless of the type. But there are extensive federal requirements to qualify these plans for deductibility. If you're buying a company, and assuming its medical plan is assumed, analyze to see if the seller has complied with the rules. If not, there could be penalties and back taxes. It is also advisable to have the seller make representations and warranties to the effect that the medical plan is in compliance.

For older companies (say, more than 20 years old), the ongoing liabilities for medical plans can be costly. As workers age, they are more prone to use medical benefits. Annual costs can be in the millions. And one trouble spot for a buyer is medical coverage for employees who have retired. Changing or terminating is not allowed unless there is a clause in an employee's medical coverage allowing that. Even so, the termination or change of such benefits often leads to lawsuits.

One approach is to cut the medical benefits of employees who have already retired. This is not allowed if the employees were promised contractually that this would not happen. But companies with strong legal teams have been successful in cutting such medical benefits for retirees. The result could be huge cost savings for the company and to make the company more attractive to a potential buyer. This is what Chiquita did when it sold its meatpacking division. The company was able to get a federal court to agree to terminate the medical benefits of 3,300 retirees.

Finally, there are more specialized benefits, such as dental, vision plans, disability, and life insurance. Compared to medical plans and pension plans, the termination of these specialized benefits is not likely to cause much employee dissatisfaction. Then again, offering such benefits can be a nice, morale-boosting bonus.

If any medical benefits are terminated, there must be written disclosure to all affected employees. The disclosure also needs to show how employees may be able to continue their coverage through COBRA options.

Organization Integration

A crucial part of an integration plan is to determine who the key employees are of the seller's organization. Of course, this is no easy feat. Then, the integration plan must deal with how to position these key people in the proper organization structure of the new company.

All companies have some type of organizational philosophy. Some may have relatively flat organizations. That is, there may be very few layers of management. Thus, employees are empowered to make many of their own decisions without having to obtain multiple levels of permission or approval. On the other hand, there are hierarchical organizations, which entail more involved decision cycles.

While the prevailing wisdom is that flat organizations are better, this is oversimplistic. In fact, an organization may be too flat—employees could be overburdened by too many responsibilities. Instead, companies need to periodically look at their overall structure and see if they need to create new divisions or management levels.

Typically, the seller's organizational structure will be made to conform to the buyer's style of organization. But a smart buyer keeps an open mind. It's not uncommon that a seller's company is better structured than the buyer is. And of course, there are opportunities for creating hybrid organizations that combine the strongest aspects of both approaches.

It is beyond the scope of this book to thoroughly detail the fine points of different organization structures. But I will offer a condensed, multistep approach to help you integrate organizations.

WHAT IS THE ULTIMATE REASON FOR THE ACQUISITION? The answer to this will guide you in determining what employees to focus on. If the main reason is to acquire innovative technology, then you'll likely focus on the company's engineers and other "idea people." Administrative, marketing, and salespeople may be expendable, assuming that the buyer accomplishes these functions superbly. But as I mentioned at the beginning of the chapter, be careful of who you discard. For example, perhaps your sales force is top-notch, and you know it, but they still might not be equipped to sell the technology you've just acquired.

DETERMINE THE KEY EMPLOYEES OF THE SELLER'S ORGANIZATION. These people are the driving forces for the success of the company and no doubt will be essential for the continued success of the new organization. Some are "rainmakers," some are the "go-to guys," some are resident departmental experts, and so on. Ask the seller's HR vice president for his or her opinion on these determinations—but don't take that to be gospel. Especially in larger organizations, HR often has an incomplete or even partly inaccurate sense of who's who.

You need to investigate further. Certainly, review employee records: Who has been promoted? What have various employees accomplished? What are their areas of expertise? Can a given employee transition to another area? How has the employee dealt with challenges? Remember that the MVPs do not *always* sing their own praises and insist on recognition. Remember, sometimes the putative head—of a project, a department, or even a company—is not the *true* leader.

Another angle is that there are some people who hold companies together by their galvanizing effect on employee morale; if you find there are any bona fide in-house mentors, realize that they could be "worth" a lot more than their job descriptions indicate.

Organizational integration virtually always involves stepping on some toes, and it rarely goes smoothly. But you must be exceptionally careful. One especially common and seriously unwise move is to let a veteran IT guy go ("our people are younger and more 'with it'"), only to have to hire him back as a consultant, for more money, when the system goes haywire. There aren't many great answers to this dilemma—there are a lot of parts you don't know, and then the consequences hit you, and you realize you goofed.

If feasible, it's a good idea to interview the key employees. You will get a feel for their background and expectations as well as advice on how to improve things.

Above all else, do not needlessly delay the process of determining the leaders and how they will fit in the organization. If the leaders feel that there is foot-dragging, they may be impelled to find other opportunities. Also, keep in mind that you might have to do such things as provide signing bonuses and reimbursement for relocation to retain these key employees.

LOOK FOR DUPLICATIONS. For example, each company probably has a sales department. Yet there may not be the need to keep all the salespeople. Who are the real performers? Sometimes being "equitable" means laying off some of your own people, but that's hardly a great solution—unless the acquisition actually presents the long-hoped-for opportunity to clean house.

A few tips follow:

- If you're struggling with this aspect of the integration, consider keeping the new company as a separate entity, at least for a while.

- Unless it's unavoidable, don't have employees training their successors. They may not train them correctly, or if they're angry enough, they might instill incorrect information. Even if you've set up these soon-to-be-ex-employees with splendid golden parachutes, there's no guarantee they'll feel motivated to do a good job once they know they're leaving.

- As a general rule, try not to place 25-year-olds in charge of 35-year-olds. Thirty-five year olds tend to be very up on current developments and have much more experience and usually *far* more business intelligence than a fairly recent grad. It's potentially humiliating to ask a pro to answer to a beginner, even a highly bright beginner.

- Make use of the key people you identified in every way you can. For example, your comptroller might be inclined to have the integrated company stop attending a trade conference because "the numbers don't make sense." That is, the conference doesn't seem to generate significant sales. Before agreeing to this move, consult the relevant key people. Ask if there are any compelling reasons to keep on attending. What you might hear is this: "This show is the industry's key venue; if any company stops showing up, everyone assumes the worst—that they're verging on failure. The contacts we maintain—and make—at this convention are crucial."

- Your company may have a philosophy of centralized control. But again, some flexibility can help. For example, it could be a bad idea to relocate a plant. If your business is cyclical, the relocation might come at an inopportune time—and might take longer than you anticipated—and disrupt orders and hence customer relations. That would create an opening for your competition to swoop in to fill. Or perhaps you'll find transportation costs will be higher when that particular plant is relocated to your main site.

Communications

For postmerger integration, communication needs to start as soon as possible—and be constant throughout the merger and integration processes. For a public company, of course, communication is limited by regulation. The merger cannot be announced to public shareholders until the LOI is signed. Before this, communications among nonexecutive employees would probably be considered insider information.

And even if both companies are privately held, it is probably still a good idea to wait until the LOI. Many deals fall apart before an LOI is signed. If you make a premature announcement to employees and the deal is nixed, this could create confusion.

But once the merger is announced, employees need swift communications. If not, expect rumors to spread. When there is an information void, it will be filled—usually by false information. (Chapter 1 covers this topic in more depth.) What's more, it is not uncommon for headhunters to try to poach employees when there is an M&A event.

When communicating, here are some tips:

- If you get a question that you cannot answer, you should say, "I don't know that, but I can get an answer for you." And be prompt with the answer.
- Never make a promise that you cannot fulfill.
- Keep your cool. An M&A event can be very stressful, but don't let this get to you.
- Employees can sense trouble.

COMMUNICATION

Integrations can easily fail because of miscommunication. The CEOs of both companies must be clear in their vision of integration; and of course, there must be an integration plan. Here are some tips for better communication:

Newsletters. With e-mail, it is not difficult to set up and send newsletters to employees. A newsletter can be an excellent communications device for a merger (as well as ongoing communications for a company). The newsletter can discuss the progress with the merger, have Q&A, and provide an opportunity to ask more questions. Another good idea is to have an employee survey. You can ask a variety of questions about the general feeling of the post-merger process. Has it been smooth? Or has it been difficult? Also, ask for suggestions. After the survey is process, disclose the results to the employees through the newsletter.

External communications. Customers and vendors may also be fearful of a merger. Will customers get their products on time? Will vendors be able to sell their products to the new company?

First of all, what customers and vendors do you want? There may be some customers that are unprofitable—and may never be profitable. This could be an opportunity to let these customers go.

Analyze the vendor deals. Can there be better deals? Also, can these vendors handle increases in volume that may result from the merger?

The vendors may also be service professionals, such as lawyers or investment bankers. In most cases, these relationships will be terminated. But don't be hasty. For example, if you are buying a company in another industry, it may make sense to retain these professionals, for they have much more specialized knowledge.

After you identify the customers and vendors you want to maintain, definitely establish communication with them quickly. Send letters and make personal calls. You may even make on-site visits. Another good idea is to have a party where you can get acquainted with everyone as well as explain the merger.

Explain it. A veteran of integrations once told me an effective technique is to say, "Now, explain it back to me."

- Listen to employees' concerns and talk them over with them.

Here are suggested meetings for communicating with employees of the seller:

THE BIG DAY. This is when the M&A deal is announced to the public for the first time. There is nothing worse than for an employee to find out about the acquisition by reading the morning newspaper. If at all possible, it is preferable to have the CEOs give a speech to all employees as well as answer questions. If this is not possible, then perhaps a CEO speech can be recorded and streamed over the Web. In fact, some companies have a large number of employees who telecommute. It is critical that they are notified of the merger and have a way to get access to the details of the transaction.

If the CEOs cannot announce the message to everyone, then get a vice president to do so. Make sure the vice president has a script or even a PowerPoint presentation. Rehearse the message several times.

Face-to-face communication is incomparably better than e-mail. However, if the CEO is a poor public speaker, an alternate route would be preferable. (CEOs who get the sweats and jitters when speaking before large audiences are advised to enroll in Toastmasters or another program that will help them overcome this hurdle.)

The message should talk about the backgrounds of the buyer and seller. What were the main reasons for the transaction? Why is this a good deal? There shouldn't be any talk about salaries or benefits at this point. Tell the employees, though, that in the next several weeks, they will be getting new information about their compensation and benefits. Then there will be another meeting to announce all these things.

At this meeting, give all employees the merger press release. Other good handout materials include a background sheet of the two companies, any SEC filings (if a company is public), and letters from the CEOs.

When sending out the benefits information, it is a good psychological device to send out employment offer letters. The letter will allay employee fears as well as clarify compensation arrangements.

SECOND MEETING. This meeting will address benefits—how they'll change or remain the same. Expect quite a few questions. It's a good idea to try to anticipate some of the questions and create a Q&A handout—like the "FAQ" so favored on-line. Tell employees that after the meeting, they should feel free to ask any questions or even have personal meetings to go over any concerns.

If the seller's employees will be getting better benefits, then of course stress this. It will definitely help with overall morale.

As for communications with people who will be laid off, this should be done in a personal meeting. Communicating this via voice mail or e-mail will anger employees.

Also, keep in mind that if the Worker Adjustment and Retraining Notification Act (WARN) applies, you must take the following steps for the notification. (In fact, even if WARN does not apply, providing the above communication is smart.)

- Written question-and-answer documents about the terms of the separation.

- Names of the contact people (HR people who can answer questions about benefits)

- Separation letters

- Exit checklists (that is, what materials an employee must return to the employer)

Finally, it is a good idea to conduct exit interviews from which you'll glean more insights into the company. Also, ask about how the transition was managed. Perhaps there were problems. This should prove helpful for the next M&A event.

CHAPTER 9

REGULATIONS

One of the more complex aspects of M&A is the regulatory dimension. You need to deal with multiple dimensions of federal agency law—and the attendant potential liabilities—when you buy or sell a company. Plus, the rules continue to shift and expand, with new horizons of regulatory impositions emerging continually. (For example, how many business leaders could have foreseen the emergence of workplace online-content-access regulations as a component of antidiscrimination law?)

And, it is not altogether clear how they may play out. Even if there are clear-cut laws, this does not mean they will be enforced aggressively. After all, the president, Congress, and the courts may be taking a pro-corporate stance and thus be lenient with enforcing business regulation.

At any rate, in case you're wondering why so many lawyers have to be involved in M&A deals, this chapter will put things straight. We will take a look at the main types of regulations you are likely to face in an M&A

transaction, especially antitrust and, to a lesser extent, labor laws. The following information is certainly not intended to take the place of expert legal counsel, but it should help M&A players understand what they need to assess and do to avoid regulatory hassles or catastrophes.

ANTITRUST LAWS

The idea that a small or medium-size deal is "below the radar" of the antitrust apparatus is not a sound assumption. In actuality, it's not a matter of whether you're large or small; it's about whether you're being anticompetitive. True, regulators *probably* won't go after you, but there are plenty of exceptions. Sometimes someone in power "has it in" for a particular person, business, industry, or geographic area. State attorneys general have been known to have axes to grind at times. A competitor can set someone up. So there are plenty of reasons to be diligent in not running afoul of this area of regulation.

The roots of antitrust go back more than 100 years. Over this period, antitrust laws have evolved, and enforcement vigor has waxed and waned in different eras. In 1890, Congress passed the Sherman Antitrust Act. There was much concern by the American public that there was too much concentration of power, especially with the Standard Oil empire. The Sherman Antitrust law allowed Congress to break up Standard Oil into a number of smaller companies.

The laws were also strengthened in the 1950s and 1960s. In the mid-1970s, however, antitrust law enforcement became much more lax. So it was no surprise that more and more companies began to merge. In fact, by the 1980s, antitrust laws were barely enforced. With the Clinton administration in the 1990s, the laws were enforced with a little more frequency. The general tenor of governmental attitude to mergers has been highly permissive, and many industries have seen a great deal of consolidation. Banking and media are two good examples.

Nevertheless, to repeat this again: If you are thinking of buying a company, you need to consider possible antitrust implications. In fact, if you have any reasons to be concerned, it is smart to hire an economist who specializes in antitrust matters. (When I refer to economists, I mean professors from nearby universities or, sometimes, consultants with doctoral degrees in the field.) He or she can be very helpful in determining the odds of the deal going through. At the same time, it's wise to retain an experienced attorney who understands the intricacies of antitrust law, which is a highly specialized field.

Keep in mind that a deal that is blocked on antitrust concerns can be devastating for both the buyer and the seller. There are significant immediate consequences: the loss of a lot of time, money, and effort; the sharing of business information; and goodwill. And there's also the damage to the reputations of those involved.

Example: Suppose that two major banks—MoolahCorp. and DoughCorp.—decide to merge. The combined market share will be 40% of the U.S. market. To do the deal, both companies spent $20 million in fees to investment bankers. There are also ongoing fees—about $1 million per month—to handle the antitrust review, which lasts six months. During this time, MoolahCorp. and Dough-Corp. have begun to integrate their operations. Clearly, they are optimistic they will receive antitrust approval. However, the FTC ultimately decides to block the merger, claiming the market concentration is too high and there is no other way to resolve the matter than to unwind the transaction. In the end, both companies spent $26 million in fees as well as millions in integrating and then deintegrating the companies. What's more, it was a waste of six months. Both companies could have done other things during this other than the merger that produced nothing.

Antitrust Analysis

When it comes to M&A transactions, the key element to focus on is Section 7 of the Clayton Act. Congress passed the Clayton Act in 1914 to deal with some of the deficiencies of the Sherman Antitrust law (for example, companies were using the antitrust laws to attack unions). The main part of Section 7 prohibits the acquisition of stock or assets if "in any line of commerce in any section of the country, the effect of such acquisition may be substantially to lessen competition, or tend to create monopoly."

As a buyer of a company, you definitely should act on the economist's and/or attorney's expert advice. However, you can do your own rough analysis first. The following step-by-step approach is not exhaustive, but it covers the prime issues associated with antitrust. A buyer should go through all the steps.

STEP 1—THE POTENTIAL FOR ANTITRUST. In Section 7 (see the quote above), the word "may" is crucial. In other words, it doesn't matter whether the merger results in less competition; rather, it only matters that it "may" lead to such a lessening. This is why economists are involved in looking at antitrust matters. They build economic models that attempt to predict if the acquisition will lead to substantially less competition—or even to a full-scale monopoly. You should have a trained economist go through this modeling, partly because the result should be useful in allaying potential concerns if the threat arises.

STEP 2—TYPE OF MERGER. For the purposes of antitrust, we'll look at M&A transactions as falling into three categories—horizontal, vertical, and conglomerate. Which one is your transaction?

- **Horizontal.** This is when two competitors merge. Horizontal mergers tend to come under the most scrutiny from federal regulators. The reason is that there is a chance of lessening competition when one competitor is eliminated from the marketplace.

- **Vertical merger.** This is when a company buys a company in its chain of distribution or manufacturing. It is rare that such deals are blocked. Although, if the intent of the merger is to block a competitor from gaining access from the products of the vertical supplier (called "foreclosure"), then federal regulators may stop the merger.

  Example: Suppose a car manufacturer, Vehicle Corp., purchases the main supplier of tires, Rubber Co. One of Vehicle's competitors needs to buy tires from Rubber, but Vehicle blocks the transaction. This would be a case of "foreclosure" and is a violation of antitrust laws.

- **Conglomerate.** Of all the mergers, this is the least likely to come under scrutiny. The main reason is that since both companies are in different industries, there is little risk of substantially reduced competition.

STEP 3—ACQUISITION. The statute covers the acquisition of stock or assets. But the intent of the statute is broader than a typical M&A transaction. For example, joint ventures or strategic partnerships also qualify. In fact, when an acquisition is not for 100% of another company, the statute applies—though the courts look primarily at situations in which acquisition results in control of another company.

If the acquisition for stock or assets is meant as a "passive investment," there is no violation. Since there is no clear-cut way of defining passive investment, the court will look at all the facts surrounding the case. The court will likely *not* accept the passive investment claim if one or more of the following five conditions prevails:

- The target is having problems.
- The stock price is relatively illiquid.
- The acquirer really does not have a diversified portfolio.
- The price for the target' stock or assets was at a premium.
- The acquirer has one or more board seats.

The court will also look at the buyer's acquisition history: In previous deals, did the company ultimately take control of most companies it invested in?

STEP 4—RELEVANT MARKET AND GEOGRAPHY. The statute prevents antitrust behavior "in any line of commerce in any section of the country." That is, you need to define the relevant product market and the relevant geography of the market.

Relevant markets are both very important and difficult to define. Many cases live or die on the basis of this analysis. First, you need to look at the goods and services that the merging companies compete in. For example, let's say that two low-price sport shoes companies (price range between $20 and $50 per shoe) decide to merge. As a result of the transaction, the combined company owns about 75% of the U.S. market for low-priced shoes. And there are two other companies that split the remaining 25% of the low-priced shoe market. In other words, the market is concentrated among only four companies—and the merger could be a violation of the Section 7.

However, a court may take a broader view of the relevant market, one based on the economic concept of "cross-elasticity." Essentially, this means there is a high correlation between quantity demanded of one product when there is a percentage increase in the price of another product. Suppose the merger reduces competition substantially and the prices for shoes increase by 10%. Consumers are dissatisfied and start to buy medium-priced shoes. So, the medium-priced shoes are a rough substitute product for the low-priced shoes. Consequently, since there is cross-elasticity, the medium-priced shoes should also be included in the relevant market.

There is another mumbo-jumbo economics concept called "cross-elasticity of supply." This indicates the relative difficulty for a company to shift its demand from one product to another. In the above example, the medium-priced suppliers may see an opportunity in the low-priced shoe market and use their production plant to make these types of shoes, thus putting pressure on the merged company. Again, if there is cross-elasticity of supply, these companies should be part of the relevant market.

A relevant geographic market is the area where the anticompetitive effect will have its impact. In many cases, the relevant market is the United States. However, the courts can narrow this—perhaps to a large city.

In defining the relevant market, a court will usually make a two-step analysis. First, it looks at the areas in which the two merging firms are located. The court determines the percentage of total output in these areas purchased by local customers. The court then looks at the percentage of output purchased by these customers from suppliers outside these areas.

Example: Suppose MoolahCorp. Bank is located in Blue County and DoughCorp. Bank is located in neighboring Red County. Both companies decide to merge. In Blue County, 90% of the residents use the banking services based in the county, and in Red County, 89% of the residents use county-based banking services. Since only a small percentage comes from outside markets, the relevant markets are Blue and Red Counties. But if the percentages were lower—say, 10%—then the relevant market would extend beyond the counties. In fact, the relevant market might be the nation. Or suppose the merger of MoolahCorp. and DoughCorp. results in higher prices and competitors from outside markets move into Blue and Red Counties. This is likely to expand the relevant market as well.

The purpose of looking at the relevant market and the relevant geographic market is to help the courts identify competitors or potential competitors. With this information, the courts can see if the merger will be anticompetitive.

Step 5—Measuring market share and concentration. Courts typically use the Herfindahl-Hirschman Index (HHI) to measure market concentration. With HHI, the court squares the market share of each firm and then adds up the squares. The HHI can range from nearly 0 to 10,000.

Let's take a look: If the industry has one firm, then the HHI will be 10,000. This is equal to 1002. If the market has two firms, both of which have 50% market shares, then HHI is 5,000, calculated as follows:

1. (number of companies with equal market share)
$\times$ (market share)^2

2. $(2) \times (50)^2 = 5,000$.

So if there are 10 firms and each firm has equal market share, the HHI will be 1,000. In the case of a merger, the court will look to see how much the HHI will increase. Suppose Gear Co. and Stuff Co. are in an industry with 10 companies with equal market share. Gear Co. and Stuff Co. decide to merge. The formula to calculate the increase of the HHI is as follows:

Before the merger, the HHI scale is as follows:

$$10 \times 10^2 = 1,000$$

Here is what the HHI looks like after the merger:

$$8 \times 10^2 + 2 \times 20^2$$

$$800 + 800 = 1,600$$

The difference between the two HHIs is 600.

How do you use HHI? In 1993, the Department of Justice and the FTC set forth guidelines. Keep in mind that these are merely guidelines (but they tend to work in most cases). These are the HHI numbers after a merger has been factored in:

- **Below 1,000.** This is relatively low concentration of the market (that is, the market probably has many competitors and potential competitors). So there is little chance of an antitrust challenge.
- **1,000–1,800.** This is a market with a medium degree of concentration. If a merger increases the HHI by 100 or more, then there is a presumption that the merger is anticompetitive. Thus, the federal regulators may challenge the transaction.
- **Above 1,800.** This is a highly concentrated market. An increase of 100 or more would alert the federal authorities, and there is a strong possibility the transaction will be challenged.

If federal regulators challenge the merger, then the merging companies have the burden of proof to show that there is no violation of Section 7. The proof is case by case; there is no magic bullet to win a case. Rather, the merging companies will present as much evidence as possible indicating the following:

- Prices will not increase (and they may even fall).
- Consumers will benefit (perhaps from better-quality goods).
- There will be more efficiencies in the marketplace (because of less duplication).
- There is cross-elasticity of demand and supply.
- The barriers to entry—manufacturing, distribution, marketing—are relatively low.

Keep in mind that it is rare for mergers to be blocked on the basis of antitrust concerns. As stated above, the courts have been lenient with mergers. Also, if there are antitrust problems, there is often a way to structure the deal to make it less harmful to competition—perhaps through the divestiture of certain assets.

Example: In June 2000, Philip Morris offered to pay $55 per share in cash to buy Nabisco ($18 billion in all). The combined entity would result in the world's largest food company. The FTC had objections to the buyout. So Philip Morris agreed to divest certain product lines. This satisfied the FTC, and the merger received regulatory approval.

FINAL TIPS. There's a saying, "Perception is reality." This is very true in antitrust matters. So, be careful what you say, write, and e-mail during the merger process.

Example: Microsoft has been under intense antitrust scrutiny and even has had to forgo its merger with Intuit because of the FTC. No question, Microsoft has extensive market power. However, it did not help that Bill Gates and other Microsoft executives had routinely e-mailed each other with talk about "destroying the competition" or "cutting the air supply of our competitors." Such evidence shows intent to violate the antitrust laws.

Meanwhile, a company such as Intel—which has a high degree of market power—has had little problems with antitrust laws. Perhaps it's because the company has an extensive antitrust policy, including employee training and even mock FTC raids and interviews.

Your merger will be critical to the growth of your company. Do not jeopardize it because of a "smoking gun."

Premerger Notification

In 1976, Congress passed the Hart-Scott-Rodino (HSR) Act, which provides that merging companies notify the FTC and the Department of Justice about the merger. The filing must be made before a deal officially closes and give federal regulators adequate time to investigate the antitrust implications of the transaction.

Within 30 days of the filing, the parties to the merger can close the deal—unless the government shortens or extends the period. (Before the law was passed, federal regulators may have blocked a merger after it was closed, which meant it was very difficult and expensive to unwind the transaction.)

However, if the federal regulators deem the transaction to violate the antitrust laws, they can issue a preliminary injunction to block the merger. The case can be litigated (which can be expensive and time consuming), or a settlement can be attempted (perhaps a division will be divested).

In 2001, Congress changed the requirements for HSR filings. Here are the new guidelines to see if your company applies:

COMMERCE TEST. Each company must be "engaged in commerce or in any activity affecting commerce." This is easy to prove. After all, it is the nature of companies to be involved in commerce.

SIZE-OF-THE-PARTIES TEST. Either the buyer or the seller must have annual net sales or total assets of at least $100 million. Moreover, the other party must have at least $10 million in net sales or total assets. However, this test does not matter if the total value of the transaction is over $200 million (in this case, an HSR filing must be made).

SIZE-OF-THE-TRANSACTION TEST. A filing is required if the value of the transaction is in excess of $50 million. If so, there is a mandatory filing fee that is based on the total value of the transaction:

- $50 million to $99.99 million: $45,000
- $100 million to $499.99 million: $125,000
- $500 million or more: $280,000

If the deal involves a public company, then the valuation is based on the price of the stock when the deal closes. But if two private companies merge, then the boards of directors of both companies must determine a fair market value. The best approach is to hire a valuation firm, broker, or investment banker to determine the valuation. The valuation also includes assumption of debt.

Actually, the FTC offers a worksheet to help determine the valuation and fee payments. You can download a copy online at *www.ftc.gov/bc/hsr/hsr.htm.*

The site also provides some guidance on what type of information must be submitted in the HSR filing. Currently, the code section is 4(c), and it is quite broad. Essentially, all documents that executives use to proceed with an M&A transaction must be provided in the HSR. To clarify this too-vague requirement, the FTC is currently developing new guidelines.

Violating HSR can be devastating. For example, in April 2001 the FTC allowed a lawsuit to unwind a 1998 merger between Hearst and Medi-Span. If Hearst did violate the statute, the company would have to disgorge any profits from the acquisition. Basically, the FTC is alleging that Hearst failed to make material disclosures in its HSR filing. There is even a $11,000 fine per day for every day Hearst is in violation of HSR.

Suppose your company's deal does not fall within the requirements of HSR. Does this mean you should not bother to contact the FTC? No, it does not. If the step-by-step process above—as well as advice from counsel and advisers—shows there are potential antitrust problems, then you should contact the FTC.

Global Antitrust Laws

Until recently, M&A deal participants would need to be concerned mostly with U.S. antitrust laws. However, there is an ongoing trend, worldwide, for megaglobal deals. One such case is the AOL–Time Warner acquisition, which took a year to complete because of the required approval from the FTC and European Union (EU), which comprises 15 European countries in the process of unification.

The attorney who handled the antitrust matters for AOL, Paul Cappuccio, complained on a variety of occasions about the difficulties with the approval process in the United States. But he is even more vocal about the EU. "The FCC is harmless compared to the European Commission. Who do you appeal to there? The intergalactic court of justice?"

During the 1990s, the FTC and the EU have been trying to unify the antitrust regulations. But this is not easy. The U.S. system is based on an intricate court system and several federal statutes. If there is to be an antitrust action, the FTC or Department of Justice needs to file a lawsuit (a company or even a private individual can as well).

Furthermore, the main goal of the U.S. antitrust system purportedly is to promote the welfare of the consumer. This was the result of the conservative thinking of the 1970s, based on the Chicago School of Economics and carried forward into the 1980s by the Reagan administration. Antitrust law should be based on the economic consequences in terms of prices for the consumers. And, yes, a merger could actually result in lower prices.

The EU, on the other hand, is not based on a court system. Rather, the EU has the final rule. There is no appeals court, nor is there a Supreme Court. Antitrust is the sole authority of the EU. True, the EU provides for the process to annul a decision, but this can take anywhere from 18 months to three years.

Thus, the Competition Commission of the EU is quite powerful. Currently, that person is Mario Monti, who has become a high-profile participant in many megamergers.

Moreover, the focus of the antitrust law is to promote not the rights of consumers but those of competitors.

That is, a large company should not have the right to stomp on another company. Ironically enough, this philosophy was the result of the influence of the United States in the aftermath of World War II. The United States did not want to see the rise of huge industrial powers in Europe—as was the case in 1930s Germany. This antitrust policy was adopted across Europe.

Then, during the 1950s and 1960s, Europe began diverging from this policy. Countries would try to create dominant companies—through subsidies—in key industries, such as computers, telecom, steel, and so on. But these state-funded cartels were not competing effectively against foreign companies. Thus, by the 1990s, Europe wanted to promote competition again. The thinking was that this would create a much healthier marketplace.

In light of all this, it makes sense that there are complications with unifying the U.S. and EU antitrust systems. It is inevitable.

Example: One of the most prominent international M&A cases is the $41 billion merger between GE and Honeywell. For GE's legendary CEO, Jack Welch, the deal would be the crowning achievement of his storied career. It's hard to believe, but the deal—the biggest in GE history—was negotiated over a three-day weekend, which broke up an agreed-on deal for the merger between United Technologies and Honeywell.

In fact, Welch did not have time to consult his European merger lawyers on the matter. But they did indicate later that there was a good chance of getting European approval. After all, there was little overlap between the businesses of GE and Honeywell.

This was a very big mistake. As a result, it would take GE attorneys three months to prepare reports for the EU, which normally would take one month.

This gave GE competitors enough time to argue effectively against the deal. For example, United Technologies hired a top antitrust attorney, Mark Leddy, a partner with the Washington firm of Cleary, Gottlieb, Steen & Hamilton. Leddy hired an American economist, Robert Reynolds. But Reynolds did not speak before the EU. Rather, Leddy hired Janusz Ordover, who was born in Poland and understood the cultural issues, to make the case. To counter this, GE hired a top economist from Yale University, Barry Nalebuff, to provide statistical evidence that competition would not be harmed.

United Technology attorneys, though, were able to come up with a theory that created an impossible stumbling block: bundling. That is, by combining similar types of products and services, GE would be able to exert substantial power relative to competitors. For example, GE provides financing for planes and also manufactures the engines. As for Honeywell, the company develops the internal electronics. Perhaps GE would be in a position to provide incentives for companies to buy electronics in order to get favorable financing.

Reynolds also had enough time to compile factual statistical studies to show that the GE deal would create the bundling effect. This came as a surprise to GE, which instead was advancing the theory that there was no overlap.

Things only got worse. In a last-ditch effort, in June 2001, Welch talked to former Clinton administration officials and even President George W. Bush to help make the case to the EU.

Then Welch took the corporate jet to Brussels to meet with Monti. Welch proposed the divestiture of about $2.2 billion in assets. Monti, though, wanted at least twice as much, which would include much of the aviation electronics business of Honeywell.

For Welch, it was a deal killer, and the EU eventually blocked the merger. It was the first time that the EU rejected a merger even though U.S. federal regulators already approved it. "You are never too old to be surprised," said Welch, who was 65 years old at the time.

LABOR LAW

Labor law can play a critical role in M&A deals. To begin with, M&A transactions frequently involve layoffs. If not done properly, there could be civil lawsuits as well as governmental penalties.

One cautionary tale from recent business history is that of the dot-coms. When these companies started to lay off many employees during 2000–2001, many of them did not realize the extent of the labor laws. Basically, the companies did not think the laws applied to them. It was a serious blunder.

To follow are some of the major factors.

Unions

True, unions have been declining since the 1970s. However, they still are an important factor in certain types of industries, such as manufacturing.

There is a patchwork of federal regulations that apply to unions: the National Labor Relations Act, the Labor Management Relations Act, and the Landrum-Griffin Act. These are collectively known as the "Labor Act," which is administered by the National Labor Relations Board (NLRB).

A union can be defined as a unit of the following: all employees of a company, employees of a division or plant, or employees of a certain craft (for example, the airline pilots union). The unit must, by majority vote, elect a union to represent it. If this happens, then the NLRB will certify the union as the exclusive bargaining agents for the unit. Thus, a company may not deal with another union.

The status of the union can be one of the following:

- **Certification bar.** After a majority election, the presumption is that the majority will last one year (unless the election was fraudulent).

- **Recognition bar.** If there was no official election but the employer believes there is a majority, then the majority is considered to last a "reasonable" amount of time (less than a year).
- **Contract bar.** If the union has entered a collective bargaining agreement with the employer, then the majority lasts for the term of the agreement (no more than three years).

Suppose Company A buys Company B, which has a union. Thus, A will be the new employer of B's unionized employees. If the union is a certification or a recognition bar, then A must negotiate with the union. After the expiration of the representation, A may not be required to bargain with the union if it can demonstrate—with strong evidence or a vote—that there is no majority.

However, if the union is a contract bar, then A does not have to bargain with the union if the collective bargaining agreement is not assumed in a merger agreement. After the agreement expires, A can challenge the status of the union.

According to the Labor Act, there are mandatory areas that must be bargained over, like "wages, hours, and other terms and conditions of employment." Does this mean that, in the case of A, it must bargain with its union about the proposed buyout? After all, the buyout may mean that there are layoffs or perhaps the union is even not recognized. The courts have ruled that there is no mandatory bargaining—unless, that is, the buyout has only one reason: to reduce labor costs. Of course, companies will list many reasons for the buyout in an effort to avoid mandatory bargaining.

Worker Adjustment and Retraining Notification Act (WARN)

This is a federal law that applies to companies that have 100 or more full-time employees who have worked at least six of the past 12 months.

As the name implies, WARN requires that companies notify affected employees 60 days before they are to be laid off. An affected employee is one who is reasonably expected to be laid off. The law does not apply to temporary workers, consultants, and contract workers. Notification must also be made to the employee's union and the state labor agency.

If an employer violates the law, then it owes 60 days' worth of back pay and employee benefits. Moreover, the penalties can be as high as $500 per day per violation, and the employer is likely to be liable for "reasonable" attorney's fees.

The rationale for the law is to give employees time to transition to the next job.

WARN applies when either of these conditions applies:

- A plant or facility is closed and results in at least 50 employees being out of work for 30 days or more
- There is a layoff of 30 days or more that results in the cuts of at least 500 employees or the cuts represent 33% of the total workforce

Suppose that ABC buys XYZ. Within a few weeks, ABC lays off 100 people but does not provide WARN notification. Who's liable, ABC or XYZ? In the event of an M&A transaction, the seller is required to make the notification no later than the date on which the transaction closes. After this, the purchaser must make the notification. However, a seller might want to protect itself in a merger contract for possible WARN liability, such as by requiring the purchaser to indemnify the seller of all liability exposure.

Likewise, ABC could also ask for indemnification. But this may not be enough. ABC may be liable anyway because of "alter ego" or "successor liability" (discussed below).

Stock Options

Stock options are no longer exclusively the province of executive compensation. Even secretaries and janitors receive stock options. At Starbucks, for example, even part-time employees receive them.

In a layoff, an employer may want to terminate the stock options. While this lessens the potential dilution for the company, there may be disgruntled employees who sue.

Example: Qualcomm is a high-flying company that designs wireless technologies called CDMA (Code Division Multiple Access). And the company had a stock option plan since 1991. The option plan had standard features, such as vesting. This means an employee must work at the company for a period of time before being able to exercise (that is, buy) the options. In Qualcomm's plan, the shares would vest in equal installments over a five-year period.

In 1997, Ericsson filed several patent infringement suits against Qualcomm regarding CDMA technology. The suit was preventing Qualcomm from commercializing its technology, so the company decided to sell its Infrastructure Division to Ericsson in 1999. But Ericsson was concerned that, if the employees of Infrastructure continued to have options in Qualcomm, there would be divided loyalty. When the deal was struck, the 1,800 employees of the Infrastructure Division had all their unvested stock options canceled. This caused considerable animosity, especially because Qualcomm's stock soared after the cancellation.

A group of Infrastructure Division employees sued Qualcomm. They claimed breach of contract, fraud, and suppression of material fact.

A year later, both parties reached a settlement in which 840 employees received $11 million.

Discrimination

Traditionally, companies have used "employment at will" contracts to justify firing any employee at any time for any reason. But during the 1990s, the laws and the courts became more skeptical of these actions. For example, there could be problems with age, race, or gender discrimination. Of these, age discrimination is particularly problematic, as older employees tend to be more vigorous in fighting for their civil rights. Also, juries tend to be more sympathetic. Moreover, older employees will typically have been with a company for many years—showing that they have been solid contributors.

The main applicable federal law is the Age Discrimination in Employment Act (ADEA) of 1967. This prohibits age discrimination against those over 40 years old. The law applies to companies with 20 or more employees.

Regardless of the discrimination, the alleged victim has the burden of proving the discrimination, which is no easy task. The plaintiff must come up with as much evidence as possible to show that the employer did actually engage in discrimination.

To avoid discrimination claims, here is a checklist for employers to consider:

DISCRIMINATORY COMMENTS. Make sure that managers of the M&A transaction refrain from discriminatory comments, such as "this old geezer must go" or "we need new blood." Although these types of comments will not usually be enough to show discrimination, it can be powerful evidence that leads to liability exposure.

DISPARATE IMPACT. A plaintiff will often use statistical evidence to show that there was discrimination. For example, suppose that Company S buys Company T. Of the 100 employees of Company T, 20 are black and 50 white. However, 10 of the black employees are fired but only five white employees. Thus, there was clearly a disparate impact on the black employees.

In this case, Company S should have conducted an analysis of the workforce in terms of protected groups (racial groups, gender, age-groups, and so on). Then look how layoffs will result in a potential disparate impact on each group.

EMPLOYEE RECORDS. Decisions to fire employees must not be rushed. First of all, review the employee records. It is a good idea to have the help of legal counsel.

Do not be inconsistent. For example, suppose Jane, who is black, and Fred, who is white, work for the same company. Both were hired two years ago for the same position. However, both had about the same low performance ratings. But in the merger, Jane was let go, and Red was retained. This would certainly raise concerns that there was discrimination.

OBJECTIVITY. Set up a procedure that bases the layoffs on objective standards. For instance, the factors could be based on sales volume for a salesperson, on efficiency for an order taker, and so on.

DEMOTION. One technique to avoid problems with discrimination is to demote a worker. Yet if the demotion is drastic (for example, going from a senior level programmer to a clerk), the court may still find discrimination.

OUTPLACEMENT SERVICES. This is a great defense to discrimination. That is, the employer will help the former employees find new jobs, such as with retraining.

COMPASSION. Dealing with the human side of layoffs is critically important. For the company, it is not easy to be responsible for layoffs.

A big mistake is to inform the laid-off employee via e-mail. This is extremely impersonal and is likely to

cause great resentment. If possible, a face-to-face termination is the best. What's more, there should be a clear
explanation of the reasons for the layoff.

Workplace Violence

In December 2000, a high-tech employee came to work
and began shooting at his coworkers. In all, seven employees died.

Sadly, workplace violence is growing. There are
many reasons. In some cases, the incidents stem from
layoffs from an M&A transaction. The threat of such
problems is especially high in bigger, restructuring-type
deals. Death threats have not been uncommon, and executives have hired bodyguards.

Some companies will have psychology tests for employees. But these are not necessarily good predictors.
Rather, promoting open communications within the
workplace is probably much better. Also, an employer
must be aware of warning signs. They can include incidents of anger, excessive blame, or deterioration of work
performance. Also useful are employee-training programs, which can be helpful to encourage employees to
report problems.

Security precautions are a good idea, of course. The
employer should have a crisis manual on how to deal
with incidents of violence (for example, whom do you
call?). There can be locks and alarm systems and in
some cases on-site security guards.

INSIDER TRADING

Suppose you are the founder and CEO of ABC. You decide to sell your company to XYZ for $45 per share—all
cash. The deal has not been announced yet, and ABC

shares are trading at $30 each. You decide to buy 10,000 shares. And, of course, when the deal is announced, you make a tidy profit.

However, this would be a violation of the federal securities laws. Basically, you committed illegal insider trading. The basic definition is buying or selling securities while knowing nonpublic material information.

Now, in the case above, if the information had been disclosed to the public, then you could have purchased stock. Then again, it probably would not have been a good investment.

Interestingly enough, you may be subject to insider trading violations even if you do not gain anything. How is this possible? If you provide a tip to another person and this person acts on the information, you are guilty. In other words, if you have nonpublic information, keep it nonpublic.

Example: James McDermott, who was convicted on insider trading charges in 2000, was the CEO of the investment bank Keefe, Bruyette & Woods. Because of the nature of his business, McDermott was privy to insider information. McDermott had tipped his girlfriend on an upcoming bank merger. His girlfriend, Katherine Gannon, was also known as Marylin Start, a famous porno star in Canada. She made about $88,000 from the transactions. She is currently in hiding.

The penalties for insider trading can be severe. The SEC can impose fines ranging from $5,000 to $100,000 per violation. Also, a violator must disgorge his profits and may be subject to paying treble damages. The SEC can also ban people from the securities industry or being an officer or director of a public company. Plus, the Department of Justice can impose criminal penalties. Fines can be as high as $1 million, and jail sentences can last 10 years.

Actually, even the company whose employee is convicted of insider trading may be liable as well. As a result, many public companies have instituted their own employee policies to warn against insider trading violations.

There is such a thing as *legal* insider trading. The SEC understands that insiders—who are officers, directors, and major shareholders of a company—will always be privy to some type of material, nonpublic information. The SEC does not want to prevent these insiders from buying or selling stock. So, the SEC has a system that requires insiders to disclose their transactions:

- **Form 3.** This must be filed within 10 days of becoming an insider. This sets forth the insider's holdings—even if the insider has no shares.

- **Form 4.** This must be filed by the 10th day of the following month in which the trade was made.

- **Form 5.** This is filed 45 days after a company's fiscal year end. This shows any trade activity in the past year.

- **Form 144.** This is a necessary filing for shareholders who have unregistered stock. This is the final step before the shares can be sold on the open market.

If you are no longer an insider, you must still abide by these disclosure rules for another six months. Moreover, insiders are subject to the short-swing rule. If an insider makes a profit from a trade within six months, then the profits must be returned.

ENVIRONMENTAL LAW

Rachel Carson grew up in the rural town of Springdale, Pennsylvania, near a large, flowing river. Carson had a great love of nature and received her M.A. in zoology from Johns Hopkins University in 1932. She then worked for the U.S. Bureau of Fisheries, becoming editor-in-chief of all its publications. Carson, who had a poetic way of expressing scientific concepts, was very concerned about synthetic chemical pesticides and wrote a book called *Silent Spring* (1962). It had a tremendous impact and helped launch the environmental movement in the United States.

A year later, Carson testified before Congress. Her warnings formed the groundwork for many federal environmental laws and the creation of the Environmental Protection Agency (EPA).

Somehow, the belief is that environmental considerations apply solely to old industries, such as steel or chemicals. But, as in the M&A field, environmental laws can affect virtually any type of business. For example, the semiconductor industry is under strict scrutiny because of the hazardous wastes that result from the chip-making process.

Here is a list of common areas where there could be environmental liability:

- **Facilities.** Have asbestos and polychlorinated biphenyls (PCBs) been checked for?
- **Fuel tanks.** Has there been any leakage?
- **Factories.** What types of chemicals are used? How are they disposed?
- **Surrounding areas.** Are there lakes or ponds near a company's facilities? If so, check to see if they have been contaminated.

It is a good idea to hire an environmental consultant to investigate these matters. The costs can be high, $25,000 or more. But it is certainly better than being hit with a lawsuit from the federal government, which can demolish a company. Some of the biggest corporate bankruptcies have been the result of environmental actions (especially with asbestos).

When hiring an environmental consultant, you should interview a number of candidates and ask for the following information and answers.

HOW DO YOU CHARGE? CAN YOU ESTIMATE THE TOTAL COST OF THE PROJECT? For the most part, the consultant will charge on an hourly basis, which can run from $100 to $500 per hour. But don't necessarily try for frugality in your selection. In fact, it is a good idea to go with a large firm (more than 50 employees), which should have more experienced people to help with the project.

HAVE YOU EXPERIENCE IN M&A DUE DILIGENCE CONSULTING? If not, then do not use the consultant.

ARE YOU FAMILIAR WITH THE STATE AND LOCAL LAWS? The legal system for environmental laws is not only federal but also state and local. If you need a consultant to analyze a facility in Dallas, then make sure he or she understands the laws in that municipality as well as in Texas. See if the consultant has actually done any projects in that area.

ASK FOR AT LEAST THREE REFERENCES. One well-established consultancy is R.T. Hicks Consulting, based in Albuquerque, New Mexico. The company not only uncovers environmental problems but also establishes regulatory strategies. For M&A deals, the firm will represent both buyers and sellers. For example, for the past 30 years, a roofing company had been releasing asphalt and water into unpaved areas of its facility. A company wanted to buy the roofer but while investigating the environmental situation found low levels of polynuclear aromatic hydrocarbons in the soil and groundwater. So, the buyer requested that $3 million be set aside to handle the remediation. Of course, this would represent a substantial reduction in the company's sale price.

The seller hired R.T. Hicks, which determined that there was no violation of drinking-water standards. The firm presented these findings to the governing regulatory agency, which agreed. The acquisition proceeded without the seller having to pay undue amounts of cash for remediation.

As stated above, there are numerous environmental laws. However, the main legislation is the Comprehensive Environmental Response, Compensation, and Liability Act (CERCLA), commonly known as the "Superfund" law. As the name implies, there is a fund behind this that helps pay for removing wastes and doing remedial actions with environmental waste sites.

Under the law, a company is required to disclose to the EPA any and all hazardous wastes on their properties. From this information, as well as independent findings, the EPA will establish a priority list on which environmental sites should be cleaned up first. A removal action is a long-term solution, while a remedial action is short-term in nature.

CERCLA sets forth a broad array of potentially responsible parties (PRPs) for liability. They include current owners and operators, former owners and operators who were present at the time of contamination, waste generators who arranged for waste disposal, and waste transporters.

The liability is strict, joint, and several. That is, if there is a link between the PRP and the waste site, there is liability even if there was no blame. As for joint and several liability, this means that each party can be liable for all the costs of the cleanup. In fact, there can be treble damages.

However, there is the "innocent purchaser defense." Thus, a buyer of a contaminated property can reduce liability or eliminate it if the buyer performed adequate due diligence. The due diligence is known as an environmental site assessment (ESA), or Phase I (defined below). Many environmental consulting firms perform ESAs, which are based on standards known as the American Society for Testing Materials (ASTM) guidelines. These can be found online at *www.astm.org*.

If contamination is found, a buyer should be able to negotiate a much better price.

Here's what constitutes an official site audit:

PHASE I. This is the initial investigation that is based on historical records to see what chemicals were used on a site as well as processes. The audit will look to see if the company is in compliance with existing regulations. Also, there should be research to see if all necessary permits are filed.

PHASE II. If Phase I indicates problems, then this phase ensues. This report will show the recommendations for cleanup. Be careful. A Phase II audit can be time consuming and expensive. It is important to have a reputable consultant handle these matters.

IMMIGRATION LAW

A common mistake is to overlook immigration laws in the M&A process, but this regulatory area can be important. For instance, it is typical of high-tech companies to have a large percentage of its workforce composed of foreign workers. Historically, the industry has had a severe labor shortage of technical workers.

Congress has changed the laws to make it easier to hire foreign workers. In October 2000, Congress increased the H-1B visa limit from 65,000 workers per year to 115,000. But this may not be enough. Also, Congress increased the fees for visas from $85 to $610.

The legal process for hiring foreign workers is complex. An employer must verify that the employee can legally work for it. This is done by filling out an I-9 form within three days of the hire. The filing goes to the Immigration and Naturalization Service (INS). An employer also needs to fill out the Labor Condition Application (LCA) for the Department of Labor.

When filling out these forms, the employer must attest that the foreign worker is being paid a prevailing wage. The reason is that the federal government wants to prevent low wages from taking jobs away from American citizens. The employer must also make a concerted effort to advertise the job.

But the process can drag on—for as much as four months or more.

It is a violation for an employer to allow the employee to work before the INS approves the application. Fines range from $200 to $10,000. There can even be prison sentences of up to six months for chronic violators. Moreover, there is the "death penalty." This means that if there are a large number of violations, an employer may be prohibited from hiring foreign workers.

If a company is involved in a reorganization, such as an M&A event, it may need to file a new or amended H-1B petition—even if the employee has the same position. According to the INS, there is no need for a new or amended petition if the M&A event only changes the name of the companies (but the company must notify the INS of the name change). But if a merger results in the creation of a new corporate entity, then there must be a new or amended petition. Basically, the employee has a new employer.

However, the law is not necessarily clear-cut. The INS has had divergent views regarding M&A transactions. For example, if the acquisition results in a company changing its tax identification number, this may be enough to require new or amended petitions.

POTENTIAL REGULATION

The adoption of new technologies usually entails the creation of new regulations. As is customary, it may take politicians some time to deal with the consequences of the new technologies. Furthermore, it may take a lot of time to see if there are any "side effects." Typing, for example, historically had not been treated as a potentially injurious activity, until the rise of computer keyboards led to more typing-exclusive jobs and the resultant spate of carpal tunnel syndrome.

Thus, when you buy a technology company, keep in mind that you could be subject to future regulation.

Example: The cell phone industry has two potential problems. First, there are rising concerns about driver safety. Several studies have shown that the use of cell phones results in higher rates of auto accidents. Some states are attempting to pass laws to outlaw the use of cell phones while driving. The laws, though, could be a benefit to the cell phone industry. How? The proposed laws allow for drivers to use headsets.

Another risk is the possibility of cell phones causing brain tumors. A variety of studies have been conducted on the subject, but the results so far are inconclusive. Despite this, there have already been several lawsuits filed against telecom companies.

The moral, if there is one, is that in our regulated and highly litigious society, M&A participants need to consider every aspect of a deal and an acquisition for potential liabilities.

CHAPTER 10

ALTERNATIVES
TO M&A

An M&A transaction is an all-or-nothing proposition. Yet many times a buyer would really prefer
to purchase a piece of another business, not the
whole shebang. True, buyers can sell off unneeded assets. But this is time consuming and entails uncertainty
about how much would be recouped. What such a buyer
wants is some creative alternatives to a full-scale M&A.
Fortunately, these do exist and are known under the collective name of "alliances."

An alliance is a relationship between two or more
companies that leverages their combined strengths and
enables them to enter new markets or build new products.
This differs from a merger in that there is less transfer of
ownership. Here's a look at the varieties of alliances (going
from the least comprehensive to the most comprehensive):

DISTRIBUTION/MARKETING AGREEMENT. A company
agrees to sell its products through another company's
marketing and distribution channels. Usually, a smaller

company with an innovative product will sign such deals with larger, established companies that are looking for growth opportunities.

LICENSING. A company pays a fee to use another company's intellectual property—such as technology or copyrighted or trademarked materials or images. There is usually an up-front fee and then ongoing royalties based on the number of units sold.

JOINT VENTURE/STRATEGIC ALLIANCE. Two or more companies enter an agreement to develop a new product or technology and to distribute the products through their existing marketing and distribution channels. The difference between a joint venture and strategic alliance is that a joint venture is a separate company (co-owned by the parties), whereas a strategic alliance is a contract between the parties.

The absolutely critical point when pursuing any M&A alternative is that you have an internal strategic plan that sets forth the types of alliances that make sense for your firm. Companies can falter if they take a scatter-shot approach to forging alliances. For one thing, it can be a great drain on resources. It may not necessarily be difficult to form an alliance, but it often takes a lot of effort to manage one successfully.

In this chapter, we'll look at how alliances are formed and make a detailed survey of the different alliances your company may engage in. At the end of the chapter, we'll present franchising (as a way to expand business or start a new business) and initial public offerings (IPOs).

THE ALLIANCE PROCESS

It's an all-too-common scenario: Two CEOs meet, instantly like each other, and start talking about their businesses. One CEO suggests, "Let's do something to-gether. Maybe we can set up some kind of alliance." They'll discuss this on a very high level, waxing about their companies' potential "strategic synergies." Then the CEOs will get senior managers to try to come up with something.

This spur-of-the-moment approach can be danger-ous. Just as with the M&A process, the alliance process should involve lots of planning. Since both companies would have to divert valuable resources to the new al-liances, it's crucial to analyze whether the alliance makes sense for everyone.

Screening Criteria

Senior management should spend at least several months setting up a list of criteria for screening alliances. Some of the key areas to cover include the following:

WHAT ARE THE GOALS OF THE ALLIANCE? Is it to tar-get new markets and distribution channels? Or to fill holes in product lines, create new technologies, pene-trate international markets, leverage brand names, or make equity investments?

WHAT TYPES OF PARTNERS DO YOU WANT? For exam-ple, do you want to deal exclusively with companies that have sales of at least $100 million? Or is your main con-cern to deal with companies that have similar corporate cultures?

WHO MANAGES THE ALLIANCE? Some companies ap-point a vice president of alliances or licensing.

WHAT RESOURCES CAN WE BRING TO THE TABLE? Will you be offering some combination of money, technical, or marketing talent, distribution channels, and/or products?

ORGANIZATION. Does your company have experience with alliances? Do you have enough qualified employees to manage future alliances? If your organization is already stretched, then it is probably not a good idea to engage in an alliance.

CONTROL/PRICING. If you form a joint venture, do you want to own more than 50%? Are you willing to own less? If the alliance will be splitting profits, what allocation is acceptable to you?

Deal Flow

Management needs to be constantly looking for possible alliance opportunities. Much of this is done by researching the industry and networking. (See chapter 2 for more information on this subject.) In fact, the best alliance partners are sometimes those you already deal with, such as suppliers, customers, and distributors.

Meeting with the Potential Alliance Partner

If there is no prior contact, then you should contact the CEO if the company is a start-up or a hypergrowth company. For all other companies, you should first contact a vice president (of business development, usually).

Once initial contact is made, a first meeting should be set up. At this meeting, no specific agreement should be made. Rather, both parties should get to understand each other's interests and backgrounds. At the end, set up another meeting and indicate who should attend. This meeting should include discussion of possible terms of a deal.

At all subsequent meetings before a deal is closed, it is smart to have an attorney present. The attorney should not be your M&A attorney but rather one who specializes in alliances.

Spend time preparing for these meetings. If you are proactively seeking alliance partners, you are in a sense pitching your company. A good way to do this is to have an information package about your company. It would include brochures, testimonials, background information, product demos (such as CDs), press releases, and so on.

Also, research the other company as much as possible and see what other alliances the company has engaged in. Find out about the other company's culture to assess whether it's a good fit. (See chapter 8.) However, keep in mind that a midsize or mature company may have a variety of divisions, some of which have cultures that are similar to start-ups or hypergrowth companies. Even if this is the case, however, you will still have to deal to some extent with the parent corporation.

If, as negotiations proceed, both parties realize there is no real fit at the time, remember that there may be a fit in the future. So be sure to keep this company in the alliance database and periodically review to see if a fit makes sense.

Terms

During the meetings, you will be negotiating terms of a deal. (See chapter 4 for tips.) Again, you want to have an attorney present.

The following key terms are general, relevant to virtually any type of alliance. In the rest of the chapter, we'll look at the terms specific to each type of alliance as we get to them.

LENGTH OF THE ALLIANCE. In many cases, both parties will want to test each other out and so prefer not to commit to a long-term agreement. This is a good idea.

Given a little time, the parties will realize either that the agreement does not make sense or that it should be broadened.

These are the three time frames:

- **Short-term.** This lasts up to three years. You typically see a licensing or distribution structure.
- **Medium-term.** This lasts between three to five years, and usually applies for a joint venture or strategic alliance structure.
- **Long-term.** This lasts five years or more. You will see in many cases an acquisition.

PRICE. If you're a start-up or even a hypergrowth company, you'll probably be at a pricing disadvantage when dealing with midsize and mature companies. After all, start-up and hypergrowth companies can benefit tremendously from the clout and distribution of midsize and mature companies. What's more, mature and midsize companies usually can pick from among a bevy of potential alliance partners.

But if you feel your company has a unique advantage (perhaps your technology is a year ahead of the rest), then you should use this leverage to negotiate the best price you can.

CONFIDENTIALITY. When forming an alliance, the same standards of confidentiality apply here as in full M&A deals. Both parties will disclose sensitive information—strategic goals, financials, and so on—that must be kept confidential. Also, it can take one to six months to set up an alliance. While this is going on, internal information should also be kept secret—you don't want to provide your competitors a recipe for structuring a deal. It is imperative to sign confidentiality agreements. (See chapter 4 for more information about this.)

DISTRIBUTION AGREEMENTS

Distribution agreements are quite common, mostly because they're fairly straightforward. Typically, one company has one or more valuable products, and the other party has established distribution channels suitable to these products. The key negotiation point is determining how to split the profits. As this varies tremendously, it's important to have an understanding of industry practices.

The main benefits from a distribution agreement include the following:

- Market share is increased.
- Credibility—Teaming up with a well-known company tends to validate your product.
- Less capital is needed for a sales force.

Disadvantages include the following:

- Quality control—Is the product being represented accurately and well? Is customer service up to snuff?
- Manufacturing—You might not have enough capacity to fill the volume requirements.
- You may be teaming up with a company that does not use its best efforts to sell your product.

We'll look at an actual distribution agreement between Inrange Technologies and Ancor Communications (signed in October 1995). Inrange designs and manufactures testing equipment for telecom networks. Ancor is a major supplier and marketer to the telecom industry. In the deal, Ancor agreed to purchase and resell the Inrange product line.

Key terms included the following:

EXCLUSIVITY. The agreement is not exclusive for both parties. That is, Inrange and Ancor can enter similar agreements with other parties. This is a good idea. It can be very damaging for a company to be locked into the distribution of one company, as it will limit the potential market size.

PROMOTIONAL MATERIALS. Ancor has the right to create and modify existing promotional materials.

CUSTOMIZATION. If the product has to be customized, Inrange must be given lead time. The standard is 90 days, but that can vary, depending on how extensive the customization is. There is also a fee for the customization.

PURCHASES. For each order, Ancor must provide Inrange with written purchase orders to make it binding. In terms of pricing, Ancor received a discount from the retail price, with this discount increasing as the volume increases. Payment is required within 30 days of the date of the invoice, which Inrange issues on shipment. Inrange gets 1.5% interest per month for unpaid balances.

ORDER CANCELLATIONS. If an order is reduced or canceled before it is shipped, Ancor is required to compensate for Inrange's expenses. However, if the order is already sent, the agreement sets forth terms for extra charges (such as shipping expenses) plus the purchase price.

PRODUCT WARRANTIES. Ancor is subject to Inrange's customer warranties (covering issues such as product returns and product defects).

LIABILITY DISCLAIMERS. These are clauses that attempt to limit the amount of liability—for example, if a product causes injury. These are standard clauses, but they may not necessarily be enough; both parties also have a variety of insurance policies, such as product liability.

PRODUCT MODIFICATION OR DISCONTINUANCE. Inrange can make any changes to its product line, including terminating a product, without incurring any liability. However, Inrange must notify Ancor with "as much advance notice as possible" for modifications. For discontinuing products, the notification must be six months, and Inrange must use "reasonable efforts" to support the discontinued product for three years.

INTELLECTUAL PROPERTY. Inrange indicates that the agreement in no way transfers intellectual property rights to Ancor.

INDEMNIFICATION. Inrange agrees to reimburse Ancor if there is any liability from Inrange's infringement on another's intellectual property. Ancor agrees to indemnify Inrange if the contract is violated or its employees have engaged in false or misleading actions with Inrange's products.

SALES PROMOTION. Ancor agrees to use its "best efforts" to promote and sell the products. To this end, Ancor will provide Inrange with a 12-month forecast of sales (updated quarterly). Moreover, Ancor agrees to maintain an adequate amount of inventory of promotional materials. Likewise, Inrange agrees to provide enough promotional materials to Ancor.

SUPPORT. Ancor agrees to handle customer service, installation, maintenance, and technical support for products sold. But Ancor can call Inrange—free of charge—for technical assistance once it has used reasonable efforts to resolve the problem. Inrange also agrees to provide training courses for its products, free of charge. During a 12-month period, there will be no fewer than three training sessions. If Ancor requests additional classes, it must pay a fee.

TERM. The contract lasts for three years. After this, if both parties agree, the contract will continue for an additional year.

TERMINATION. This happens if one of the parties breaches the contract and does not cure the breach within 30 days, there is a bankruptcy, Ancor merges with a direct competitor, Inrange discontinues its products, or both parties agree to end the agreement. In the event of a termination, all money owed to Inrange is immediately payable. The remedies are limited. Excluded from the calculation are loss of future compensation, loss of goodwill, and expenditures used to prepare for the agreement (hiring employees, leases, and so on).

LICENSING

It is common for people to confuse franchising and licensing. First of all, a franchise is identified by the franchiser's trademark. For example, McDonald's is the trademark for the parent company as well as the franchisees.

A franchisee usually is restricted to selling the products or services of a franchise on an exclusive basis (that is, you cannot have both a McDonald's and a Burger King franchise). But licensees usually can deal with a variety of competing products or services. And whereas a franchisee gets a lot of training and ongoing support, this is typically not the case with a licensee. For the most part, the licensee must do much of the work to set up and market a product or service using the license.

With licensing, a company lets other companies use its intellectual property for a fee. But there is no transfer of ownership; rather, the intellectual property is heavily protected by copyrights, trademarks, or patents. There are two types of licensing: merchandising (for example, using the likeness of Donald Duck) and technologies.

Why license? Here are the main benefits:

- Potential to attain more market share
- Annuity stream of royalty income
- Building a standard
- Lowers capital outlays for expansion

Of course, there are disadvantages:

- Legal complexities
- Administration of many customers
- Screening good licensees
- Difficulty of providing quality control standards

In December 1999, Handspring licensed operating system software from Palm Computing. Both companies develop handheld devices to keep track of information as well as to browse the Internet and read e-mail.

Here's a look at the key elements of their licensing agreement:

TYPE OF LICENSE. It is nonexclusive and allows Handspring the ability to modify the software code of the Palm operating system (this is known as "derivative works"). For this, Handspring agrees to pay a royalty to Palm.

STANDARDS. Palm has very rigorous technology quality standards that a licensee, such as Handspring, must comply with. If Handspring fails to do so, then either it must cure the problems or the license is terminated. Also, Handspring has the right to specify the following message on its products: "Palm Computing Platform Compatible."

INSPECTION RIGHTS. A big risk for licensing agreements is ensuring that the licensee is not cheating. For example, perhaps Handspring sells many devices but underreports this to Palm.

This can be handled with inspection rights. Thus, Palm can inspect the facilities and records of Handspring as long as it provides reasonable notice. What's more, Palm has the right to hire an independent CPA to audit Handspring's royalty records. If there is more than a 5% underreporting of royalties, Handspring must pay for the audit.

SUPPORT. There are several pages of specifications for handling different levels of support. For example, Palm will help Handspring deal with programming the operating system. Handspring, on the other hand, is responsible for providing general technical support to its own customers. Palm also agrees to provide training courses to the Handspring technical staff.

UPDATES. All upgrades, bug fixes, modifications, enhancements, and new versions will be provided to Handspring within 10 days of beta release.

WARRANTIES/INDEMNIFICATION/DISCLAIMERS/TERMI-NATION. These are similar to the ones discussed above.

TERM. The agreement lasts for five years. After this, the agreement may be renewed on successive one-year terms (if both parties consent).

JOINT VENTURES AND STRATEGIC ALLIANCES

In terms of goals, joint ventures and strategic alliances are very similar. They allow two or more companies to join forces to engage in a substantial undertaking. In fact, the alliance will often involve distribution and licensing agreements.

But there is much more than this involved:

- Research and development for a new product
- One party makes an equity investment in another party
- Use of manufacturing capacity
- Ability to enter new line(s) of business without incurring much financial risk
- Gain access to supplies

If the alliance is a strategic agreement, then the form of the relationship is a contract. This is much easier than joint ventures, which require the establishment of a new company.

In some cases, however, forming a joint venture makes sense. Here are several reasons:

Psychological impact. It seems more permanent and committed.

Spin-off. By being a separate company, with its own assets, liabilities and employees, the joint venture can be spun off as an IPO or sold to another company.

International. A foreign country may require a new company be set up and that the foreign company own more than 50% of the entity. Essentially, this can be the price to pay to enter foreign markets.

Regardless of the form of the alliance, joint ventures and strategic alliances share the same types of advantages and disadvantages.

First the advantages:

- Market share is expanded.
- Credibility is gained.
- Shared resources—The companies involved can leverage cash, technology, and employees.
- Access to foreign markets that may be difficult to penetrate.

- Opportunities to learn new management techniques, processes, or technologies. This knowledge can be spread to other parts of the company beyond the alliance.

Disadvantages include the following:

- Cross-purposes—It is not uncommon for alliance partners to be competitors in other lines of business. This can definitely cause a great degree of friction.
- Leadership confusion—Who's in charge? What are the rules? Many alliances fail because there are no clear standards for dealing with major decisions.
- Inadequate capacity—For a big company, it may be dependent on a small company that may not have the resources to carry out its side of the contract.
- There may be much hype and enthusiasm when the deal is announced. If the alliance does not meet or exceed expectations, Wall Street will be disappointed, and the stock price may fall.

Strategic Alliance

In June 1999, Maxygen and Zeneca signed a strategic alliance contract. Maxygen is a biotech company, and Zeneca is a global pharmaceutical company.

Let's take a look at the key terms:

PURPOSE. Both companies jointly agree to engage in research and development of a new biotech drug. This drug is extremely complex and was described in great detail in the contract.

STAFFING. Maxygen agreed to devote an average number of full-time employees (FTEs) for the project. There was also a research committee established to monitor the progress of the agreement and make the necessary adjustments for the staffing and budgeting. There were three members from Maxygen and three from Zeneca. Meetings are conducted, at a minimum, on a quarterly basis (attendance can be in person or by phone), with at least two members from each company in attendance. Minutes must be taken at each meeting (that is, all actions must be recorded), and decisions must be made on a unanimous basis. If this is not possible, then there is a policy for handling disputes (which is fairly extensive).

The dispute resolution clause calls for the following process:

Step 1. Refer the problem to the CEO of Maxygen and Zeneca's business director for agricultural biotechnology.

Step 2. Mediation.

Step 3. Binding arbitration.

EXCLUSIVITY. This takes up several pages of the contract. In some cases, Maxygen must deal exclusively with Zeneca on specific applications of the drugs developed. However, Maxygen was able to make other uses or research areas nonexclusive.

TERM. The agreement lasts for five years.

CONSIDERATION. The compensation structure is very detailed. First of all, Zeneca purchased preferred stock in Maxygen. There is also an option to purchase more shares in the future (at a fixed price). Next, Zeneca agrees to pay agreed-on payments to fund the research effort of Maxygen (this is based on the average FTE level). These payments are made on a quarterly basis. In addition, Zeneca agrees to make specific payments when milestones are achieved (as an incentive for Maxygen to hit its targets). For all this, Zeneca has negotiated a comprehensive compensation system that allows it to commercialize the products developed.

LICENSES. This is another lengthy section. It delineates what party owns the technology and specifies licensing agreements between the parties. The licensing terms include exclusivity, royalty payments, and territorial coverage. There are also inspection rights to see if each party is complying with the royalty requirements.

DILIGENCE. Zeneca agrees to provide "commercially reasonable efforts" to commercialize the products for the alliance. To this end, Zeneca and Maxygen agree to form a Commercial Development Committee, which consists of two representatives from each party. The committee meets twice a year.

INTELLECTUAL PROPERTY. All intellectual property developed solely by Maxygen belongs to Maxygen, as is the case with Zeneca. Intellectual property developed by both parties is considered jointly owned.

REPRESENTATION AND WARRANTIES/INDEMNIFICATION/ DISCLAIMERS/TERMINATION: These are similar to the above agreements.

Joint Venture

In the case of a joint venture, all the above terms would be specified. But there would be some other elements as well (especially in regard to starting a new corporate entity), such as these:

CAPITAL CONTRIBUTION. At least one party must contribute cash to the venture. If a party is cash starved, it can provide other types of assets, such as intellectual property. For the investment, each party will have equity ownership in the new company.

MANAGEMENT TEAM. The company will have its own employees, management, and board of directors. This management group will run the day-to-day operations of the company. Typically, however, the parties that set up the joint venture will have ultimate control. They usually will represent the majority of the board. Moreover, the parties will be able to vote their shares for major corporate decisions, such as to allow a new shareholder or even do an IPO or sell the joint venture.

RESTRICTIONS. There are likely to be resale restrictions on the stock. For example, one party cannot sell any interest to a competitor.

RIGHT OF FIRST REFUSAL. Suppose one of the joint venture partners goes bust or does not want to be a part of the venture anymore. In this case, the other venture partner(s) can have the right to buy out the interest.

Finally, keep in mind that a strategic alliance or joint venture is no way to escape antitrust scrutiny. Such alliances are included in the federal laws. Thus, you should use the same process for seeing if there is an antitrust violation as in chapter 9.

Example: Covisint is a joint venture created in December 2000 that plans to develop a sophisticated business-to-business exchange for the automotive supply industry. The partners include DaimlerChrysler AG, Ford Motor Co., General Motors, Nissan, and Renault; the technology partners were Commerce One and Oracle. In order to launch, Covisint had to receive approval from the FTC and the German antitrust authorities.

FRANCHISING

The law defines a franchise as a business relationship that involves a trademark, a predefined marketing plan, and a franchise fee. If you decide to use franchising to expand your business, you should seek expert advice—not only in setting up the infrastructure but also in complying with the myriad of regulations.

Because of many fraudulent franchises, Congress passed major legislation in 1979 to provide for all material disclosure for franchisees (the person who buys the franchise). The disclosure document is called the Uniform Franchise Circular Offering (UFCO). Moreover, some states require that a franchise be registered with the state (there is no federal registration requirement).

By establishing a franchise, you are shifting the capital costs of expansion to others. In exchange, you receive franchise fees and a percentage of the overall revenues. However, franchising is not appropriate for every business. Some of the factors for successful franchising include the following:

REPLICABILITY. You need to have a business that can be duplicated almost anywhere. This is typically the case with such formula-type businesses as restaurants, printing, tax preparation, and so on.

BRAND STRENGTH. A franchisee is relying on an established brand to make it easier to sell products or services. Often, a strong franchise will spend lots of money on advertising to create a meaningful brand.

SUPPORT PERSONNEL. Inadequate support personnel could lead to major problems with quality or even fraud. A proven way to provide enough support is through franchisee training. In fact, some franchise companies have their own universities.

ONGOING IMPROVEMENT. The franchise should be taking steps to improve the product line or service. Franchisees want to know that they belong to a competitive organization.

STANDARD PROCEDURES. There needs to be uniformity among all franchises. One part of ensuring this is by creating an extensive manual, specifying procedures for dealing with site selection, facilities decor, and so on.

FRANCHISEE SCREENING. The company should have techniques to screen and monitor franchisees. This can be done with a field staff as well as computer systems.

Now, as for the pros and cons: A franchise can be an effective way, in a sense, to buy a new business. As the business becomes successful, profits can be parlayed into buying another franchise and then another and so on.

As I said, most franchises are laden with rules. So, if you truly want to run your own show, then a franchise is probably not a good idea. Then again, if you want to lower the risk of a new venture, a franchise with a proven track record is a viable alternative.

Also, the costs of a good franchise are not cheap. Your annual fees could top $50,000. And the percentage you generated from revenues that you must pay to the franchise could be as high as 10%. And there are other costs to consider. For example, you might have to buy or lease the land. There will probably be expenses for equipment, signage, and inventory.

It is smart to do lots of research before buying a franchise. Is the product or service really a fad? What's the reputation of the franchise? Is the support good? How strong is the brand? How strong is the competition? Is there potential competition?

Example: Ray Kroc was a master (some would say the master) of franchising. At the age of 52, Kroc visited a fast-food restaurant in San Bernardino, California. At the time, he was a milkshake machine salesman, and one of his top clients was this eatery, known as Mc-Donald's. Kroc knew that the restaurant was a gold mine as he stared at the long lines of customers. What's more, the restaurant was an example of extreme efficiency—basically a hamburger factory. He quickly cut a deal to franchise the restaurant. The company grew at a rapid pace and by the early 1960s, he purchased the equity interest of the McDonald brothers for $2.7 million. Obviously, he kept the name because he understood that brand is critical for a successful franchise. Next, he engaged in aggressive national advertising—first on radio and then on television.

Kroc also understood that a franchise needs strong discipline and standards. If not, it becomes almost impossible to replicate the concept. Kroc established a research lab to perfect the most efficient fast-food methods. He also set up an extensive training program for franchise managers (called Hamburger University). Interestingly, some of the franchisee owners became sources of innovation. For example, a Pittsburgh operator developed the Big Mac.

IPO Option

An IPO is the ultimate for an entrepreneur. An IPO is when a company issues shares for the first time on an exchange, such as the New York Stock Exchange or the Nasdaq.

Example: Glen Meakem and Sam Kinney co-founded FreeMarkets in 1995. The company provides reverse-auction services to allow businesses to buy and sell supplies. Meakem had the idea for the business while he was an employee at General Electric in 1994. He even proposed the idea to GE, but the company rejected it. By 1999, FreeMarkets was growing quickly.

About $630 million worth of purchase orders were
processed by the company's systems as customers realized cost savings of 2% to 25%. In all, FreeMarkets had
30 clients in 50 product categories—in such areas as
metal fabrications, chemicals, printed circuit boards,
and even coal. The client list included such biggies as
General Motors, United Technologies, and Pepsico.
Sales surged from $400,000 in 1998 to $21 million in
1999. But losses were $13.5 million. There were 300
employees. In September 1999, when FreeMarkets
filed to go public (both Meakem and Kinney were 35
years old), the major investment banks Goldman
Sachs and Morgan Stanley agreed to underwrite the
offering. By December, FreeMarkets shares were sold
to the public. The company issued 3.6 million shares at
$48 each, raising about $172.8 million. On the first day
of trading, the stock price reached a high of $293 and
closed at $280, with about 7.8 million shares trading
hands. Meakem and Kinney were worth hundreds of
millions.

Sounds, great huh? Yes, besides wealth, there are
many advantages for going public. They include the
following:

CAPITAL. With the IPO, FreeMarkets was able to raise
enough money to execute on its business plan. By 2000,
the company had revenues of $91.3 million and had auc-
tion volume of $9.8 billion.

LIQUIDITY. The founders of the company have the
ability to cash out some of their equity holdings. For
example, in July 2000, Meakem sold 100,000 shares for
$4.7 million.

PRESTIGE. Becoming a public company is very helpful
for a company's overall image. Public companies appear
to be much more permanent. There also tend to be more
PR opportunities.

EMPLOYEES. A company can issue stock options to employees. This can help hire and retain key employees.

ACQUISITIONS. A public company can use its stock as currency to buy other companies. For example, in February 2001, FreeMarkets purchased Adexa, a privately held company that provides collaborative commerce solutions. In the deal, FreeMarkets issued 17.25 million shares for all the outstanding shares of Adexa. The price amounted to about $340 million. The deal expanded the customer base to over 160.

But, of course, there are drawbacks as well. They include the following:

DISCLOSURE. A public company is required to make quarterly and annual reports to the public. If there are any special events—such as mergers—then there must also be a disclosure (if it is material). The purpose of these disclosures is to protect investors. Unfortunately, compiling the necessary information can be time consuming and involves the help of a variety of advisers, such as attorneys and CPAs. Thus, the costs of the disclosures can be substantial.

COSTS. The cost of an IPO is significant. See the table "Fees for the FreeMarkets IPO."

The underwriters' compensation was based on a percentage of the proceeds raised from the IPO. The total amount was $12 million.

CONTROL. In most cases, the founders will lose voting control of the company. Meakem, for instance, has less than 10% ownership of FreeMarkets. Thus, his company could be susceptible to a hostile takeover, or, if Meakem's performance falters, he could be booted as CEO.

SELLING RESTRICTIONS. If you are suddenly worth hundreds of millions, it certainly would be tempting to

FEES FOR THE FREEMARKETS IPO

SEC registration fee	$45,905
NASD fee	17,888
Nasdaq National Market listing fee	94,000
Printing expenses	350,000
Legal fees and expenses	800,000
Accounting fees and expenses	550,000
Transfer agent and registrar fees	3,500
Miscellaneous	306,707
Total	$2,168,000

sell everything. However, this would disrupt the stock price. Therefore, the underwriters will impose restrictions on how many shares can be sold from the offering. One mechanism is the "lockup period," denoting that directors, officers, and employees cannot sell the stock for a certain period of time—usually about six months after the IPO.

Finally, keep in mind that an IPO is a rare event for a company. In any given year, there may be 300 to 400 IPOs.

CHAPTER 11

HOSTILE
TAKEOVERS

A ny company—regardless of size—is a potential
target of a hostile takeover. In a nutshell, there is
a tremendous amount of liquidity in the world financial system. And if a deal makes sense, sufficient
capital usually can be found to make the deal happen.

As a significant part of the 1980s deal world, hostile
takeovers acquired a nasty reputation indeed. The buyers, who were known as "corporate raiders," were extremely aggressive in their tactics. For example, it was
not uncommon for a target to find out about a hostile
raid by reading the morning *Wall Street Journal*. Also,
in many cases the raiders wanted only to bust up the
company and liquidate it at a profit.

However, there has been a change in hostile deals
since the 1980s. One reason is the legal landscape. For
example, the minimum amount of time that a tender
offer can be open is 20 days. Besides, many companies
have takeover defenses in place (explained in more detail below). Companies learned some lessons from the

1980s, and they're better prepared to ward off unwanted suitors.

Ironically, a hostile acquirer may start its offer on friendly terms. But there is a big risk to that tack. That is, the target might require that the prospective acquirer sign a "standstill agreement." Essentially, this means the acquirer can do the deal only on friendly terms. But what if, after review, the target does not want to do a friendly deal? Depending on how the standstill agreement is set up, the prospective buyer may not be able to do a deal.

Rather, a more popular approach is the so-called bear hug. In this situation, the acquirer sends a confidential letter to the board of directors of the target. Since the board has a fiduciary responsibility to shareholders, it will be pressured into considering getting the best value from a deal—regardless of how management feels. After all, the board could be subject to shareholder lawsuits.

The third option is that a company can do a traditional hostile takeover. This is no easy feat and can be very expensive and stressful.

HOSTILE TAKEOVER FACTORS

To be successful, a hostile acquirer needs to do some in-depth analysis. If you're considering such a move, here are some factors to look at:

CASH IS KING. No question, cash is very important in hostile takeovers. And the price should be at a significant premium. If you can satisfy those two conditions, you are likely to convince shareholders to sell out.

DEFENSES. You need to look closely at what the company has set up to deflect a hostile offer, such as poison pills and staggered boards.

SHAREHOLDER BASE. You need to have a strong understanding of the composition of the target's shareholders. How do they feel about management? Are they showing discontent? Is management isolated from shareholders? Has management been taking huge salaries even though the company has been losing traction against competitors? How many shares does management control? Do they have the support of the employees?

Basically, you want a sense of how shareholders will vote. If the company is successful, management has substantial ownership, and employees are happy, then a hostile bid will be practically impossible. But if the company is in serious trouble and shareholders and employees are disgruntled, the chances are much better.

INDUSTRY. Some industries are less than amenable to hostile takeovers. The high-tech industry, for instance, has had very few. First of all, high-tech companies rely heavily on the talent of its knowledgeable workforce. If there is a hostile takeover, key people are likely to leave—severely reducing the value of the company. Another consideration is that high-tech companies usually have most of their assets in intellectual property, not hard assets like real estate and equipment. So there are not many opportunities to sell off assets to pay down the debt from a hostile takeover.

Example: Charles Wang takes exception to the rule that high-tech hostile takeovers do not work. In fact, he built his software empire, Computer Associates (CA), by hard-hitting acquisitions. He bought the company in 1976 and focused primarily on infrastructure software tools for major corporations. While his company has grown internally, he also has completed more than 200 acquisitions. Wang believes that CA needs a unified management voice. So, when he buys a company, he usually fires top management (although he provides them with lucrative severance packages). He is also not afraid to fire programmers if they are not willing to keep up with the fast-paced work ethic of CA. But not all Wang's deals work out. In February 1998, CA made a hostile bid for Computer Sciences (CSC) for a whopping $9 billion. But CSC did a tremendous job in defending the company from the bid. CSC filed lawsuits and also did an extensive PR campaign, arguing that the price was too low. In less than a month, CA withdrew its offer.

BUYING SHARES. If a hostile acquirer loses the contest to buy the target—say, because a white knight intervened—the hostile acquirer is likely to be left with large amounts of expenses, such as legal fees and financial advisory fees. To lessen this problem, a hostile acquirer may want to buy shares in the target before the offer is made.

There are strict regulations for these types of transactions, however. There is Section 13(d) of the Securities and Exchange Act of 1934, which requires that the acquirer disclose purchases that exceed 5% of any class of the company's stock. The filing must be made within five days of the purchases. In the filing, the acquirer must indicate its future plans.

But if the transaction comes under the Hart-Scott-Rodino law, then the buyer must disclose the transaction if it is $35 million or more. The only way to avoid this is if the purchase is for investment purposes only (which, in a hostile takeover, is definitely not the case).

Nevertheless, purchasing a company's stock could be critical in terms of a shareholder vote. It may be just enough to win the war.

PROXY FIGHT. A proxy fight is when a hostile acquirer goes directly to the shareholders to vote (via a proxy statement) on matters such as changing the composition of the board or even terminating a poison pill. A proxy fight can be the prelude to a tender offer to buy the whole company. Or, in some cases, the proxy fight is a way to stir interest in the company and attract a buyout by a white knight at a good valuation.

Example: Carl Icahn, who was involved in a variety of hostile takeovers in the 1980s, has frequently employed proxy-fight tactics. In October 2000, Icahn wrote a letter to VISX Inc.'s CEO Mark Logan, indicating that he wanted the company to be sold. Here's the letter:

Dear Mr. Logan:

On October 20, 2000, I called you as a courtesy to advise of our impending filing of a Schedule 13D reporting the acquisition by my companies of 9.9 percent of the outstanding stock of VISX.

In your absence, I spoke to Elizabeth Davila, President and Chief Operating Officer of VISX. We discussed both (i) my desire to acquire additional shares which could be accomplished if your newly adopted poison pill were amended to raise the threshold higher than 10 percent and (ii) my view that the shareholders of VISX would be well served if the Company's business could be sold to a better capitalized company with a broader product base in the ophthalmologic field. Ms. Davila indicated that she understood both issues and would take them under advisement.

Since that conversation, I placed a number of calls to you to further discuss these matters and have not even received the courtesy of a return call.

As I indicated to Ms. Davila, I strongly believe that the poison pill's threshold is unreasonably low at 10 percent and should be raised, if the poison pill is not eliminated which would be even more preferable. Furthermore, VISX's business and, therefore, stockholder value would be greatly enhanced, in my opinion, if VISX actively sought a merger partner fitting the description set forth above. The time to take this action is now. You and the Board of Directors have a duty to VISX stockholders to affirmatively seek to enhance values and not take a non-committal attitude while VISX's market value continues to erode.

I continue to look forward to hearing from you so that we may discuss these matters.

Very truly yours, Carl Icahn

No doubt, Icahn was aware that a company in the same industry, Summit Autonomous, was purchased for $900 million by Nestle. The price amounted to 10 times sales. Applying this multiple to VISX would give it a valuation of about $32.75. Icahn purchased shares between $22 and $29 per share. But in May 2001, Carl Icahn withdrew his proxy. Basically, he was unable to garner enough shareholder support.

TENDER OFFER. While a bear hug is an offer made to the board, a tender offer is made directly to shareholders. In a tender offer, the acquirer proposes to pay a premium for the shares. The shareholders can either keep their shares or sell out.

If there is a tender offer, the acquirer must meet a variety of securities regulations. The key elements of the regulations come from a law passed by Congress in 1968 called the Williams Act, of which Section 14(d) covers tender offers. Congress wanted to prevent acquirers from pressuring public shareholders into accepting a tender offer.

The rules include the following:

- After the offer, the acquirer cannot buy any more shares on the open market.
- If the price of the offer goes up, those shareholders who have already tendered their shares will also receive the additional increase in value.
- An offer may not discriminate; it is open to all shareholders.
- The acquirer must file a Schedule 14D-1 with the SEC. The document must disclose such information as negotiations, contracts, or transactions between the acquirer and target during the past

three years, the source of the funds for the tender offer, the purpose of the transaction (for example, to sell off assets), the advisers retained to do the solicitation of securities, and the regulatory requirements. The shareholders, however, do not receive a 14D-1—although it is smart for them to read it anyway by downloading it from the EDGAR database. Instead, the acquirer sends shareholders an "Offer to Purchase." This has the material information from the 14D-1 as well as the pricing information for the proposed transaction.

But that's not all. In response to the breakup hostile deals of the 1980s, a number of state governments also have passed their own laws to deal with tender offers. These laws apply to companies that are incorporated in the given states or do a substantial amount of business in the given states.

Some of the elements of state laws include the following:

- **Merger moratorium.** This prevents a transaction from happening unless there is a supermajority vote (say, 60% or more) of the shareholders or approval of the target's board of directors.

- **Fair price rule.** Sometimes a hostile acquirer will make a two-tier deal. That is, the buyer will purchase the first 50% with cash and the remainder in stock or other types of securities. A fair price rule prevents such types of deal structures.

COMMUNICATIONS. Clear communication can make all the difference in hostile takeover situations. The hostile acquirer needs to effectively communicate the benefits of the transaction to current shareholders. Meanwhile, the target must be able to explain to shareholders that the acquirer is not paying a good price and will be unable to manage the company properly. There also needs to be communication with employees, who may fear losing their jobs.

POISON PILLS

There are several defensive mechanisms to ward off hostile takeovers. The best known is the poison pill defense, which was invented in 1982 by securities lawyer Marty Lipton. Within a few years, more than 200 public companies adopted the defense. Of course, this helped catapult Lipton to become the top attorney for companies defending against hostile acquirers, such as T. Boone Pickens and Carl Icahn.

Essentially, a poison pill plan (also known as a shareholder rights plan) makes it prohibitively expensive for a hostile bidder to buy the target company.

Example: At Viant, a computer consulting firm, its board of directors adopted a poison pill plan in March 2001. In the plan, Viant issued a dividend to all shareholders. For each share owned, the shareholder can purchase another share for $0.001. This is activated if either of the following occurs:

- A person or group buys 15% or more of the common stock of Viant.

- A person or group announces its intention to acquire 15% or more of the common stock of Viant.

Of course, the group or person that triggers the above does not have the same right to buy shares at $0.001. Most of the rest of the shareholders will, though, since they are getting new stock at an extremely steep discount. The result is that the hostile acquirer is substantially diluted.

Devising Pills

Here are factors to consider with poison pills:

RENEW. There is an expiration date for poison pill plans. Oddly enough, not all companies remember this, and they fail to renew. Also, company officers should periodically check the plan to see if there can be any improvements made.

PERCEPTION. When executives adopt a poison pill, investors may see this move as management's attempt to insulate itself from market forces. In fact, some shareholders—such as major institutional investors—will fight the company's decision to adopt poison pill plans.

As a result, some companies are adopting watered-down poison pills—known as "chewable pills." For example, Texaco adopted a pill wherein if a hostile deal is an all-cash tender offer open for 45 business days, then the board would not be able to oppose it. (Whereas this pill did not require that the price of the offer be at a certain premium, some chewable pills do so.)

Another approach is TIDE, which stands for Three-Year Independent Director Evaluation. This is a committee of the company's board that will, every three years, review the poison pill plan and see if changes should be made.

By and large, poison pill plans last for 10 years. However, some companies are shortening the length of these plans—say, to five years.

AGGRESSION. If a poison pill is too strong, the courts may disallow it. This was the case with the "dead hand" poison pill. Essentially, this meant that a poison pill could be eliminated only by the votes of the directors who adopted it.

Other Defenses

Other ways to fortify against a potential hostile takeover include the following:

WHITE KNIGHTS. A white knight is a company that is friendly to management and buys the company instead of the hostile acquirer.

If a company thinks it is a takeover candidate, it should not waste any time in trying to identify its white knights. Management could then communicate with these companies, so if a hostile bid occurs, the company can react more quickly.

JOINT VENTURES AND STRATEGIC ALLIANCES. Suppose Pebble Inc. and the Rock Group invest huge sums to create a joint venture. However, Boulder Corp. makes a hostile bid for Pebble and wins. What if Rock Group does not want to engage in the joint venture with its "new" partner? Contracts can be drafted to allow joint venture partners to buy out the hostile bidder.

GOLDEN PARACHUTES. This provides a predefined payment to managers in the event of an acquisition. And the payments can be high. For example, in March 2001, MGM purchased Mirage Resorts for $6.4 billion. Mirage Resorts' CEO Steve Wynn agreed to leave the company. For this, he received the tidy sum of $12 million. He also received other perks, such as a car and chauffeur and office support for three years. MGM also agreed to pay Wynn's excise taxes. He still gets to receive $523,633 per month for having his art on display at the Bellagio casino—not to forget his options, which were worth about $501 million, and his wife, who was on the board of directors and had options worth another $5.4 million or so.

However, a golden parachute must be adopted before a hostile bid is made.

REAL-LIFE EXAMPLE

To illustrate some of the previous points, I'll offer the following chronology of a hostile bid:

March 2001: On March 1, Shell Oil sent a letter to Barrett Resources to buy the company for $55 per share

ARE YOU VULNERABLE TO HOSTILE TAKEOVER?

All companies are vulnerable to a hostile takeover—even billion-dollar businesses. Thus, it is important to be vigilant for a possible hostile bid. But there are some factors that could make your company particularly susceptible. Here's what to look at:

Has the stock declined significantly? If so, has the decline been larger compared to the industry group? This is perhaps the most important sign. After all, a hostile acquirer is looking for a company that represents a quick turnaround.

Is the industry consolidating? If so, the big consolidators likely will be knocking on your door.

Is growth slowing, yet cash flows are still good? To a hostile acquirer, the cash flow can be the way to finance the deal.

What are the views of institutional shareholders? If the major shareholders have lost confidence in the company, then there is a good chance they will vote in favor of a hostile takeover. One good idea is to hire a proxy solicitation firm to help you monitor share activity. A high level of activity may indicate that a hostile acquirer will make a bid for the company.

in cash. In the letter, Shell indicated that if there were no negotiations within four days, it would make an unsolicited tender offer. The offer was announced in a press release.

Within a week, Barrett's board met three times and analyzed the offer with the assistance of legal and financial advisers (respectively, Petrie Parkman and Goldman

Sachs). The board decided to reject the offer but also to look for other ways to maximize shareholder value.

The financial advisers began the process of contacting 45 qualified potential buyers of Barrett. The advisers also set up a "data room" on the premises of Barrett, which contained nonpublic information about the company. In all, 12 qualified potential buyers entered confidentiality and standstill agreements. Of these, nine visited the data room. However, Shell did not sign a confidentiality agreement or a standstill agreement and was unable to visit the data room.

On March 12, Shell launched its unsolicited tender offer for $55 per share and also filed preliminary proxy materials—for Barrett shareholders—to vote out all the company's directors and replace them with Shell-appointed directors.

For two weeks, the board of Barrett studied the Shell offer.

One company that showed particular interest in buying Barrett was Williams, which visited the data room and did due diligence in the middle of March.

In late March, Barrett's financial advisers rendered an opinion indicating the Shell offer was inadequate. The company's board again rejected Shell's offer and recommended that shareholders not tender their shares.

April: During the second week of the month, Barrett sent to each company that had signed a confidentiality agreement and visited the data room a detailed letter requesting proposals and merger agreements, due by May 2.

In late April, Shell announced that it would increase its offer from $55 to $60 per share and that the deadline for the tender would be May 9. Barrett's financial advisers considered this to be still inadequate, so the board rejected the new offer and recommended that shareholders not tender their shares.

May: Williams submitted its proposal by the deadline and offered $71 per share, of which half would be cash and the other half stock. The proposal also provided

Williams with a termination fee of 3% of the value of Barrett. Two other companies (whose names were not disclosed, so let's call them Companies A and B) made offers.

On the same day, Shell announced it would keep its offer at $60 per share and there would be no termination fee. However, the company said it was willing to negotiate.

Over a three-day period, Barrett's board reviewed the offers. Finally, it agreed to contact Williams and Company B to see if the offers could be increased. Shell and Company A were not notified to increase their offers.

The Barrett Board set May 5 (a Saturday) at 2:00 P.M. as a deadline for revised offers. The board wanted more certainty regarding the equity portion of the Williams' deal. Moreover, the board wanted Company B to lower the termination fee.

By the deadline, Williams had increased its offer to $73 per share (keeping it half cash, half equity). Company B did not change its price (which was lower than Williams' proposal) but did reduce its termination fee—however, not to the level of the Williams proposal.

The Barrett Board accepted the Williams proposal and began negotiating the merger agreement. Senior management flew to the headquarters of Williams to do its own due diligence.

As of May 7, Barrett's financial advisers considered the Williams proposal to be fair, and the board approved the merger. Each company published press releases announcing the deal. Shell published a press release announcing it would terminate its offer.

CHAPTER 12

GOING
PRIVATE

Going private could be seen as a form of acquisition—self-acquisition, as it were. But a primary reason for covering the subject in this book is that it is part of an overall M&A strategy. The going-private marketplace is cyclical. Whenever the markets fall, these types of transactions can be expected to proliferate. There is little going-private activity, however, when markets are hot because that's when management can take advantage of their high stock price to buy companies (using the stock as currency) and even raise more money (with secondary offerings). Also, because valuations are high, it would be expensive to take a company private.

I'll illustrate this with a common scenario:

Three years ago, your company—ChipSwitch Digital— went public on Nasdaq. The company had a strong opening for its IPO, as it was a leading high-tech firm. At one point, the company was trading at $150 per share. You were worth—on paper—about $500 million. Unfortunately, the high-tech industry went into recession—well, it seemed more like a depression—and ChipSwitch plunged. Now, the stock is trading for a mere 50 cents per share. The Nasdaq has given your company notice that it is to be delisted. The trading volume of the stock is dismal, with a meager 10,000 or so shares exchanged on a daily basis. The analysts that covered your stock have abandoned the company. But you still believe in the company's long-term prospects, and there is that $80 million still in the bank. You ponder if it would make sense to go private, and after deliberation and seeking advice you go for it.

As I said, such decisions are common when the stock market collapses. For example, during the late 1970s, the stock market was so depressed that many companies were selling well below their cash values. As a result, many companies went private. And when the markets came back, these companies then did public offerings or were sold to bigger companies.

Further, many of the same considerations and activities are involved in going private as in standard M&A deals. Yet there are significant pitfalls for the going-private process. If it's not done properly, it can quickly fall to pieces.

WHAT IS IT REALLY?

Many people think that going-private transactions are a recent phenomenon. Actually, they have been used for many years—even in the 1880s. However, with the emergence of high-profile leveraged buyouts in the 1980s, the concept of going-private transactions became mainstream.

A going-private transaction is when an existing public company buys out public shareholders in order to transform the company into a private entity. However, not all shareholders are bought out. Rather, it is the so-called unaffiliated shareholders that are cashed out. An affiliated shareholder is someone that has control over the company, such as a major stockholder or an executive officer. When a company goes private, typically affiliate shareholders will retain their equity.

Example: Widget Corp. decides to go private. The company currently trades for $10 per share on the New York Stock Exchange, with 10 million shares currently outstanding. Of these shares, about 3.5 million are owned by the executives of the company, and the family of the founder owns 2 million. The remaining 4.5 million shares are owned by individual investors and institutions. In the going-private transaction, the company borrows $54 million to buy the 4.5 million shares for $12 each.

Actually, this financing mechanism is known as a leveraged buyout (LBO). Typically, an investor group and management will borrow the money using the assets of the company as collateral. The financing structure is typically as follows:

SENIOR DEBT. This consists of loans from banks. The loans are backed by specific assets of the company, such as accounts receivables, inventory, and plant and equipment. They have a first priority to claim these assets if the company is liquidated. These loans may account for from 20% to 50% of the purchase price of the private-going transaction.

MEZZANINE FINANCING. This is called "mezzanine" since it is between the senior debt and common stock financing. This debt is not secured by specific assets. Rather, in the event of a liquidation, the senior debt holders are paid off first, and then the mezzanine financing is paid off. For the most part, mezzanine financing is in the form of junk bonds, which have an interest rate that is 3% or 5% higher than the senior debt.

COMMON STOCK. This is the amount of equity financing. This may be anywhere from 5% to 20% of the purchase price. In the event of a liquidation, the common stockholders are the last in line to get any proceeds. (In fact, common shareholders usually get nothing.)

Then again, if the company eventually goes public or is bought out, the common shareholders stand to make substantial profits.

Example (continued): Suppose that in the Widget Corp. financing, about $16.2 million (30%) are senior, $27 million (50%) are junk bonds, and $10.8 million (20%) are common stock. The company is delisted from the New York Stock Exchange and is now officially private. Two years later, the stock market rebounds with a vengeance. Widget decides to go public again. In the offering, the company raises $50 million, and the market value of Widget is now $500 million. The IPO resulted in dilution of the existing equity holders to 15%. However, this equity stake is still worth $75 million. This is not bad, considering the original equity investment was $10.8 million. Does this sound far-fetched? Maybe not. A classic example of this is the Gibson Greetings transaction (see chapter 13.)

WHY GO PRIVATE?

As stated above, a big reason to go private is the huge upside. But there are other reasons as well. Here are the factors a CEO is likely to consider when thinking about taking his or her company private:

EXPENSES. Being a public company is expensive. Quarterly and annual filings are required. Also, under Rule FD a company must make public its conference calls with analysts. It is not uncommon for a company to spend $100,000 per year complying with federal securities disclosure laws.

DEFENSE. If your company is the subject of a hostile takeover, you might decide to take the company private instead. This is the case if you feel the hostile acquirer is not paying an adequate price for shareholders.

QUARTERLY MADNESS. As a public company, management is under a microscope. If the company reports results that are slightly worse than expected, there could be a plunge in the stock price, and investors will move on to the next stock. It could take years to return to the prior stock price. In fact, there is a temptation to "manage" earnings, such as by recognizing sales earlier than they should be. Such practices could alert the SEC, which may require the company to restate earnings as well as pay fines.

A private company, however, faces little pressure for short-term results. So, if you want to invest in a new product, you can do so without being penalized by public investors.

Also, as a public company the management and board of directors are potentially subject to expensive lawsuits, known as derivative lawsuits. There are law firms that specialize in these types of suits—many of which are unfounded. But in most cases it makes sense to settle because going to court is even more expensive.

FEW BENEFITS. One of the major benefits of a public company is that the stock can be used as currency to buy other companies. But if the stock price is low, it is difficult to do stock-for-stock acquisitions. The target may be reluctant to take your stock. Also, the acquisition will likely be very dilutive since the valuation of the company is already low.

COMPETITIVE INTELLIGENCE. As a public company, you need to disclose all material information. This can be very useful for competitors. If you're private, however, there is no disclosure requirement.

IS YOUR COMPANY RIPE FOR GOING PRIVATE?

If you run a public company and want to go private, you should realize that not all companies have the necessary characteristics for this type of transaction. Here are some factors to consider:

ASSETS/CASH FLOW. If a company has a large amount of cash in the bank, there may not be a need to borrow. But in many cases, a company will indeed need to borrow money—lots of it. To qualify for the borrowing, a company will need to demonstrate the following:

- The business can generate enough cash flow— even if there is a recession—to pay its annual interest payments (look at chapter 3 to see how to construct cash flow projections).

- It has a strong portfolio of assets—say, real estate, plant and equipment, and divisions—that can be readily sold off to pay down debt or meet interest payments.

Note: Interestingly enough, when dot-com stock prices plunged in 2000, there was no strong trend toward going-private transactions. Why? Because most of these firms did not have cash flows. Instead, they were losing money. Second, those companies had few hard assets. Most of the assets were intellectual property, such as software and patents. And there was not enough value in these types of assets to justify a going-private transaction.

OUT-OF-FAVOR BUT SOLID COMPANY. When dot-coms were flying high, the so-called brick-and-mortar companies were largely ignored. The future was all Internet, right? Of course, this was not the case. But when the dot-coms were hot, there was an uptrend in brick-and-mortar companies going private. They saw their stock prices as too low, but they also knew their companies had solid business models that would eventually be in favor in the future.

CONFLICTS OF INTEREST AND FAIRNESS

During the 1970s, going-private transactions became much more common. However, the SEC had concerns. The agency thought that the transactions were unfair to minority shareholders. After all, the reason these shareholders bought stock was to make a big payoff. But with the going-private transaction, these shareholders are shut out from this possibility. Rather, they will probably get a premium of only 20% to 50% of their stock's current value. They will not have the opportunity to make the big gains.

The SEC was also troubled by potential conflicts of interest. In a going-private transaction, the management is usually on both sides of the table. On one end, the management has a fiduciary responsibility to all shareholders. Then again, management is negotiating a deal to get rid of certain unaffiliated shareholders and remain in control of the resulting company—at a good deal, it is hoped. In other words, is management representing the general interests of shareholders or the interests of management?

So, in 1979, the SEC adopted Rule 13e-3. The rule did not require that a going-private transaction be fair; rather, it required disclosure of all material information for shareholders.

Here's the process for 13e-3:

QUALIFICATION. There are three main ways in which a company will have to comply with 13e-3:

1. The transaction results in the number of shareholders of any class of equity to fall below 300.

2. The transaction results in the company being officially delisted from a national securities exchange.

3. The company is ineligible for quotation on an interdealer quotation system of a registered national securities (that is, the company is no longer eligible for Nasdaq).

But the above events need not actually occur for 13e-3 to be triggered. Instead, there must be a "reasonable likelihood" of the event occurring. Thus, practically speaking, most going-private transactions are required to comply with 13e-3.

PROXY. If 13e-3 applies, then there must be additional disclosure in the proxy statement sent to shareholders (see chapter 11 for more information about proxies). That is, there must be disclosure of the following:

- Employment contracts and profit-sharing agreements with management
- Actual and potential conflicts of interests
- Dissenters' rights
- Reasons for the going-private transaction
- Discussion of fairness (such as a fairness opinion)

For an example of a 13e-3 form, go to *www.sec.gov /divisions/corpfin/forms/13e3.htm.*

Fairness Opinions

Most M&A transactions that involve public companies solicit a fairness opinion. The buyer retains an independent firm—usually an appraiser or investment banker—that investigates the seller and determines if the price of the acquisition is fair for the seller's shareholders.

And when a company is going private, the buyers should definitely secure a fairness opinion. Although a fairness opinion does not recommend the deal or indicate the tax ramifications, it does provide safety for the board of directors. That is, the price tag the buyer is willing to pay is in line with an independent valuation. With such support, it is difficult for shareholders to win a lawsuit claiming that the buyer was unfair. Proceeding without such an opinion can create dangerous exposure.

Example: In the merger between Travelers and Citigroup, there was no fairness opinion. Shortly after the deal, there were four lawsuits filed against the directors of both companies.

A fairness opinion comprises the following elements:

- Analysis of how the price and terms of the deal impact the economics of the transaction
- Analysis of the historical data
- Analysis of the industry and macroeconomic trends
- Perhaps a summary of on-site visits of the company and management interviews
- The disclosure of any potential conflicts of interest

Note: Make sure you give an investment banker or appraiser enough time to perform the fairness opinion.

Besides protecting the board of directors from liability, a fairness opinion should make it easier to get shareholder approval. In fact, it could be particularly helpful in a transaction for a private company. The reason is that the shareholders may be more intransigent than public shareholders (for example, when family members are at odds with each other).

Tip for the seller: It's usually a good idea to get a fairness opinion early. Doing so gives you more time to allow for other bidders.

Appraisal Rights

Besides the 13e-3 disclosure requirements, you must also be aware of appraisal rights when you take your company private. All states have appraisal rights, which mandate that if a shareholder dissents on a transaction, he or she can force the company to repurchase the shares at a "fair price." This amount is left up to a jury to decide. And, as is often the case with juries, there is no way to predict how they will rule.

As we take a look at appraisal rights for going-private transactions, we will look at Delaware's laws. This is because most corporations are incorporated in that state. (In fact, many states use Delaware as a model).

Weinberger v. UOP

The landmark case for appraisal rights—which set the standard—is *Weinberger v. UOP* (decided in February 1983).

Background

Signal and UOP were both conglomerates listed on the New York Stock Exchange. In 1974, Signal purchased a controlling interest—50.5%—in UOP for $21 per share. After the transaction, Signal nominated six members to the UOP board. Of these, five were either directors or employees of Signal (UOP had a total of 13 directors). When the CEO of UOP retired, he was replaced by another Signal employee.

By 1977, Signal wanted to buy the remaining minority interest in UOP. Two Signal officers (who were also board members of UOP) did a feasibility study for the transaction. The conclusion was that $24 would be a fair price. However, when the chairman of Signal, William Walkup, notified the CEO of UOP (who was on the board of Signal), James Crawford, he said to him that Signal wanted to buy the rest of the company for

$20 to $21 per share. Crawford thought the price was "generous." At that time, the stock price was $14.50.

From February 28 to March 6, Crawford had meetings with the non-Signal board members of UOP and retained Lehman Brothers to conduct a fairness opinion. Six days later, Lehman Brothers finished its fairness opinion and said the deal was fair. Then, at a special meeting, the boards of Signal and UOP approved the deal.

Analysis

Eventually, some of the minority shareholders sued, and the case went to the chancery court in Delaware. The court was troubled by the conflicts of interest. Perhaps this explained why the $24 price was not disclosed in the "negotiations" for the deal between Signal and UOP.

Now the "business judgment rule" provides management and the board much discretion when making the decision to merge with another company. But in the Weinberger case, the court thought that going-private transactions were much different and required a higher standard, which is the following:

> [W]here a self-interested corporate fiduciary has set the terms of a transaction and caused its effectuation, it will be required to establish the entire fairness of the transaction to a reviewing court's satisfaction.

There are basically two elements to the standard:

FAIR DEALING. This involves the timing of the transaction and how it was negotiated and disclosed to the directors. The officers and directors have a duty to disclose all material information. Thus, in this case the feasibility study should have been disclosed. Other relevant issues were timing (only six days for the deal), the absence of any attempt to find alternative buyers, and the inadequacy of discussion about increasing the price of the deal.

FAIR PRICE. This looks at the financial aspects of the transaction, such as the assets of the company, market value, and future prospects. The court declared that valuation techniques that are "generally considered acceptable in the financial community" be used. These include the following (discussed in chapter 3):

- Discounted cash flow
- Asset value
- Comparable analysis

Over the years, companies have developed procedures to deal with Weinberger. They include the following:

APPOINTMENT OF A SPECIAL COMMITTEE. The committee must comprise directors free of any conflicts of interest. This helps ensure that the transaction is in the best interest of all shareholders.

Moreover, the committee should have at least two individuals (as was the case with the going-private transaction of CB Richard Ellis, which is detailed at the end of this chapter). It is critical that the special committee have its own legal counsel, which will determine if there are any potential conflicts of interest and set forth the responsibilities of the special committee.

Furthermore, the special committee will hire its own financial firm—usually an investment banker—to provide the necessary valuation. Keep in mind that the special committee will need to take all steps to minimize conflicts of interest. Thus, if the special committee hires an investment banker that already had performed services for the company, it could pose a problem if the transaction is litigated.

Also important is that the special committee has the power to negotiate the deal on behalf of shareholders— such as by getting a higher price or better terms. Also, the special committee has the power to reject any transaction. Whenever there is a special committee meeting, the discussions must remain confidential. Management or the rest of the board cannot attend.

The special committee also has the right to access any internal company information. Legal counsel and the financial adviser will analyze this information. Basically, this is an extensive due diligence process.

If you are on the committee, do not feel that you must rush the deal or that you must accept the advice of the financial adviser. The ultimate decision is yours. You must consider the interests of the shareholders at all times.

The activities of the special committee can be extensive, sometimes taking more than a hundred hours in total. Therefore, it is appropriate to pay a fee to the special committee (perhaps on an hourly basis). The board of directors must approve this compensation.

FAIRNESS OPINION. In most deals, the price is within the range specified by the fairness opinion.

SHOPPING THE DEAL. A company is not required to find alternative buyers, but it is nonetheless a good idea. This is more evidence that there was fair dealing and that the best price for shareholders was sought. For example, in the CB Richard Ellis deal (see below), the transaction was shopped to over 30 third parties.

SHAREHOLDER VOTE. Once the board of directors signs the merger agreement, the shareholders need to approve the transaction. To this end, a proxy statement is sent out to all shareholders of record. The vote is held at a shareholder meeting. (See chapter 11 for more information about proxy statements.)

REAL-LIFE GOING-PRIVATE TRANSACTION: CB RICHARD ELLIS

I think the best way to grasp all the above rigmarole— especially how the actions play out on a time line—is with an actual anecdote. So here's a behind-the-scenes look at a going-private transaction.

CB Richard Ellis is a diversified real estate services firm (brokerage, consulting, and valuation), with more than 10,000 employees and offices in 44 countries.

Mid-1999: The board of directors of CB Richard Ellis studied the possibility of merging with another publicly traded real estate services company. But the company did not pursue this.

November: RCBA Strategic Partners, which takes companies private, purchased 1.2 million shares of stock of CB Richard Ellis (a 7.7% ownership stake). (Note that Richard Blum was a board member and a general partner of RCBA.)

January 2000: RCBA purchased another 1.6 million shares (increasing its stake to 15.8%).

July: Representatives from RCBA met with Ray Wirta, the CEO of CB Ellis, to discuss a going-private transaction.

August: RCBA talked with CS First Boston to look at ways to finance the acquisition.

September: CS First Boston delivered a commitment letter to do the debt financing for the deal. However, RCBA also talked to other investment firms.

The CS First Boston commitment letter involved the following terms: senior debt of up to $375 million and junk bond (mezzanine) debt of $225 million. If the junk bonds couldn't be raised, then the senior debt would include that $225 million. There were several conditions to the commitment letter. One of the key provisions was the "market out" clause. If there was "material disruption or material change in the conditions of the financial, banking or capital market, including the high-yield market," then CS First Boston could withdraw its commitment letter.

RCBA hired Bain & Company, a strategic consulting firm, to do an in-depth study of the real estate services industry and look at the relative position of CB Richard

Ellis. Next, RCBA retained Arthur Andersen to look at the accounting and tax implications and hired the law firm of Simpson, Thacher & Bartlett to do legal due diligence of CB Richard Ellis. CB Richard Ellis provided nonpublic information to these service providers. There were also a variety of interviews with the senior management of CB Richard Ellis.

RCBA contacted representatives of Freeman Spogli, an investment company. One of the partners is Bradford Freeman, who was a director of CB Richard Ellis. Freeman Spogli indicated that it might want to invest in the transaction.

October: Discussions started between RCBA and Freeman Spogli. There were also talks with Wirta and the CFO of CB Richard Ellis, Brett White, concerning employment agreements and equity participation. Two other directors (Gary Wilson and Frederic Malek) were notified via telephone conference.

November: Blum made an official proposal to the board to buy all the outstanding stock of the company except that common stock that would be owned by continuing shareholders. The price was $15.50. The offer would terminate by December 1.

At the board meeting, a special committee of the board was established with two outside board members, Stanton Anderson and Paul Leach. The board also approved a press release that announced the proposed offer (it appeared in a few days).

Within a month, there were five class-action lawsuits filed by various shareholders against the directors and continuing shareholders. Of course, the suits called the offer "unfair."

The special committee interviewed a variety of law firms and hired McDermott, Will & Emery. There were several interviews with financial advisers, and the special committee selected Morgan Stanley.

Next, there was a board meeting, and the special committee reported its findings. Afterward, Morgan

Stanley talked to senior management to get the necessary financial information. McDermott lawyers drew up confidentiality and standstill agreements for the continuing shareholders.

RCBA extended the deadline until December 31.

December: Morgan Stanley briefed the special committee on matters of valuation and contacted third parties who might be interested in buying CB Richard Ellis. The special committee authorized Morgan Stanley to contact third parties.

The continuing stockholders executed confidentiality and standstill agreements. The standstill prevented shareholders from purchasing or soliciting proxies to vote shares of common stock until at least April 15, 2001. Also, the standstill had a provision that extended the expiration another nine months if a third party intervened to buy CB Richard Ellis. The special committee considered this to be favorable to the company, as third-party offers would not be thwarted.

CB Richard Ellis filed an 8-K filing with the SEC showing the details of the transaction.

Morgan Stanley met with Wirta and specified that the share price should be increased. Morgan also expressed concerns that the financing was not a strong commitment. RCBA recommended that CB Richard Ellis make a presentation to the corporate rating agencies of Moody's Investors Services and Standard & Poor's Rating services. Ratings from these agencies would be helpful in getting a better financing commitment.

January 2001: In a meeting with the special committee, Morgan Stanley indicated there was little interest from third-party bidders. As a result, the special committee would focus on the CB Richard Ellis deal and had McDermott, Will & Emery draft a merger agreement.

RCBA and Simpson, Thacher & Barlett began their due diligence (it would last until late February).

There was a board meeting in which Writa presented to Morgan Stanley CB Richard Ellis' preliminary

2000 operating results and the final 2001 operating plan (budget for the new year).

An 8-K was filed with the SEC to show the progress in the going-private transaction.

In late January, Simpson, Thacher & Bartlett and McDermott, Will & Emery began making comments to the merger agreement draft. Also, senior management met with Moody's and S&P.

The special committee had a meeting in which Morgan Stanley said it contacted 33 potential strategic and financial buyers. Yet there was still little interest.

February: CS First Boston introduced a revised financing structure. There would not be any junk bonds but instead would involve debt from DLJ Investment Funding. There would also be an increased amount of equity from continuing shareholders. Also, Morgan again indicated that the price of the deal should be increased.

The special committee contacted the continuing shareholders and informed them the deal would not happen unless the price were increased. The special committee recommended $17 per share.

RCBA said it could raise the bid to $15.75 but no higher. The special committee was not satisfied. But on the next day, RCBA raised the bid to $16, which was enough for the special committee to recommend that proposal to the board.

A board meeting was held at which the special committee distributed copies of the current draft of the merger agreement and summarized the key points of the deal. After this, the board members—who would be continuing shareholders—left the meeting, and the special committee and the rest of the board stayed (these other board members were represented by the law firm of Pillsbury Winthrop).

Several days later, the continuing shareholders made an official offer of $16 per share. The special committee had a meeting with Morgan Stanley, who indicated that the price was fair.

At a board meeting, the special committee recommended the offer, and the board agreed unanimously.

A day later, the company issued a press release announcing the transaction.

The price of $16 per share was a premium of 28% over the closing price before the deal was announced in November. The price tag came to $750 million (an all-cash deal). Here's the financing structure:

SENIOR SECURED CREDIT FACILITY. CS First Boston acted as an agent for a senior secured credit facility. This is essentially bank debt and, in the event of bankruptcy, has the highest priority.

The debt had three parts:

Tranche A. Up to $150 million. The interest rate is LIBOR plus 3.25%. The loan matures in six years.

Tranche B. Up to $250 million. The interest rate is LIBOR plus 3.75%. The loan matures in seven years.

Revolving line of credit. Up to $100 million.

To get the financing, CB Richard Ellis used its assets as collateral.

16% SENIOR NOTES. For $75 million, DLJ got a senior note earning an annual interest rate of 16% maturing in 10 years (interest is paid quarterly). However, the debt is not secured by the assets of the company. However, in the event of bankruptcy, the note will be in second priority. Moreover, DLJ got 3% of the total outstanding stock.

EQUITY. RCBA agreed to make an equity investment of $109.9 million.

EMPLOYMENT AGREEMENTS. Wirta and White signed employment agreements for three-year terms. Wirta's salary was $519,000, with an annual bonus with a maximum of 200% of salary. White's salary was $395,000, with a 200% potential bonus. The employment agreements had noncompetition clauses (applicable two years after termination). Also, Wirta and White signed nonsolicitation agreements (again, applicable for two years after termination).

CHAPTER 13

HISTORY
OF M&A

A s this book is focused on the here and now—in short, the "how"—of M&A, the vast majority of our examples have been contemporary ones, which are the most useful in many ways. However, most people interested or involved in M&A presumably would appreciate some overall historical perspective on the subject.

It should be obvious by now that M&As have been a (if not *the*) primary propulsive force in American business. If you're interested in reading further about the fascinating role M&As have played, there are many excellent books available. I would recommend *The 50 Best (and Worst) Business Deals of All Time,* by Michael Craig (Career Press, 2000) and *Wall Street: A History,* by Charles R. Geisst (Oxford University Press, 1997) as excellent places to start.

ROBBER BARONS (1860S TO 1880S)

Until the Civil War, the United States was an agrarian society. This changed abruptly afterward, though, as the country quickly industrialized during the last 30 years of the eighteenth century. The key technology and industry that drove economic growth in the United States was the railroad.

There was a group of profit-seeking entrepreneurs—called robber barons—who took advantage of the rail-centric situation and made huge fortunes in the process. Robber barons like Daniel Drew, Jay Gould, Jim Fisk, and Cornelius "Commodore" Vanderbilt fought each other (sometimes literally, in the case of the two-fisted Vanderbilt) to buy up the railroad industry. Their push-and-shove efforts involved bribes of public officials, and the robber barons were known to pillage corporate treasuries to enrich their own lifestyles (some would say that things have changed little since then.)

All this cross-purposed activity was detrimental to the railroad industry. The economics of the industry were daunting, with enormous capital costs. The existence of multiple, competing lines added to the expense. Why not merge instead?

The financier that engineered this consolidation was J. P. Morgan. He set up a meeting with the railroad barons at his New York home, where he told the group that competition was ruinous. The solution, he said, was to merge. Ultimately, the railroad industry saw the wisdom in Morgan's advice. After the ensuing wave of massive consolidation, J. P. Morgan was the de facto ruler of the railroads.

But Morgan did not stop there. He wanted to consolidate many more industries, such as steel. He eventually bought out Andrew Carnegie—himself one of the greatest industrial consolidators in U.S. history—to form U.S. Steel.

TRUSTS (1880S TO EARLY 1900S)

Everyone knows that John Rockefeller made his fortune in oil. But his focus wasn't on drilling but rather on the refining industry, which he deemed better suited to his purposes. As long as the oil industry was growing, he reasoned, so would the need for refining. Like J. P. Morgan, Rockefeller pursued a strategy of consolidation—though many would say monopolization. He created the Standard Oil Company, which ultimately controlled about 80% of the nation's refining industry.

The concentration of power among a few captains of industry caused widespread concerns—primarily about the potential for abuse of such power. Did this pose a threat to democracy? Could other businesses possibly be successful? A variety of influential writers—known as muckrakers—wrote about the problems of unrestrained capitalism. One of the most prominent was Ida Minerva Tarbell, who wrote investigative pieces about trusts for *McClure's* magazine. She also authored a book about the anticompetitive practices of Standard Oil called the *History of the Standard Oil Company* (1904).

In 1890, Republican Senator John Sherman crafted the Sherman Antitrust Act to deal with the growing monopolization. Although it ultimately had little power, the law represented a start for the federal government's moves against concentration of economic power. It fell to President Teddy Roosevelt to set in motion the process to break up Standard Oil as well as other trusts. Roosevelt was a staunch critic of industrialists, whom he called the "malefactors of great wealth."

The case against Standard Oil went to the Supreme Court. In a lengthy opinion delivered on May 14, 1911, the Court ruled against the company (in an 8-to-1 vote). As a result, the company was split into 33 parts, with Rockefeller owning 25% of each. Ironically enough, Rockefeller's wealth continued to grow year after year.

THE ROARING '20S

Business during the 1920s was undoubtedly good. Tremendous technological developments—including the radio and automobiles—were spurring growth. And rampant speculation goosed the stock market to new heights as well. Investors typically borrowed large sums of money to buy as much stock as possible. Many brokerage firms allowed borrowing at a 10-to-1 ratio. Today's margin investing is tame in comparison. Many influential people—including President Herbert Hoover—expressed concern about these speculative practices, but no one heeded their warnings.

Also during the 1920s, there was a huge amount of M&A activity—more than 7,000 transactions. One industry heavily involved was automobile manufacturing.

But Henry Ford—who had founded the Ford Motor Company in 1908—was not a believer in M&A. His approach was to build everything internally, with his famous mass production techniques. Ford's sales burgeoned from about 18,000 in 1909 to over a million cars a year a decade later. Moreover, prices fell from about $1,000 to $355 during this interval.

While Ford grew internally, another automobile visionary took the M&A route: William Durant. In 1903, Durant met David Buick, an inventor, with whom he founded Buick Company, and in 1908 he contacted the major automobile companies to sound them out for interest in merging. He even approached Henry Ford: a futile effort. Durant was able, however, to convince Olds and Cadillac to sell out. The new company became known as General Motors.

Even though GM had 22% of the auto market in 1910, the company experienced extreme difficulties—mostly because of Durant's high-flying nature. GM had to be recapitalized with a restrictive bank loan. What's more, the creditors removed Durant as the CEO.

Undeterred, Durant bought a small car company called William H. Little, which then became the Chevrolet Motor Company. Wasn't this a conflict of interest with GM? It apparently didn't matter to GM, which didn't see the smaller company as a threat. Chevrolet thrived, however, as GM hit hard times. In 1916, Durant had the last laugh—nearly—as Chevrolet and GM merged and he regained control of the company he'd created.

When the stock market plunged in 1929, so did the stock price of GM. Durant was wiped out and had to resign as president.

But of course, GM would become the dominant auto company worldwide, thanks mostly to the superior business and managerial acumen of one Alfred P. Sloan.

CRASH AND DEPRESSION (1930S)

On October 28, 1929, the stock market crashed, falling about 12.8%. The next day, the market continued to crash, diving another 11.7%. President Hoover's efforts to instill confidence—declarations that the economy was "fundamentally sound"—had little effect. By 1933, the stock market was down about 90% from its 1929 peak.

The upstanding, solid reputation that bankers enjoyed during the 1920s suffered a thorough reversal in the 1930s. Americans came to consider the moneymen greedy and a major cause of the economic downturn.

With Wall Street at a dismal low, the federal government became much more intrusive in the securities markets. This shift would have a major impact on M&A, as Congress passed key legislation, such as the Securities Act of 1933 and the Securities Exchange Act of 1934.

Up until the 1933 law, the securities industry was regulated exclusively by state rules. These "blue sky laws" were easy to circumvent, allowing securities firms great leeway. The Securities Act changed that by requiring companies to disclose material information to investors before offering their securities to the public.

The 1934 bill established the Securities and Exchange Commission, which remains the main federal regulator of the securities industry. The agency originally had five commissioners, who were empowered to enforce the regulations of the Securities Act of 1933. The first chairman of the SEC, ironically enough, was Joseph Kennedy—who had been notorious as a big-time speculator during the 1920s.

CONGLOMERATES (1950s TO 1960s)

During the 1950s and 1960s, the U.S. economy grew at a spectacular rate. Although companies saw M&A as a way to accelerate their growth plans, there was a hitch: Federal antitrust laws were being strongly enforced at the time. This made it difficult for companies to buy other businesses in the same (or a related) industry.

So they devised a logical solution: Why not buy unrelated companies? Companies that own a variety of unrelated businesses are called conglomerates. And conglomerates were all the rage during the 1960s.

One of the key players in the conglomerate industry was Harold Geneen, a gifted number cruncher who became president of International Telephone and Telegraph (ITT) in 1959. At that time, ITT lived up to its name—the company had significant operations overseas. Unfortunately, when Castro took power in Cuba, he nationalized ITT operations. Understandably wanting to avoid such events in the future, Geneen focused on domestic markets.

Geneen also wanted to pursue an aggressive M&A policy, which he described in a paper he wrote called "Acquisition Philosophy." He did in fact go on a spending spree, snagging such companies as Avis Rent-a-Car, Levitt Homes, Continental Baking, Sheraton Hotels, and Hartford Insurance. He even tried to buy the American Broadcasting Company system but was rebuffed.

Another flamboyant conglomerate player was James Ling, a high school dropout who had worked as an electrician and saved up about $2,000 to start his own business. In 1955, Ling convinced several small investment banks to take his company public. By 1961, he purchased a variety of companies in the aircraft manufacturing industry and renamed his company Ling-Temco-Vought (LTV). LTV was ranked 158th on the Fortune 500 list at the time.

The company incorporated such far-flung holdings as sporting goods, pet food, meatpacking, and even pharmaceutical companies. In 1966, LTV purchased Wilson & Co. Another acquisition was Greatamerica, which owned National Car Rental and Braniff Airlines, for about $500 million. Ling consistently showed rising profits, which captivated Wall Street and spurred LTV's stock price to soar from $10 in 1960 to $170 at its height in the late 1960s.

LTV's undoing came in 1968, when the company purchased Jones & Laughlin Steel for $465 million. That was a premium price, which the Jones management was more than happy to accept. After all, Jones was a struggling steel company, beset with high labor costs, slowing demand, and intense foreign imports. Interestingly enough, the Justice Department tried to prevent the purchase on the grounds that conglomerates could be anticompetitive. A similar suit was brought against ITT. However, the cases were ultimately settled. The steel industry went into a tailspin, taking LTV along with it. In 1970, the company suffered a net loss of $38 million, its stock price fell to $10, and Ling got booted. The conglomerate era had come to an end.

THE 1970S

Throughout much of the 1970s, the U.S. economy was mired in turmoil. In 1973, the Organization of Petroleum Exporting Countries (OPEC) doubled the price for oil. With skyrocketing inflation in the United States, the per-barrel price eventually went from $3 in 1971 to more than $30 by 1980.

The economy went into recession, and a new term was coined: stagflation (the combination of inflation and stagnant growth). Meanwhile, an onslaught of foreign competition produced a growing trade deficit—and a budget shortfall as well. The dollar was falling. Meanwhile, America's political system was under intense pressure, as Watergate and the Vietnam War fomented deep distrust.

Under such turbulent conditions, M&A activity was subdued. But still, there were signs of things to come— such as a smattering of small leveraged buyouts (explained in more detail below). There were also a variety of hostile takeovers in the 1960s. But these were different from later hostile takeovers in that the hostile parties were not blue-chip companies. It was still considered taboo for a blue chip to behave in such a fashion.

But these taboos started to evaporate. In 1974, blue-chip International Nickel made a hostile bid for Electronic Storage Battery (a $157 million deal). Who represented International Nickel? None other than the blue-chip investment bank of Morgan Stanley. The bid was a success.

The tide for antitrust policy was also shifting. In 1978, Robert Bork published a book called *The Antitrust Paradox: A Policy at War with Itself,* which was a harsh critique of the antitrust laws. Essentially, he claimed that the laws are, for the most part, nonsense. Instead of promoting competition, he claimed, they result in less efficiency and higher prices for consumers.

THE LBO YEARS (1980s)

By the late 1970s, many Americans wanted radical change. The economic environment was intolerable. The new chairman of the Federal Reserve, Paul Volcker, wanted to purge the U.S. economy of inflation. To this end, Volcker imposed a very tight monetary policy but allowed interest rates to skyrocket. Furthermore, Americans resoundingly voted in Ronald Reagan as president. Reagan was an unabashed supporter of free-market policies.

At every chance, the Reagan administration sought to institute free-market ideology into government. For example, he nominated conservative justices to the Supreme Court and the federal judiciary and appointed right-wingers to the SEC and the Justice Department. As a result, the federal government became very lenient on any mergers.

Interestingly enough, a big concurrent economic trend was the unraveling of the old conglomerates. Wall Street believed that these conglomerates were stifling innovation with bureaucracy and lack of focus.

The deal that sparked the phenomenon of leveraged buyout (LBO) was the purchase of Gibson Greetings, which was masterminded by two veteran investment bankers, William Simon (a former Treasury secretary) and Raymond Chambers. Both saw tremendous opportunities to buy undervalued companies—especially divisions of underperforming conglomerates. The two launched an investment firm called Wesray.

One company that caught their attention was RCA, which contained a fetching division called Gibson Greetings. In 1982, Wesray bought the division for $80 million, of which about $79 was borrowed.

The transaction was known as an LBO since it involved a huge amount of debt. Although debt historically had been considered very risky, that attitude began to diminish in the 1980s—especially since companies were selling at low valuations. In addition, investors realized that once they purchase a company, they could instruct management to sell off assets and thus significantly reduce the debt load. Moreover, management would have a substantial equity stake—that is, a major incentive to improve the performance of the company. Plus, the company could write off the interest payments.

How did the Gibson deal fare? Within 14 months of the transaction, each partner made a profit of $70 million.

Of course, a critical element in the LBO trend was access to debt financing. This was made possible by Mike Milken, an investment banker with a boutique firm called Drexel Burnham Lambert. While a student at the Wharton Business School, Milken had become fascinated with so-called junk bonds, which have a high risk of default. He read W. Braddock Hickman's *Corporate Bond Quality and Investor Experience,* a lengthy book that analyzed junk bond performance between 1900 to 1943. Milken also found another study by T. R. Atkinson, which covered 1944 to 1965. The findings were very revealing for the young student, who found that over the long history of junk bonds, their rates of return outweighed the potential default risk. In other words, junk bonds were a good investment.

Steadily, Milken won over insurance companies and savings and loans to buy his junk bonds. These bonds helped finance such companies as MCI, CNN, and McCaw Cellular.

By 1984, Milken started to wield his junk bond empire for corporate takeovers. One of his biggest clients was a firm called Kohlberg, Kravis & Roberts. Jerry Kohlberg, Henry Kravis, and George Roberts were investment bankers at Bear Stearns, where they carried out several small LBOs. Seeing the potential for tremendous profits, they formed KKR in 1976.

The firm's big break came in 1978, when it pulled off the Houdaille Industries LBO. Houdaille's chairman,

Gerald Saltarelli, had grown up in the Depression era and was fiscally conservative. His view of debt was decidedly skeptical. A machine tool and pump manufacturer with 7,700 employees, Houdaille was a $400 million company with about $40 million in cash and only $22 million in debt. KKR built a strong rapport with the chairman and management. They also drew up a convincing business plan to show how the deal would succeed. The deal involved $48.1 million in equity and $306.5 million in debt. It was a success, and as a result KKR was the undisputed leader of the LBO game.

Consequently, KKR had no problem raising money. By 1983, it was doing billion-dollar deals.

The ultimate deal occurred in 1998 with the LBO of RJR Nabisco, an event that even became an HBO movie. No question, greed was running rampant. The CEO of RJR Nabisco, F. Ross Johnson, announced that he and management would purchase the company for $75 per share. Seeing this as a lowball offer, KKR intervened, offering $90 per share. KKR won the bidding battle, but at a steep cost. The final price tag was $109 per share, or $30 billion. The equity was $1.5 billion.

Although the deal almost collapsed within a few years, KKR rallied to restructure the operations and raise more money.

THE END OF THE LBO DECADE

By 1990, the junk bond market was rapidly coming undone. Because of the extensive federal bailout, the S&L industry was required to liquidate its portfolios of junk bonds. As prices plummeted, insurance companies, pensions, and other institutions also unloaded most of their junk bonds.

Junk bond deals like Southmark Corp. and Eastern
Airlines fell into bankruptcy. Finally, in February 1990,
Drexel Burnham went bankrupt. In light of all this, the
U.S. economy slipped into a recession during the early
1990s. Very few analysts thought the M&A game would
return any time soon. But it did.

DECADE OF THE MEGAMERGERS (1990S)

In the 1990s, the stock market had a tremendous bull
surge. Instead of using cash, companies used their high
stock prices to buy other companies. It was the decade of
the megamerger, and it affected many industries, including media. Essentially, media companies wanted to control every part of the chain: distribution, production, and
merchandising. It was not uncommon to see megadeals,
like Disney's $19.5 billion purchase of the American
Broadcasting System.

A key player in media megamergers was Sumner
Redstone. He understood that the media industry was
about to change drastically. In a tough buyout battle in
1987, Redstone leveraged his empire to the hilt and purchased cable operator Viacom for about $3.4 billion. Red-
stone was not an expert in this industry, so he hired top
people, such as Frank Biondi (who helped establish
HBO), to run Viacom—which owned properties including MTV and Nickelodeon. Then in 1993, Redstone purchased Paramount Communications for $10 billion and
Blockbuster Video for $8 billion.

Faced with a stifling debt load, Redstone sold off a
variety of Paramount's assets—Madison Square Garden
for $1 billion and the education publishing division of
Simon & Schuster for $4.6 billion. Then in 1999, Red-
stone merged with CBS for a deal worth about $35 bil-

lion. By 2000, Viacom had revenues of $20 billion and cash flow of $2.5 billion.

Many other megadeals have transpired, and others are in the pipeline. Our economy seems to be enthralled with M&As, with no letup in sight. I hope this book has prepared you to play a meaningful role in this crucial business activity.

WEB RESOURCES

In short order, the Web has become an incredible
source for all varieties of information, including a
wealth of business news, knowledge, and insight.
The trick, of course, is sifting through the dross to find
the bookmarkable jewels. Here's my highly selective list
of the top-notch online M&A resources:

BOWNE & CO.
www.bowne.com / newsletters
Interestingly enough, Bowne was founded in 1775 (before there was the United States!). Since then, the company has become a global powerhouse for content and
technology for corporations. In fact, Bowne is the world's
largest financial printer.

In the past few years, the company has been developing Internet publications. One is an e-mail newsletter
called "The Bowne Review for CFOs & Investment
Bankers," which always has several articles about M&A.

THE DAILY DEAL
www.thedeal.com
The Daily Deal is an online and print journal for professional deal makers. There is extensive coverage of M&A
events as well as IPOs, venture capital, private equity,
and bankruptcies.

The company consists of 190 employees who write timely and engaging articles. There is also international coverage, with correspondents in 15 countries.

Actually, the company is the brainchild of a well-known M&A star, Bruce Wasserstein, who manages the investment bank of Wasserstein Perella.

The Web site has many great features:

- **Deal Research.** Links to research sites to help with due diligence. A section called Score Card has charts for recent M&A deals and metrics.

- **Career Center.** Listings of jobs for deal makers (called the DealJobs Database). A Tip of the Day helps you improve your abilities in the deal game. The site even has a career coach whom you can ask questions. A section called A Day in the Life shows what top deal makers do in a typical day.

- **Networking.** Using chat technology, you can interact with other deal makers.

- **Tools of the Trade.** Here you'll find the latest cool gadgets to make your business life easier (Palm Pilot, software, cell phones).

- **Event Calendar.** Listings of upcoming conferences.

Currently, the Web site is free. However, there are plans to charge for certain value-added services in the future.

HR INTEGRATION TOOLS
www.hr-integration-tools.com
Patti Hanson has spent more than 18 years dealing with merger integration issues. A senior human resources consultant with FBD Consulting, she is also the author of *The M&A Transition Guide: A 10-Step Roadmap for Workforce Integration.* On her Web site, you can download for free her integration Excel spreadsheets.

Mergerstat

www.mergerstat.com

Since 1963, Mergerstat has been tracking the M&A marketplace. The criteria for the database is any formal transfer of ownership of at least 10% of a company's common equity in which the purchase price is at a minimum of $1 million and at least one of the parties is based in the United States.

The company provides custom research reports (the minimum is $300). The reports include market intelligence, trend analysis, and valuations.

On the Web site, there are free and premium resources. The free e-mail services include overall activity (on an annual basis), industry stats (deal volume for 49 industries), top deals, top financial advisers (their fees), and top legal advisers. The information is updated weekly.

The premium service has information about private and public U.S. and international transactions. The information is updated on a daily basis.

WRHAMBRECHT

www.wrhambrecht.com / wrhco / ma

WRHambrecht is an investment bank founded in 1998 by William Hambrecht, the cofounder of Hambrecht & Quist (another investment bank). Originally, the company focused on initial public offerings but has since entered other services, such as M&A.

This site has a section on M&A that is rich with useful information. It also has a collection of newsletters from the top law firms like Skadden, Arps and Gibson, Dunn & Crutcher. The subject matter is broad, including antitrust, cross-border transactions, accounting, SEC rules, and taxes.

The site also has a section that has charts of recent M&A transactions, covering a variety of valuation metrics (for example, revenue multiples). The charts cover the high-tech industries.

CFO MAGAZINE

www.moneysoft.com

CFO Magazine is a detailed magazine that often has articles about M&A. The magazine is published monthly and was founded in 1985. If you are a "qualified senior financial executive in the United States," the subscription is free. The Web site, which is also free, features a comprehensive section on M&A.

LAW.COM

www.ljextra.com / practice / mergers / index.html#links
Law.com is a top legal site. While it is geared for attorneys, there are still useful articles for those interested in M&A. The site is divided into various practice areas, of which there is an M&A section.

MONEYSOFT

www.moneysoft.com
Founded in 1991, MoneySoft develops software analysis tools for M&A transactions. (These tools are useful for both buyers and sellers.) The software also applies mainly for small to medium-size acquisitions (below $100 million in sales). The software is comprehensive and top-notch:

- **Buy-Out Plan.** Allows you to perform valuation, pricing, structuring of terms, and financing.
- **Corporate Valuation.** Guides you through the process of valuing a closely held company.
- **Lightning Deal Reviewer.** Helps evaluate prospective acquisition candidates, looking at strategic and financial objectives.

MERGERFORUM

www.mergerforum.com
My own site. I will post any updates to my book, and there will also be M&A resources, such as service providers, and lots of articles to help with your M&A transactions.

INDEX